STEP BY STEP THROUGH THE OLD TESTAMENT

Waylon Bailey and Tom Hudson

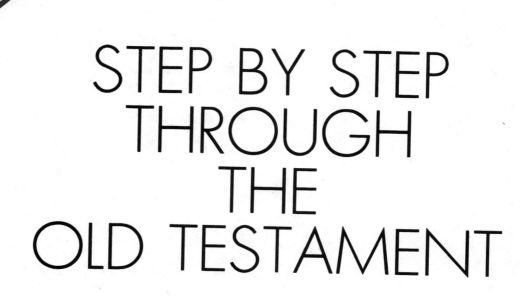

ISBN 0767326199

Dewey Decimal Classification: 221
Subject Heading: BIBLE. OLD TESTAMENT

This book is the text for Course CG-0104 in the subject area Bible Studies
in the Christian Growth Study Plan

Printed in the United States of America

Produced by the
Discipleship and Family Adult Department
LifeWay Christian Resources of the
Southern Baptist Convention
127 Ninth Avenue, North
Nashville, TN 37234-0151

ACKNOWLEDGEMENTS

Unless otherwise indicated, biblical quotations are from:
The HOLY BIBLE. *New International Version*, copyright
© 1973, 1978, 1984 by International Bible Society. Used
by permission.

Cover design by artist Paula Savage
includes a painting by Dutch painter
Jan I. Lievens (1607-1674) entitled
Abraham's Offering.

TABLE OF CONTENTS

THE AUTHORS

D. WAYLON BAILEY wrote the content for *Step by Step through the Old Testament*. Waylon has been professor of Old Testament and Hebrew at the New Orleans Baptist Theological Seminary since 1978. Before joining the faculty at New Orleans Baptist Theological Seminary, he served 12 years as pastor of churches in Alabama and Louisiana. In addition to his seminary responsibilities, he serves as a pastor of First Baptist Church in Covington, Louisiana.

Waylon, who is a native of Brantley, Alabama, is a graduate of Samford University and holds a master of theology and a doctor of theology from the New Orleans Baptist Theological Seminary.

He is no stranger to Southern Baptists. Since 1981 Waylon has been widely used as a conference leader and teacher at state and national conference centers, and he has written for journals and denominational publications. He has written one book entitled *As You Go*.

TOM HUDSON is the author of the learning activities in *Step by Step through the Old Testament* and also for the companion study *Step by Step through the New Testament*. Tom is manager of Adult Bible Book/Convention Uniform Series materials in the Sunday School division of the Southern Baptist Sunday School Board. He joined the board in January 1986 after 21 years as pastor of Oak Forest Baptist Church in Jackson, Mississippi. He also has served as pastor of First Southern Baptist Church, Anaconda, Montana, and assistant pastor of Broadmoor Baptist Church, Jackson, Mississippi. While in Mississippi, he served in numerous positions in the Mississippi Baptist Convention.

Tom, who is a native of Jackson, Mississippi, is a graduate of Mississippi College and holds a master of divinity degree from Southwestern Baptist Theological Seminary and a doctor of ministry degree from New Orleans Baptist Theological Seminary.

INTRODUCTION

The Lay Institute For Equipping

Step by Step through the old Testament is a course in the Lay Institute For Equipping or LIFE. LIFE is an educational system designed to provide quality education to laypersons in the areas of discipleship, leadership, and ministry. All Life courses have some common characteristics. These also apply to *Step by Step through the Old Testament*.

- Participants interact with a self-paced workbook (this is your workbook) for 30 to 60 minutes each day and do life related learning activities.
- Participants meet for a one-and- one-half to two-hour small-group learning session each week.
- The course leader (or facilitator) guides group members to reflect on and discuss what they have studied during the week and then make practical application of the study to everyday life. This small group becomes a support group for participants as they help each other come to understand and apply the Scriptures to life.
- A Christian Growth Study Plan diploma is awarded for those who complete a LIFE course in a small-group study. (See p. 223 for course credit request information.)

Studying *Step by Step through the Old Testament*

This book is different from most books in that it is not intended simply to be read from cover to cover. To get the most out of this course you must take your time by
studying only one day's lesson at a time. Do not try to study through several lessons in a single day. You need time to let these thought "sink in" to you understanding and practice. Do not skip any of the learning activities. These are designed to help you develop a framework for the Old Testament.

▶ **The activities will begin (like this paragraph) with an arrow pointing you to indented type. Follow the instructions given. After you have completed activity you will return to the content.**

Normally you will be given answers at the bottom of the page, so you can check your own work. Write your own answer before reading mine. Sometimes your response to the activity will be your own response or opinion, and no right or wrong answer can be given. If you have difficult with an activity or you question the answers given, write a note about your concern in the margin. Discuss it with your leader or small group.

Once each week you should attend a small-group session designed to help you discuss the content you studied the previous week, share insights and testimonies, encourage each other, and pray together. Small groups should not have more than 10 members for maximum effectiveness. Larger groups will experience less closeness, less intimate sharing, more absenteeism, and more drop-outs. If more than 10 people want to study the course, enlist additional leaders for each group of six to ten.

6

If you have started studying *Step by Step through the Old Testament* and you are not involved in a small group, enlist a few friends to study through the course with you. You will discover that others can help you learn and apply the teaching of this course. You will miss much of the intended learning from this course apart from a small-group study.

Resources for *Step by Step through the Old Testament* include:
- Member's book: *Step by Step through the Old Testament* (ISBN 0-7673-2619-9)
- Leader's guide: *Step by Step through the Old Testament Leader's Guide* (ISBN 0-7673-2620-2)
- Step by Step Through the Old Testament, Video (ISBN 0-8054-8429-9)

Orders or order inquiries may be sent to Customer Service Center, MSN 113, 127 Ninth Avenue, North, Nashville, TN 37234, or call 1-800-458-2772; Fax# (615) 251-5933; email to customerservice@lifeway.com. The books are also available at your local Baptist Book Store or Lifeway Christian Store.

A similar set of resources are available for *Step by Step through the New Testament*.

God and His Revelation

In this unit you will take a brief look at the groups of people involved in the process of God's revealing Himself and the places where that process took place.

WordWatch

Watch for these words as you study this unit.

Canaan—refers to the area we commonly call Palestine and the terms are used interchangably. The area is called Canaan because Noah's grandson, Canaan, and his descendants settled in that area (Gen. 10:15-19).

Canon—means "reed" or "measuring stick." It came to mean "a rule of faith," and eventually "a catalog or list." Today, when we use the word *canon*, we are referring to the books of inspired Scriptures that make up the Old and New Testaments of the Bible.

Torah—word the Hebrews used to refer to the five books of the Law. These books also are called the Pentateuch, a word which means "five-volume book."

Books of Wisdom—also are known as the books of poetry in the Old Testament. Wisdom is the preferred term because the books in that division of the Old Testament contain prose as well as poetry.

DAY 1   The People of Palestine

UNIT   1

Nothing excites me quite as much as taking a trip. If my family has planned a vacation or special trip, I think about it long in advance. I usually look at a map and find the route we will take. Even during the trip, the road map is as much entertainment as a necessity to help us get to our destination.

Think of this study of the Old Testament as a journey. Look for the exciting experiences and events.

The Old Testament contains a myriad of people, places, circumstances, and stories. You will find high drama and excitement. You will find people whose lives are filled with sorrow and sadness. Most of all, you will experience God through the pages of the Old Testament.

▶ **What do you want to gain from this study of the Old Testament?**

_____

_____

These learning activities will be the key to your success along the way. Don't skip any of them.

This unit on "God and His Revelation" gives a brief look at the groups of people involved in the process of God's revealing Himself and the places where that process took place. So many names and places may seem confusing, but you will find that some of them are familiar to you already. When you have completed this unit, you will be able to identify on a map the major population groups and significant places in the Old Testament. That may not seem possible, but remember that runners complete a marathon one step at a time. These are the first steps you will take in your journey through the Old Testament.

The People of Palestine

This small area was made up of many groups of people including the Canaanites, Hittites, Amorites, Perizzites, Hivites, and Jebusites (Ex. 3:17).

Hivites were a tribe mentioned in the Old Testament as being in various locations in Palestine. The Jebusites lived in Jerusalem. By the time the people of Israel entered Canaan, the Jebusites had lived in Jerusalem for many years. Joshua could not capture Jerusalem. David eventually took it by stealth and made it his capital.

The term *Perizzites* may refer to a class of people who lived outside the walls of the inhabited cities. *Perizzite* means "villager." This term also may have referred to a group living in central Palestine.

The Hittites came from an ancient kingdom north of Palestine in the area of modern Turkey. The kingdom of the Hittites ended about 1200 B.C.

The Amorites probably were people who lived in the central hill country of Palestine. The designation Canaanites refers to general inhabitants of the land, especially to those who lived west of the Jordan River.

► Match the following tribes on the left with the correct description on the right. Using a pencil, write the correct letters in the blanks. Answers are at the bottom of the column.[1]

_____ 1. Jebusites
_____ 2. Perizzites
_____ 3. Hittites
_____ 4. Canaanites

A. Inhabitants of the land west of the Jordan River
B. Lived in Jerusalem for many years
C. From Turkey/in Central Hill Country
D. Villagers/central Palestine

Check your answers at the bottom of the page. Did you miss some? If so, don't worry; simply erase the errors and write in the correct answers. This is an introduction. You will meet most of these folk again as you move step-by-step through the Old Testament. In later units you will be asked to refer to the map on the inside of the front cover. By the end of this course, many of these nations will be familiar to you.

Palestine is an extremely small area, only 145 miles from north to south and 90 miles across at its widest point. Since Palestine occupied an area about the size of Vermont, the groups were well-acquainted with one another. They were not divided into isolated districts with border guards. Through much of Old Testament history, the people of Israel and the other groups lived together. They knew each other's customs and they influenced one another for both good and evil.

Major Enemies

► Use the map on the inside of the front cover to locate Egypt and her primary enemies. Place a check (✓) beside each country as you locate it:

_____ Egypt; _____ Syria; _____ Babylon; _____ Assyria.

You discovered that Egypt's enemies lived to the north with Palestine in between. This location affected Israel throughout its history because Egypt attempted to use Palestine as a buffer state.

The people of Syria lived immediately to the north of Palestine. Early in Israel's history, the Syrians proved a formidable force.

Assyria, with its capital at Nineveh, covered the area between the Tigris and Euphrates Rivers. These militaristic people sought to dominate the area of Palestine.

Babylon, also known as Chaldea, lay at the mouth of the Tigris and Euphrates. Under Nubuchadnezzar they oppressed Palestine for several years beginning in 605 B.C.

► Match the following nations on the left with the correct description on the right. Using a pencil, write the correct letters in the blanks.[2]

_____ 1. Egyptians
_____ 2. Syrians
_____ 3. Babylonians
_____ 4. Assyrians

A. North of Palestine
B. Between Tigris and Euphrates Rivers
C. Used Palestine as a buffer
D. At mouth of Tigris and Euphrates

Semitic Peoples Surrounding Palestine

The Semitic peoples who surrounded Palestine were related generally to the Hebrews and observed similar practices and customs. To the south of Palestine was

---

[1] Answers to matching exercise: 1-B; 2-D; 3-C; 4-A.
[2] Answers: 1-C; 2-A; 3-D; 4-B.

Edom. The Edomites were descendants of Esau, twin brother of Jacob.
The Moabites, descendants of Lot, lived in the high country east of the Jordan River and the Dead Sea. The Ammonites also lived east of the Jordan River to the north of Moab.

The Philistines lived in the southwestern part of Palestine. The Philistines were sea traders who migrated to Palestine about 1200 B.C., about the same time that the people of Israel came to Canaan. Early in their history, before the time of David, the Philistines dominated the Israelites who lived in the adjacent territories.

On the northern coast of the Mediterranean Sea, the Phoenicians made their living by trading. They were known for trading in purple, a color associated with royalty. Tyre and Sidon are in Phoenician territory.

▶ **Match the following tribes on the left with the correct description on the right. Using a pencil, write the correct letters in the blanks.**[3]

_____ 1. Edomites	A. East of the Dead Sea
_____ 2. Moabites	B. Southwestern part of Palestine
_____ 3. Ammonites	C. Northern coast of Palestine
_____ 4. Philistines	D. East of the Jordan River
_____ 5. Phoenicians	E. South of Palestine

You may feel a bit overwhelmed with so many tribes or nations. But again, you probably were familiar with some of them. Match the names and descriptions below. After you finish, check the answers at the bottom of the column.[4]

_____ 1. Jebusites	A. Villagers/central Palestine
_____ 2. Perizzites	B. Inhabitants of the land west of the Jordan River
_____ 3. Hittites	C. Inhabitants of Jerusalem
_____ 4. Canaanites	D. North of Palestine
_____ 5. Egyptians	E. Between Tigris and Euphrates Rivers
_____ 6. Syrians	F. From Turkey/in Central Hill Country
_____ 7. Babylonians	G. Used Palestine as a buffer
_____ 8. Assyrians	H. East of the Dead Sea
_____ 9. Edomites	I. Southwestern part of Palestine
_____ 10. Moabites	J. Northern coast of Palestine
_____ 11. Ammonites	K. East of the Jordan River
_____ 12. Philistines	L. South of Palestine
_____ 13. Phoenicians	M. At mouth of Tigris and Euphrates

RESPONDING TO GOD'S WORD

★ Focusing on the various nations and tribes mentioned in the Old Testament can remind you that nations influence each other. Can you think of some modern nations that have had a significant impact on your nation in recent years? Recite to yourself or read John 3:16 and Acts 1:8. For Christians, what are some implications of these verses? Pause now and pray for the people in other nations.

In light of this study, how should you pray and whom should you pray for?

_____

_____

---

[3]Answers: 1-E; 2-A; 3-D; 4-B; 5-C.
[4]Answers: 1-C; 2-A; 3-F; 4-B; 5-G; 6-D; 7-M; 8-E; 9-L; 10-H; 11-K; 12-I; 13-J.

DAY 2   The Land of Palestine

U N I T   1

Name and Location

The Greek form of the term *Philistine* is Palestine. An older name for Palestine is *Canaan*. The descendants of Canaan, a son of Ham, occupied Palestine west of the Jordan (Gen. 10:6,15-20). These people were conquered by the Israelites under Joshua. To be such a small area, the land of Palestine played a large role in the ancient world. It continues to dominate much of contemporary history.

Palestine is a land bridge between the three continents of Europe, Asia, and Africa. Any movement of goods or people by land between the continents must move through Palestine. For this reason, Palestine continues to play a significant role in world history.

Boundaries

Palestine's boundaries have differed throughout history. Generally, the boundaries have been the Mediterranean Sea on the west, called the sea or the Great Sea in the Bible; the mountains of Lebanon on the north; and the Negeb desert on the south. The eastern border has been the most fluid. During the New Testament period, the eastern border was the Arabian desert. Today it is the Jordan River.

▶ **Identify these boundaries on the map. Write the letter on the map for the corresponding boundary. Check your answers with the map on the inside front cover.**

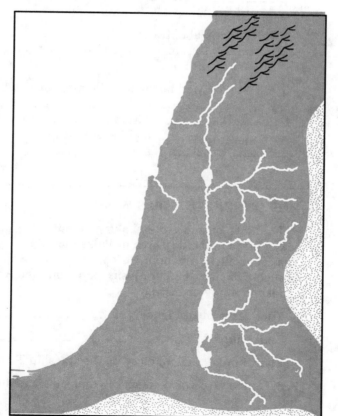

Mediterranean Sea - M

Mountains of Lebanon - L

Negeb Desert - N

Arabian Desert - A

Jordan River - J

Size

▶ **As you read, write the distances on the map.**

Recall from session 1 that the land of Palestine is small, about the size of Vermont. With a modern interstate system, you could travel from north to south in about three hours and from east to west in less than two hours even at the widest point.

In Galilee (in the north), the east to west journey may cover only about 20 miles. But in the south, the east to west traveler would journey about 90 miles. From north to south the distance is approximately 145 miles.

Climate

The land of Palestine enjoys the subtropical Mediterranean climate. The rain comes in the winter and spring while the summer is dry. Almost no rain falls during the summer months. Thus Palestine is brown in the summer and green in the winter. Crops such as grain and barley are planted in the fall and harvested in May or June. Grapes are harvested in October. The coldest month in Palestine is February. The warmest month is August.

▶ **Take a quick memory check by filling in the following blanks. Look back at the material you just read if you need to do so.**

1. Palestine played such a large role in the ancient world because it is a
_____ _____ between _____,
_____, and _____.

2. Palestine is the Greek form of the word _____.

3. Biblical boundaries for Palestine were _____ on the
west, the mountains of _____ on the north, the
_____ desert on the south, and the Arabian
_____ on the east.

4. Palestine is about the size of _____. It is about
_____ miles wide in the north; and in the south about
_____.

5. Palestine's Mediterranean climate consists of rain in
_____ and _____; dry in
_____. Grain and barley are planted in the
_____ and harvested in _____ or _____.
_____ and _____ are harvested in October.

RESPONDING TO GOD'S WORD

★ Meditate on the earth-shaking significance of biblical events that have taken place in the tiny area of Palestine. In that small area God chose to reveal Himself to a people He chose as His own. Through those people He brought His Son, the Lord Jesus Christ into the world. What does the size of Palestine imply concerning:

Your place of residence? _____

Your church? _____

Your Sunday School class or Discipleship Training group? _____

Ask God to give you a vision of what He wants to do in the place where you live.

DAY 3   The Divisions of the Land and of the Old Testament

U N I T   1

Natural Divisions of the Land of Palestine

▶ As you read the first part of today's lesson, locate the following geographical features and draw an arrow to the correct location on the map below. You also may check your answers by the map on the inside front cover.

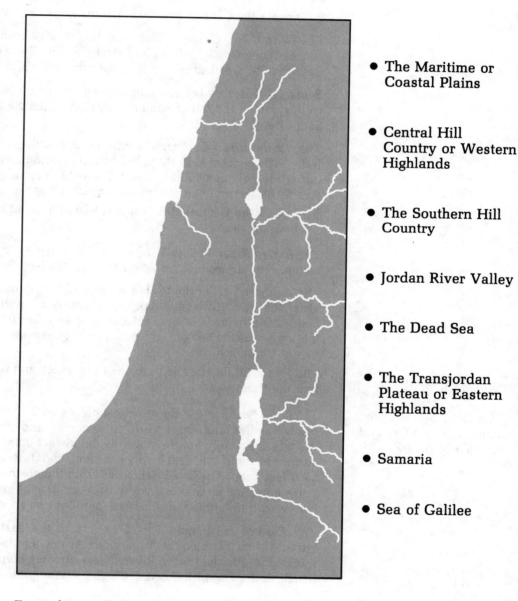

- **The Maritime or Coastal Plains**

- **Central Hill Country or Western Highlands**

- **The Southern Hill Country**

- **Jordan River Valley**

- **The Dead Sea**

- **The Transjordan Plateau or Eastern Highlands**

- **Samaria**

- **Sea of Galilee**

For such a small area, the geography of Palestine is varied. Looking at Palestine's four natural divisions helps us understand the land. We will look at these from west to east.

The Coastal Plains. Running adjacent to the Mediterranean Sea are three plains: The Plain of Acre in the north, the Plain of Sharon in the center, and the Philistine Plain in the south.

The Plain of Acre is about five to eight miles wide extending north from Mt. Carmel. The Plain of Sharon lies between Mt. Carmel and Joppa. It is about 50 miles long and six to twelve miles wide. In ancient times, this plain was mostly marsh and forests and probably never was settled.

The Philistines controlled the plain to the south. They made their living by trading with other sea-faring people. Because the Philistines felt uncomfortable in the hills, they usually did not extend their sphere of influence beyond their coastal plain.

▶ Locate the Coastal Plains on the map.

The Central Hill Country. The "backbone" of Palestine is an almost continuous range of rough, rocky hills in western Palestine. Galilee is a mountainous area cut from the Plain of Jezreel and several other plains.

Samaria. This area lay south of Galilee and made up the central part of the hill country. After the fall of Samaria in 722 B.C., people in this area were known as Samaritans.

The Southern Hill Country. At different times this area was known as Judah or Judea. The eastern half of the hill country could be cultivated. The west is desolate wilderness much like a desert. The wilderness of Judea in which Jesus experienced His temptations is a rocky, dry desert area.

▶ Locate the Central Hill Country, Samaria, and Southern Hill Country on the map on page 13.

The Jordan River Valley. The Jordan cleft is a great geological rift that splits Palestine, running from Syria down through the Red Sea.

The northern part of the Jordan River Valley is dominated by the Sea of Galilee. This "sea" is really a small lake about seven miles wide and twelve miles long. It lies 682 feet below sea level at its surface and runs 600 feet deep. In the Scripture, it is known as the Sea of Galilee, the Sea of Gennesaret, the Sea of Tiberias, or the Sea of Chinereth.

The Jordan Valley begins at the Sea of Galilee and runs 65 miles south emptying into the Dead Sea.

The Dead Sea is also known as Salt Sea and the Sea of Arabah.

The Dead Sea is one of the strangest places on the face of the earth. Although this sea is 50 miles long, averages 10 miles across, and contains rich mineral deposits, there is absolutely no life in it. It is the lowest point on the face of the earth. Its surface is about 1300 feet below sea level, and its deepest point is almost another 1300 feet deep. The Dead Sea is fed from the north by the Jordan River, runs 50 miles long, has an average width of 10 miles, but has no outlet. The water is so heavy with minerals that a person can float on its surface with no effort at all.

The Eastern Highlands. This area lies to the east of the Jordan River. Four streams—the Yarmuk, the Jabbok, the Arnon, and the Zered—flow west through this region into the Jordan River. These streams divide the area into five regions (from north to south): Bashan, Gilead, Ammon, Moab, and Edom.

▶ 1. Locate the Jordan River Valley and Eastern Highlands on the map on page 13.

2. Circle all the correct answers in the following statements. Each statement may have more than one correct answer. Answers are at the bottom of the column.[5]

A. Another name for the Dead Sea is the (Salt Sea) (Sea of Arabah) (Floating Sea).

B. Another name for the Sea of Galilee is the Sea of (Gennesaret) (Tiberias) (Chinnereth).

The Nature of the Old Testament

▶ What do you already know about the nature of the Old Testament? On the following practice questions mark the statements as T (true) or F (false).

——— 1. The Old Testament was written over a period of more than 5,000 years.

——— 2. In our English Bibles, the Old Testament usually is divided into seven major parts.

——— 3. The Books of Law also are known as the Pentateuch.

——— 4. Books included in the poetical division also are described by the term wisdom literature.

——— 5. The Major Prophets division contains writings of the four most important Old Testament prophets.

See if you can confirm your answers in the following section.

Old Testament Divisions

The Old Testament is a complex and diverse group of books written over a one-thousand-year period. In our English Bible, the Old Testament has five divisions, each of which contains a different kind of material.

OLD TESTAMENT DIVISIONS

1. Law
2. History
3. Wisdom
4. Major Prophets
5. Minor Prophets

▶ Before reading any further, open your Bible to the table of contents for the Old Testament. You will need this list for several activities as you complete this chapter.

---

[5]Answers to multiple choice: A-Salt Sea or Sea of Arabah; B-All three are correct. See the map on the inside front cover for correct locations.

THE BOOKS OF LAW

Genesis

_____

_____

Deuteronomy

THE BOOKS OF HISTORY

Joshua

_____

_____

_____

_____

_____

_____

Esther

THE BOOKS OF WISDOM

Job

_____

_____

Song of Songs

THE MAJOR PROPHETS

Isaiah

_____

_____

Daniel

(continued)

The books of Law. The first five books in the Bible are called the books of the Law because they record events leading up to and surrounding the giving of the Law. These books also are called the Pentateuch, a word which means "five-volume book."

▶ Turn to Genesis 1. Now turn to Joshua 1. Notice how much material is between your fingers. Those are the five books of Law. The first of the five books of Law is Genesis; the last is Deuteronomy. Use your Bible's table of contents to write in the other books in the table in the margin.

The books of History. A large portion of the Old Testament is contained in the books of History. These books tell the story of Israel from the time they entered the promised land until their return from exile and the rebuilding of the temple. These books are not history for the sake of history. Rather, their purpose is to show the purposes of God in history.

▶ Find Joshua 1 and Job 1 and place a finger at each. The material between your fingers is the division of history. Note that the first two divisions include slightly more than half the Old Testament. The first of the books of history is Joshua; the last is Esther. Use your Bible's table of contents to write in the other books in the margin table.

The books of Wisdom. The books of Wisdom are also called books of Poetry. These books contain a wide variety of materials. Job contains both poetry and prose. The Book of Proverbs may be considered optimistic wisdom while the Book of Ecclesiastes appears quite pessimistic. The Book of Lamentations can fit in this section or in the prophetic section.

▶ Now, in your Bible find Job 1 and Isaiah 1. This is the wisdom section. The first of the books of Wisdom is Job; the last is Song of Songs. Use your Bible's table of contents to write in the other books in the margin table.

The books of Prophecy. The books of prophecy contain both prose and poetry. The first section of the prophets is known as the Major Prophets not because they are more important, but because they are longer.

▶ Compare the size of the last two divisions. Find Isaiah 1 and Hosea 1. Now find the end of the Old Testament. Notice the contrast in the amount of material in those last two divisions. You can see clearly why the first group of five books is called the Major Prophets and the latter group of 12 books is called the Minor Prophets. Now use the table of contents in your Bible to list the Major and Minor Prophets in the margin table.

A. Cover the margin table and number the major divisions listed below in the proper order from 1 (first) to 5 (last).

_____ Minor Prophets

_____ Wisdom Literature

_____ History

_____ Law

_____ Major Prophets

Use the margin table to check your work.

B. Now see if you can list all five divisions of the Old Testament in order without looking back.

1. _____

2. _____

3. _____

4. _____

5. _____

THE MINOR PROPHETS
Hosea

_____

_____

_____

_____

_____

_____

_____

_____

Malachi

Understanding the Old Testament

The Old Testament contains the record of God's revelation of Himself to humankind. Through His written word, God reveals Himself to His people and helps them live the best lives possible. The Old Testament was written to real, live human beings in earlier times. It is a living word spoken to people in times of crises and need.

Since the Old Testament was written over almost a one-thousand-year period, it had to be collected and preserved by people of faith. Through the centuries, people told the message of God and retold the wonderful things God had done. Later, the accounts of these experiences and messages were written down and preserved carefully by scribes who revered each account.

As God spoke to people in the earlier days, He continues to speak through His Word today. However, the writings of the Old Testament differ in a number of ways. Understanding the message of the Old Testament requires careful study and interpretation. Future sessions will help you know how to read and study the Bible, giving careful and prayerful consideration to what God is saying to you through His Word.

▶ **Did you discover in your reading which answers for the practice questions (p. 15) were true or false? Compare your answers with these: 1. False. It was written over a period of more than 1,000 years. 2. False. The parts are Law, History, Poetry, Major Prophets, Minor Prophets. 3. True. 4. True. 5. False. The Books of Isaiah, Jeremiah, Ezekiel, and Daniel are called major because they are the longest prophetic books.**

RESPONDING TO GOD'S WORD

★ **Meditate for a few moments on the role that the Bible has played in your life.**

★ **Thank God for His Holy Word.**

DAY 4 The Canon of the Old Testament

UNIT 1

Canon = authoritative books

Recall the 39 books you listed in the margin table yesterday. Baptists and most Protestants believe that those books make up the canon. Most Roman Catholics, however, include additional books called the Apocrypha between the Testaments. For our study, we will use *canon* to refer to the 39 Old Testament books and the 27 New Testament books listed in your Bible's table of contents.

We believe that the books included in the canon are authoritative because they came from God. They were written by persons whom God had inspired. The Bible simply says that inspiration is a fact without explaining how it happened.

▶ **Using your own words, how would you explain to a Sunday School class member the meaning of the term *Old Testament Canon?* Write your response in the following space.**

_____

_____

_____

_____

_____

Evaluate your answer:
● After hearing your explanation of *Old Testament Canon*, would your class member know that the literal meaning of the word *canon* is a reed or measuring stick?
● Would the member understand that God's people have accepted the books included in the canon to be God's authoritative Word?
● Would the member be aware that protestants do not have some books in their canon that Roman Catholics have in theirs?

▶ **What would you need to add or change in your explanation in order to improve your member's understanding?**

_____

_____

_____

Languages of the Old Testament

Of course, you know the Old Testament was not written originally in English. But do you know what the original languages were?

▶ **Which two languages do you think were the original languages used in the Old Testament? Check two.**

☐ English   ☐ Greek   ☐ Latin   ☐ Aramaic   ☐ Hebrew

Almost all the Old Testament was written in Hebrew. However, some sections were written in Aramaic, a language related to Hebrew and popular late in the Old Testament period and during the ministry of Jesus.

Confirmation of the Old Testament Canon

Do you remember the five major divisions of the Old Testament you learned yesterday? They are listed in the margin. This is not the way the Hebrews divided the Old Testament canon before the time of Christ. The Hebrew Bible contains three parts. These three sections make up the canon of the Old Testament. The way anything is constructed determines how it is used and how it is understood. This fact is certainly the case with the Old Testament. Looking at the way the Old Testament was divided will help us understand how we received our Bible and how we ought to understand the individual books.

▶ **As you read about these three divisions, circle the Bible books included in each. Place a star beside the date when the books were considered authoritative.**

The Law (Torah). The first section of the Hebrew canon is the Torah and contains the books of the law--Genesis, Exodus, Leviticus, Numbers, and Deuteronomy.

We do not know when these books were written, but we have two reasons for believing that the people of God accepted them as authoritative by 400 B.C. First, the Samaritans accepted the Torah but denied the inspiration of any other books

---

Divisions of Our Old Testament Canon

1. Law
2. History
3. Wisdom
4. Major Prophets
5. Minor Prophets

Divisions of the Hebrew Old Testament Canon

1. Torah (the Law)
2. Prophets (former and latter)
3. The Writings

The Law (Torah), 400 B.C.

of the Old Testament. By 400 B.C. the Samaritans had broken away from the Jews. Therefore, the Law--but only the Law-- must have been considered authoritative by 400 B.C. Otherwise, the Samaritans would have taken the other books with them.

Second, Nehemiah 8 records Ezra's reading the Law. The traditional date for this event is sometime shortly after 450 B.C. If Ezra read the Law as we know it, then the Law must have been considered authoritative by that time. How much earlier the five books received authoritative status remains unclear, but by 400 B.C. they were considered canonical.

The Prophets. The prophets make up the second section of the Hebrew canon. The rabbis divided the prophets into former prophets and latter prophets. Each division contains four books. The former prophets were Joshua, Judges, Samuel, and Kings with Samuel and Kings being considered one book each.

The Prophets, 200 B.C.

We consider Joshua, Judges, Samuel, and Kings to be historical books. However, the Hebrews called them prophecy because they were written by persons considered to be prophets and tell about what prophets did.

The Books of Isaiah, Jeremiah, Ezekiel, and the Book of the Twelve make up the latter prophets. The Book of the Twelve consists of the twelve prophetic books of Hosea through Malachi. Notice that Daniel is not among the prophets in the Hebrew canon.

We know that the prophets were considered canonical by 200 B.C. or shortly thereafter. At that time, a man named Ben-Sirach wrote a book entitled *The Wisdom of Solomon* in which he mentioned the Law and the Prophets. So, by this time (180 B.C.), both the Law and the Prophets must have been authoritative for people of faith.

The Writings, 132 B.C.

The Writings. In 132 B.C. a grandson of Ben-Sirach translated his grandfather's work and added a preface in which he mentioned the Law, the Prophets, and the *other books*. Thus, a third section had been added to the canon. The *other books* later were called *the Writings*. The Writings include everything in the Old Testament not found in the Law and the Prophets. The Writings include the five scrolls of Judaism which were connected with the feasts and fasts of Judaism. These were the Books of Ruth, Song of Songs, Lamentations, Ecclesiastes, and Esther. One of the notable inclusions in the Writings is the Book of Daniel. The Writings also included Chronicles, Ezra, Nehemiah, Job, Psalms, and Proverbs.

By the time of the New Testament, the Old Testament canon looked much like it is today. In Luke 24:44, Jesus referred to the Law, the Prophets, and the Psalms. In the Hebrew Bible, the Writings began with the Psalms. By mentioning the Psalms, Jesus may have been alluding to all the Writings. If this were the case, Luke 24:44 may refer to the three-fold canon of the Old Testament.

Council of Jamnia

Council of Jamnia A.D. 90

In A.D. 90, a council of rabbis met to discuss the Scriptures. They met at a place called Jamnia. A few Old Testament scholars believe that this council determined which books would be in the canon. Most biblical scholars believe this group did not determine the books of the canon but that new books would not be added. They probably acted in response to the number of Christian writings loved and revered by Christians. Almost all of the New Testament had been written by the time of the Council of Jamnia.

The council did not determine the canon; that had been done by people of faith through the centuries. While they affirmed all the books in our Old Testament canon, they questioned whether five of them should be used in synagogue worship for these reasons: (1) the Book of Esther does not contain the name of God; (2)

the Song of Songs is erotic in nature; (3) some passages in Proverbs such as 26:4 and 26:5 appear contradictory; (4) in Ezekiel, chapters 40—48 appear to be in conflict with the law of Moses; and (5) Ecclesiastes is pessimistic in its outlook.

In the end, the council affirmed a canon already chosen by the common decision of faithful people.

▶ **In order to highlight the significant points in the material you have read today, match the following items on the left with the correct items on the right. Write the correct letters in the blanks. Answers are at the bottom of the page.[6]**

_____ 1. Ezra's reading the Law, 444 B.C.	A. Prophets accepted in canon
_____ 2. Luke 24:44	B. Closed Old Testament canon
_____ 3. Ben-Sirach's "The Wisdom of Solomon," 180 B.C.	C. Law accepted in canon
_____ 4. Council of Jamnia, A.D. 90	D. Referred to books later called "the Writings"
_____ 5. Preface to a translation of "The Wisdom of Solomon," 132 B.C.	E. Jesus' mention of the law, prophets, and Psalms

---

RESPONDING TO GOD'S WORD

★ The canon was affirmed by a council meeting at Jamnia, but the books of Scripture had proven themselves to be God's Word in the lives of God's people. How has God spoken to your heart and life through His Word? Are you giving God a regular opportunity to speak to you through His Word? Commit yourself to doing that by filling in the blank lines below:

I will let God speak to me through His Word by regularly reading from His Word:

When: _____

Where: _____

---

[6]Answers: 1-C; 2-E; 3-A; 4-B; 5-D.

DAY 5   The Text and Interpretation of the Old Testament

The Text of the Old Testament

The Jews loved and revered the Law. For these reasons, they took extra care to preserve and protect it. What do you do with an old Bible? Chances are that you do not throw it away. If you have been a believer for a long time, you perhaps have several Bibles stacked up somewhere because the bindings have worn out.

The Jews showed their reverence for the Law by making copies of it to preserve it, not by saving worn and tattered manuscripts. When an old manuscript became worn and frayed, they made a new copy and destroyed the old one. For this reason, we do not have hundreds of old Hebrew manuscripts. We do have many New Testament manuscripts because those Scriptures were preserved by people with a different mindset than the Hebrews.

The oldest complete Old Testament manuscript dates back to A.D. 1008, over a thousand years after the close of the Hebrew canon.

Recent discoveries assure us that our Bible is the same as the original manuscripts of the Old Testament. The Dead Sea Scrolls are the best example. In 1947 a number of ancient manuscripts were discovered in a cave near the Dead Sea at a place called Qumran. These manuscripts dating from 250 B.C. to A.D. 68 contained a complete manuscript of the scroll of Isaiah and fragments from every other Old Testament book except Esther. The scroll of Isaiah dated from near the time of Jesus; when translated, it overwhelmingly agreed with the text of Isaiah from A.D. 1008. The only differences were extremely minor in nature.

Through the centuries, faithful scribes preserved the integrity of the Old Testament. Certainly, God worked among His people to preserve His word substantially as it was first written by the people of God.

▶ **Take a moment to answer these two questions:**
   A. Why are ancient copies of the Old Testament so rare?

   _____

   _____

   B. What is a major significance of the Dead Sea Scrolls?

   _____

   _____

Did you answer that the Jews showed their reverence for the Scriprures by destroying old manuscripts after making new copies, and that the Dead Sea Scrolls contained copies of Old Testament Scriptures that were 1,000 years older than any other copies?

Ancient Versions of the Old Testament

Because other people in the the ancient world also wanted to read the Scripture, the Old Testament was translated, even in ancient times, into other languages.

▶ **As you read, circle each translation or paraphrase mentioned. I have circled the first one for you.**

The best known translation of the Old Testament is the Septuagint. This text was a Greek translation of the Old Testament for Jews living in and around Alexandria, Egypt. This translation was made around 300 B.C.

Because Jews in the time of Jesus and before spoke Aramaic, a language similar to Hebrew, a number of Aramaic paraphrases were made of the Old Testament. These were known as the Targums. About A.D. 404, the Latin Bible called the Vulgate was translated by Jerome.

John Wycliffe made an English translation of the Latin Vulgate. William Tyndale made an English translation from the original languages. Later, the translations which we recognize began to appear. The first popular translation was the King James Version in 1611 (though many people of its day would not read the KJV because they preferred some of the older versions).

▶ **Mark the following statements as T (true) or F (false).**
   _____ 1. The Septuagint is a Latin translation of the Old Testament.
   _____ 2. The King James Version of the Bible always has been a favorite of English readers.
   _____ 3. The Targums are Greek paraphrases of the Old Testament.

If you marked all three false, you were right! The Septuagint is a Greek translation of the Old Testament; when the King James Version first came out, many people preferred older translations with which they were familiar; and the Targums are Aramaic paraphrases of the Old Testament Scriptures.

Who Wrote the Old Testament?

Through the centuries, God spoke through many individuals. Their messages were brought together to become our Old Testament. Many of the people who spoke the words of God did not record their own messages. Other people recognized the importance of the messages and preserved them--sometimes after the messages had been passed orally from one generation to another.

We cannot be sure how most of the books of the Old Testament were put into written form. We assume that Isaiah's disciples preserved his messages (Isa. 8:1).

▶ **Read Jeremiah 36:1-4 and describe how Jeremiah's messages were recorded.**

_____

_____

_____

We do know that Jeremiah dictated many of his messages to his scribe Baruch. Baruch possibly recorded other messages of Jeremiah which were not dictated. Jeremiah 36 describes how the first scroll of Jeremiah came to be written. God told Jeremiah to dictate to Baruch all the words he had preached for a number of years. Baruch faithfully recorded the words which were then taken to noblemen in Jerusalem. When King Jehoiakim read the words, he cut them into pieces with his knife and tossed them into the fire. After Jehoiakim destroyed the first scroll, God told Jeremiah to dictate a second scroll. Baruch faithfully recorded these words as well.

In this way, or in a variation of this way, other biblical books may have been put into written form. We do know that God worked to preserve the wonderful messages for His people. We can give thanks to those people who repeated the words they heard, to those who recorded these messages, and to those scribes who through the centuries tediously preserved the message of God.

Basic Principles for Interpreting the Old Testament

▶ **In each of the principles in the box circle a key word that will help you remember the principle.**

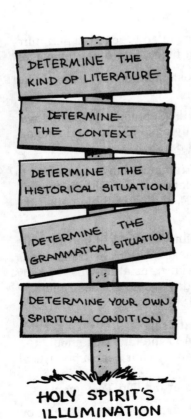

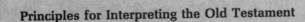

Principles for Interpreting the Old Testament
1. Determine the Kind of Literature
2. Determine the Context
3. Determine the Historical Situation
4. Determine the Grammatical Meaning
5. Determine Your Own Spiritual Condition

Every day we interpet what we see and what we hear because understanding is impossible apart from interpretation. The question is not whether or not to interpret. The question is how well we interpret the communication all around us.

How we understand the message of God depends on our ability to interpret it correctly. You will study several principles for interpreting the Old Testament.

However, you must understand that the key to understanding God's Word is the Holy Spirit; He is the One who guides us into all truth (John 16:13). My prayer is that all of the people of God will study diligently and open themselves in every way to the leadership of God's Spirit. Apart from His presence to guide us in the application of the principles and to illumine our understanding to the truth of what we see, there can be no understanding.

DETERMINE THE KIND OF LITERATURE

1. Determine the Kind of Literature. To know how to interpret any text, you must understand the kind of material you are reading. For example, a comic strip demands a short attention span and ends with a "punch-line." On the other hand, a scientific journal communicates technical data in a precise manner. Therefore you read the two differently with different expectations.

▶ **The Bible contains many different kinds of literature. How many can you list?**

1. _____   5. _____

2. _____   6. _____

3. _____   7. _____

4. _____   8. _____

Your list could include poetry, history, sermons, instruction, narratives, letters, philosophy, and prophecy. You must understand the kind of literature you are reading and interpret it accordingly. History and instruction must be taken much more factually than poetry and philosophy. We must also understand and be alert to biblical writers' frequent use of analogies and figures of speech such as Jesus referring to Himself as the door and the psalmist referring to Israel as the vine that God brought out of Egypt.

DETERMINE THE CONTEXT

2. Determine the Context. Any word or idea must be understood in its context to be interpreted correctly. The context helps determine the meaning.

To interpret Scripture correctly, you must determine the context of the passage you are studying. These steps will help.

Context of a word or idea means:

-The words or ideas that surround it

-The kind of literature that contains it

-The historical setting

Determine the Context

1. Ask yourself what is the context of the biblical book in which the passage is found.
   - What is the major theme of the book?
   - To what events and historical situations does it refer?
2. What is the context of the chapter?
   - What subject is being discussed?
3. What is the meaning of the surrounding verses of the particular verse or passage you wish to interpret?

▶ **What are two Principles of Interpretation?**

1. Determine _____

2. Determine _____

DETERMINE THE HISTORICAL SITUATION

3. Determine the Historical Situation. Understanding the historical situation is important to interpreting a passage of Scripture. For example, to understand the Book of Jeremiah, you must understand who the kings of Judah were. To whom does Jeremiah refer when he preached about Jehoiakim or Zedekiah? Only when you understand the historical background, can you make an accurate interpretation of Jeremiah's message.

In our study of the Old Testament, we will present the historical situation reflected in each biblical book. This background will help us understand the wonderful message the Lord has for His people.

4. Determine the Grammatical Meaning. Word meanings change. Understanding what a word or idea meant at the time it was expressed is important to interpreting Scripture. We have to understand the usage of words in particular time periods. Note how the meaning of "rap" has changed. In 1900 it meant to strike or hit; in 1930 it meant the punishment for a crime; in 1960 it meant a discussion; in 1990 it meant a kind of music. What certain words meant in 1611 when the King James Version of the Bible was translated may be different from the meaning of the same words today. Bible dictionaries, word studies, commentaries, and Bible encyclopedias will help us understand the meaning of words and their relationship to one another.

5. Determine Your Own Spiritual Condition. The Bible should be interpreted by people of faith who have a living, meaningful relationship with Jesus Christ, our Lord. As you study, think of your own spiritual condition and seek to hear the Word of God for you personally. Pray that God will give you wisdom to understand the Scripture. Ask the Holy Spirit to reveal God's Word to you.

▶ **Fill in a key word in the Five Principles of Interpretation.**

1. Determine the _____ of literature.

2. Determine the _____.

3. Determine the _____ situation.

4. Determine the _____ meaning.

5. Determine your own _____ condition.

As I have written these units of Old Testament study, I have prayed for God to help me make my words clear and meaningful. As we study, let us pray that God will use His Word to reveal Himself to us. One key in interpreting the Scripture is an openness to hear a fresh word from God. God wants to reveal Himself to us and tell us what we ought to do in response to His revelation.

▶ **Read the following Scriptures and determine which principle of interpretation would help answer the question. Answers are at the bottom of the column.[7]**

1. "The Israelites groaned in their slavery and cried out . . . God heard their groaning and he remembered his covenant with Abraham, with Isaac and with Jacob" (Ex. 2:23-24).

What covenant did God have with Abraham, Isaac, and Jacob?

Principle: _____

2. "Your right hand, O Lord,
       was majestic in power.
    Your right hand, O Lord,
       shattered the enemy" (Ex. 15:6).

If God is a Spirit, how can He have a right hand?

Principle: _____

3. For thou wilt not leave my soul in hell; neither wilt thou suffer thine Holy One to see corruption (Ps. 16:10, KJV).

Does this verse teach that the Messiah would actually be in hell?

Principle: _____

4. Blessed is the man who does not walk in the counsel of the wicked or stand in the way of sinners or sit in the seat of mockers. But his delight is in the law of the Lord, and on his law he meditates day and night (Ps. 1:1-2).

Why does this not sound like a "blessed" life-style to me? Why do I find understanding the Bible so difficult?

Principle: _____

▶ **SUMMARY REVIEW**

To review this week's study of the Old Testament, see if you can mentally answer the following questions. You may want to write the answers on a separate sheet of paper. Mark your level of performance on the left: circle "C" if you can answer correctly and circle "R" if you need to review.

C R 1. What are three of the tribes who lived in Palestine?

C R 2. Describe the geographical size of Palestine.

C R 3. Name two of the four boundaries of Palestine?

C R 4. Name three of the five divisions of the Old Testament.

C R 5. In what two languages was the Old Testament written?

C R 6. What happened at Jamnia in A.D. 90?

C R 7. What does canon mean?

C R 8. List three principles for interpreting the Old Testament.

Review this week's material to find the answers.

---

[7]Answers to exercise: 1- Determine the Historical Situation or Determine the Context; 2- Determine the Kind of Literature; 3-Determine the Grammatical Meaning; 4-Determine Your Own Spiritual Condition. (See 1 Cor. 2:12-14; 3:1-3.)

UNIT 2 God and His Creation *(Genesis 1—11)*

Where do you start when you discuss the meaning of life? When God gave guidelines for life, He began in the beginning. The creation tells us about our God, our world, and ourselves. When we look at creation, we see what God wants for His people and how He wants us to live.

Theme

In the outline below you can see that the Book of Genesis covers two periods of Old Testament history. You will study the first major division in this unit.

Genesis:

Outline

    I. Beginnings (Gen. 1—11)
       A. Creation
       B. The Fall
       C. The Flood
       D. The Tower of Babel
    II. The Patriarchs (Gen. 12—50)

WordWatch

Watch for these words as you study this unit.

Pentateuch—means "five books" and refers to the first five books of the Old Testament.

Patriarchs—means "fathers" and refers to Abraham, Isaac, Jacob, and Joseph as a group.

DAY 1 The Book of Genesis (Gen. 1:1—2:3)

UNIT 2

genesis (jen'esis) n. Borrowning of Latin Genesis, from Greek genesis origin, creation. General meaning: origin, creation, inception, beginning.

The Pentateuch is made up of the five books of Genesis, Exodus, Leviticus, Numbers, and Deuteronomy.

Pentateuch from the Greek:
penta--meaning five
teuch--meaning book

bara=bring into existence

▶ **Before you begin studying, check to see how much you already know. For each of the following questions check the correct answers (more than one may be correct). Answers are at the bottom of this column.[1]**

1. Genesis gets its name from
   - ☐ a. Moses
   - ☒ b. the Latin word for "beginnings"
   - ☐ c. the Latin word for "create"

2. Pentateuch means
   - ☐ a. Genesis, Exodus, Leviticus, Numbers, and Deuteronomy
   - ☐ b. "the Torah"
   - ☒ c. "five books"

3. The name most often associated with writing the first five books of the Bible is
   - ☐ a. Adam
   - ☒ b. Moses
   - ☐ c. Joshua

In this unit we will focus on the activity of God during "The Beginnings." In Unit 3 we will study "The Patriarchs."

The Book of Genesis is the first book of the Pentateuch (meaning five books), the *Torah*, or the Law. By reading through these books, you quickly recognize that the Pentateuch tells one continuous story—the story of God's people. Genesis tells the beginning of that story: the creation of the world, the creation of human beings, human sin, and God's desire to make for Himself a people who would carry His Word to all the world.

The Book of Genesis does not identify its author, but many Christians associate Genesis and the other books of the Pentateuch with Moses. Some of the Pentateuch certainly came from Moses (especially the Law) while other parts were written by others. For example, the account of Moses' death and burial in Deuteronomy 34 surely was written by someone else.

Creation in Genesis 1—2:3

Genesis 1 pictures creation from the perspective of the universe. God created everything and proclaimed that it measured up to His purpose (Gen. 1:31). God is the central figure in Genesis 1. Everything came into existence because God wanted it to exist. God spoke, and the world and all that is in it was created.

The Old Testament was written in Hebrew except for a few chapters written in Aramaic. In Genesis 1, the Hebrew word *bara* is used for *create* and means to bring into existence. Throughout the Bible, *bara* is used only to describe God's creative activity. Human beings may form, fashion, and make; but only God creates.

---

[1]Answers: 1-b, 2-c, 3-b.

▶ *Bara* **is used three times in Genesis 1. Read the following verses and describe what God created in each one:**

Genesis 1:1; God created _____heaven & earth_____

Genesis 1:21; God created _____

Genesis 1:27; God created _____

The third use of *bara* relates to the creation of human beings. In Hebrew thinking the number *three* contained the idea of completeness. The third use of *bara* to indicate the creation of humans shows the importance of human beings. God did His supreme work of creation when He created human beings.

▶ **Fill in the blanks. Use the preceding paragraphs to check your work.**

1. Bara means to _____create_____.
2. The verb bara always has only _____God_____ as its subject.
3. Bara is used _____3 X_____ times in Genesis 1.
4. The number three in Hebrew thinking signified _____completeness_____.
5. The use of bara in Genesis 1 indicates that humans were God's _____supreme_____ creation.

God spoke the world into existence. By His word He created the heavens and the earth. God said, "let there be" and "there was." The manner of creation shows the power of God—He merely spoke, and the world and its contents appeared. In the Book of Revelation, we see a similar phenomenon. At the end time God will overcome His enemies with a word (symbolized by a sword from His mouth, Rev. 19:15,21).

▶ **Carefully read Genesis 1, then complete this matching activity. Write the corresponding letter in the box by each day of creation to show the major creative act on each day. Answers are at the bottom of this column.[2]**

☐ Day 1, Gen. 1:3-5   A. Land
☐ Day 2, Gen. 1:6-8   B. Fish, Birds
☐ Day 3, Gen. 1:9-13   C. Light
☐ Day 4, Gen. 1:14-19   D. Animals, Humans
☐ Day 5, Gen. 1:20-23   E. Sky
☐ Day 6, Gen. 1:24-31   F. Sun, Moon, Stars

Genesis 1 moves to a grand crescendo. The height of creation came when God created human beings. The word "man" means human beings in general. God created all life, but He created only human beings in His own image. This does not mean that God has physical characteristics like we do. God is spirit. We are like God in that we have intellect, emotions, and will. We are created in such a way that we can have a personal relationship with God. This certainly implies that each person is a special object of God's love. We are created in the image of God and for divine purposes.

God blessed the male and the female with the power of reproduction. God made the sexual nature of human beings part of His plan. Sex, in the proper context of the marriage relationship, is pleasing to God.

God blessed both sexes with dominion over the remainder of the creation. To "rule over" (1:26) means to use the creation for the common good of humanity and according to the purposes of God. To use the creation for selfish, exploitative purposes violates God's purpose. God gave us, His supreme creation, the responsibility of caring for His world. We are to exercise that responsibility in a way that brings honor to God.

---

[2]Answers: Day 1-C; Day 2-E; Day 3-A; Day 4-F; Day 5-B; Day 6-D.

When God had finished, He surveyed His world and pronounced it very good. It was exactly the way He intended for it to be.

▸ **Mark the following statements as T (true) or F (false).**[3]

_T_ 1. The height of creation came when God created human beings.

_T_ 2. God made the sexual nature of human beings part of His plan.

_T_ 3. God blessed both sexes with dominion over His creation.

_T_ 4. The world as God created it was consistent with His purposes.

RESPONDING TO GOD'S WORD

★ List two specific ways that you are obeying God's command to "rule" over His creation:

1. _Eat food_

2. _Pets_

★ How well do you think humanity is handling the stewardship of ruling over God's creation? Give your answer and your reasons here:

awful = cloning, extinction of animals/spec.
waste way too much.

DAY 2 Creation (Gen. 2:4-25)

Do you recall the broad outline of the Old Testament you learned in yesterday's study? It is reproduced in the box in the margin.

▸ **Can you recall and write the title of the first event in the beginnings period on the blank line?**

As you continue to study God's creative activity, read Genesis 2:4-25. Then number the following events in the Creation in the correct order. Answers are at the bottom of the column.[4]

_5_ God created the woman.

_7_ Man and woman were naked and were not ashamed.

_3_ God prohibited eating from the tree of the knowledge of good and evil.

_1_ Streams watered the surface of the earth.

_6_ The man stated that the woman was "bone of my bones and flesh of my flesh."

_2_ The Lord God formed the man of dust from the ground.

_4_ God stated that man needed a helper that corresponded to his needs.

---

[3]Answers: All statements are true.
[4]Answers: Your numbers from top to bottom should read: 5, 7, 3, 1, 6, 2, 4.

Two Accounts of Creation

Genesis 1—2:3 and 2:4-25 present different accounts of the same event. The two perspectives of the one event complement each other. While each has its own focus, they both develop the same central themes. Both testify to God's creation of the world. Each emphasizes that creation is an act of God alone. No outside agent participated in the creation. Each chapter testifies to the strategic role of human beings in the world.

Genesis 1 focuses on God's creation of the universe; Genesis 2 on God's creation of human beings. Both chapters emphasize God's unique work to create for Himself a people to relate to Him in a personal way and to carry out His purpose in the world.

▶ **What title would you give to Genesis 1 and 2 if you wanted to describe the most important focus of the two chapters?**

_____ God's and Creation _____

The primary focus of Genesis 1 and 2 is not just that creation occurred. The focus is on *God*. God created the universe, it did not just come into existence on its own.

For the purpose of understanding the way the two creation accounts are related and how they complement each other, consider two different ways you might describe a great historical event. One time you might slowly build your story from the lesser to the greater. You might introduce all the important characters, describing the features, characters, and peculiarities of each one. You would describe events as they developed and show how they led up to the climactic event. On another occasion, you might begin by describing the event itself. Then you would describe characters, events, and movements that led up to that great historical event.

From this example, you can see the differences in Genesis 1 and Genesis 2. Genesis 1 builds day-by-day from the lesser to the greater. Finally, God reached the heights of creation when He created human beings. Genesis 2, however, immediately tells of God's creating the man. The essential details concerning man's work and creation of woman, are added later in the chapter. Genesis 2 emphasizes that the man and the woman complement each other. Woman is described as "a helper suitable for him" (2:18). That phrase carries the idea of one who corresponds to him, who is like him in human personhood.

▶ **In your own words, how would you explain the relationship between the two Creation accounts in Genesis 1 and Genesis 2?**

_____

_____

_____

_____

_____

Key Teachings

Much of what we understand about the family comes from Genesis 1—2. Our views of man and woman are greatly influenced by these chapters. Genesis 2 particularly focuses on the needs of male and female. What can we learn about ourselves from these passages?

▶ **After each of the five sections, write a one-line summary for the key teaching.**

(1) God created human beings for **companionship**. Whether married or single, we need friends. God did not create or equip human beings to live in isolation from other human beings. The animals simply would not do for a companion for the man. Only another person could satisfy the need for companionship.

▶ Summary: *humans weren't meant to be alone*

(2) Male and female need each other. Each **complements** the other. Though some people will not marry (see 1 Cor. 7:7-9), they need friends of the opposite sex.

▶ Summary: *Opposites attract*

(3) In chapter 2 we begin to see the importance of the marriage relationship. God ordained marriage. He brought the man and the woman together. He made marriage the permanent, monogamous (one man and one woman) relationship that fulfills God's ideal. God intended marriage to be a life-long, exclusive, and God-sealed **commitment**. Only when marriage fulfills these ideals can any marriage meet the needs of the marriage partners. God intended to propagate the human race through men and women who were married to each other.

▶ Summary: *Marriages are blessed w/ God*

(4) God gave human beings freedom of **choice**. God made human beings free. He gave them specific instructions about what they were to do and not do, but He left them free to make significant choices that would determine their future. Every person is free. We are not tied to fate. No outside force determines our lives. We choose to serve God and to obey His will, or we choose to follow our own destructive ways. These choices remain before each of us.

▶ Summary: *We have our own will*

(5) God gave human beings **work** to do in caring for and protecting the world in which they had been placed. Meaningful, productive, satisfying activity was a part of God's plan for us from the beginning. In return, the earth would willingly yield sustenance. By their sin, Adam and Eve not only corrupted their relationship with God but also their relationship with the world He had given them for sustenance and fulfillment. Without the perspective gained through a right relationship with God, the world becomes an object to be exploited. Work becomes a monotonous drudgery, often filled with frustration and hardship while withholding satisfaction and fulfillment.

▶ Summary: *After fall work isn't satisfying*

As Christians, we have learned that having our relationship with God restored also restores our relationship with work. Work that is done unto the Lord (Eph, 6:5-9) is filled with a sense of purpose and fulfillment even in the midst of toil and drudgery.

▶ **Write the five key words that capsule some key teachings about human beings in Genesis 2.[5]**

Companionship
Comlements
Commitment
Choice
Work

---

[5]Answers: companion or companionship, complements, commitment, choice, work.

DAY 3   Choosing to Rebel (Gen. 3)

UNIT 2 ▶ Remember, the Book of Genesis covers two periods of Old Testament history: "The Beginnings" and "The Patriarchs." Fill in the first blank in the following Genesis overview chart:

GENESIS

The Creation

The Fall
The Flood
The Tower of Babel

In the first part of Genesis called "The Beginnings," you have completed a study of "Creation." Today's study covers "The Fall."

In Genesis 3 we see the sorrow caused by rebellion against God and the tragic consequences of a life devoted to satisfying self. The sin of the first two humans is often described as "The Fall."

The Decision to Rebel (Gen. 3:1-6)

▶ Read Genesis 3:1-6 to see the progressive nature of temptation to rebel against God. Write the verse number in the blank beside each statement to which it applies:[6]

1. God was quoted as making a prohibition He never made. _3_

2. God's warning was contradicted. _4_

3. God was accused of withholding something good from humans. _5_

God placed the man and the woman whom He created in a perfect environment and provided them with all the necessities of life. Then the serpent questioned the instructions God had given and exactly contradicted what God had said. He started Adam and Eve thinking that God chose to deprive them of something that would be good for them. They rebelled against God because of their selfish desires.

God's commands, prohibitions, and instructions are not intended to restrict or deprive. Rather, these were intended to preserve their relationship with Him and the quality of life for which He created them. What Adam and Eve *did* was to eat the forbidden fruit. However, their sin was much more profound: rebellion against God and rejection of His commands. Disobeying His commands destroyed the

---

[6]Answers: 1-v. 3; 2-v. 4; 3-v. 5.

very things God had intended to preserve for Adam and Eve. They believed the serpent's lie, that they would be like God, but sin made them less like God. Such a desire to exalt self over God may well be the basis for all sins.

▶ **How do we destroy the things God wants for us today by disobeying Him in order to attain them?**

Doing it our way

Sin Destroys Relationships (Gen. 3:7-13)

When they sinned, Adam and Eve destroyed their relationship with each other. However, their most serious loss was their relationship with God. The previous chapters in Genesis show how God cared for Adam and Eve, how He communicated with them and provided for all their needs. Can you think of a more beautiful picture than that of God walking with them in the garden in the cool of the day? The Bible also pictures the purity and innocence of the relationship between the man and woman. But sin changed all that.

▶ **Examine Genesis 3:7-13 and list the evidences you find of changed relationships between Adam and Eve and between them and God.**

hid their bodies from each other, blaming each other, hid from God, made excuses for sin

After rebelling against God, Adam and Eve were afraid of Him and hid from His presence. Their rebellion also caused them to turn on each other. The man accused the woman of deceiving him, and in a sense, blamed God for his failure. The woman blamed the serpent. Everyone seemed quite able at turning on and blaming someone else.

▶ **To be sure you understand, explain in your own words why it was so serious for Adam and Eve to destroy their relationship with God.**

God hates sin, because they sinned God wasn't pleased

In destroying their relationship with God, Adam and Eve destroyed themselves. When they separated themselves from God they forfeited all that God had created them for: blessings, life, and His presence. In that act they passed from fullness and life to emptiness and death.

Sin Brings Consequences

Three characters were involved in the rebellion against God: Adam, Eve, and the serpent. With that rebellion, human nature and all God's creation became corrupted with sin. Certain consequences would follow because of that corruption. God told the three what consequences to expect.

▶ **Study Genesis 3:7-13 again and list each person's consequences in the chart on the next page.**

SIN'S CONSEQUENCES	
PERSON	**CONSEQUENCE**
Adam	*painful* Work of land, working all days of life
Eve	pain @ childbirth, subservant role
Serpent	eat dust, crawl on belly

Each sin brings its own
consequences.

The serpent experienced "dusty diet and belly travel" as its punishment for encouraging the woman and man in their sin. Some understand this to mean that part of the serpent's punishment involved perpetual enmity between the humans and the animals that slither on the ground. Many Bible students see in 3:15 a foregleam of the gospel of Christ. The seed of the woman is singular while the seed of the serpent is plural. Though this verse does not identify the woman's "seed," they understand it to mean Christ and the crushing of the serpent's head is understood to mean His triumph over sin.

Though faint at this point, God gave hope to the man and woman that through His faithfulness, there would ultimately be a triumph over the problem of sin. Genesis 3:15 reminds us of the ultimate victory over sin, which comes through Christ.

▶ **What do you think is the most significant part of the serpent's punishment? Write your answer below.**

A - cursed above all
T - Crushing of head

The man and woman's punishment related to the basic or elemental aspects of life. For the man, punishment affected his work. For the woman, sin affected childbirth. God originally intended for Adam to work and to take joy in the labor as well as the fruit of his labor. While some pain had been a part of childbirth, God had meant for the woman to rejoice in the opportunity to be fruitful and multiply as God had commanded. Now work would be toilsome and childbirth would be accompanied by greatly increased pain. No other members of the animal kingdom seem to experience the severe pain in childbirth that humans experience. God's original intent was for the man and woman to be co-equal as persons and full partners in the stewardship of His creation. He had created them as complementary counterparts of each other. Now because of the corruption of human nature she would be in a position of subjection.

The final part of the woman's punishment was: "Your desire will be for your husband, and he will rule over you" (3:16). In Genesis 1—2, men and women are both presented as persons made in God's image. Women are given a full partnership in humans' dominion over creation. This ideal was changed; because the woman sinned, she would be subordinate to her husband. (Eph. 5:21-33 states the Christian ideal of mutual submission. In Christianity, the role of the husband as "head of the wife" is shown not to be one of dominating power but of selfless love.)

Lest the humans also take of the fruit of the tree of life and live forever, God sent them out of the garden. The cherubim and the flaming sword guarding the tree of life emphasized the loss the man and woman faced. Their sin, far from bringing Godlikeness, resulted in godlessness. This is why we call this event in Old Testament history "The Fall."

▶ **What do you think is the most significant part of the woman's punishment? Write your answer below.**

desire for husband

What do you think is the most significant part of the man's punishment? Write your answer below.

painfully toil his entire life

List the first two events in "The Beginnings":

Creation   _Fall_

God's Grace

God tempers His judgment by His grace. God graciously protected the man and the woman by giving them skins to wear. They worried about their nakedness. They would soon have to worry about the elements and the animals as well. Some Bible students see in God's providing animal skins a picture of the sacrificial atonement of Jesus Christ to cover the sins of humankind.

Throughout the early chapters of Genesis, the Bible reveals God as a God of grace and mercy. He cares for those whom He has created.

RESPONDING TO GOD'S WORD

★ All of us have sinned, thus all of us are sinners. Those who have received the fullness of God's grace by receiving Christ as Savior and Lord are saved sinners. Those who have not received Him are lost sinners. If you are saved, express your gratitude to God for His forgivenss and for the relationship with God that you have through Him. If you are lost, today repent of your sins and by faith take Christ as your Lord. Your *Step by Step* study leader or pastor will be glad to give you further guidance.

DAY 4   The Sorrow of Sin (Gen. 4—5)

U N I T   2

1. The Beginnings

The Fall
The Flood

The Tower of Babel

▶ **Begin by filling in the blank in the overview chart at the left.**

In the first part of Genesis, "The Beginnings," you have covered the "Creation" and "The Fall." Today's study shows the spreading sorrow that came to humanity because of sin.

Sin's Sorrow for the Family (Gen. 4:1-18)

▶ **Read Genesis 4 to discover the main characters of the chapter. When you have done so, match the character on the left with the correct letter on the right. Answers are at the bottom of the column.[7]**

_D_ 1. Cain	A. Wives of Lamech
_E_ 2. Abel	B. Third son of Adam
_F_ 3. Lamech	C. Son of Cain
_C_ 4. Enoch	D. Killed Abel; lived in Nod
_A_ 5. Adah and Zillah	E. Son whose sacrifice pleased God
_B_ 6. Seth	F. Killed others who injured him

Eve bore two sons, Cain and Abel. Cain tilled the ground and Abel herded sheep. At this time God had not commanded people to bring offerings as an act of worship. However, Cain and Abel apparently felt the need to do so. Each man brought what he produced. Abel brought an offering from the flock, while Cain gave God an offering of the fruit of the ground. Although the Bible does not explain how God showed His acceptance and rejection, we are told that He did accept one offering and reject the other.

▶ **Before you read further, study Genesis 4:1-7, noting the way the words are sequenced and placed in relation to one another. A commentary will be helpful, if one is available. Then formulate your own idea of why God accepted one offering and rejected the other.**

Some believe that God accepted Abel's offering because it was associated with blood while Cain only brought the produce of the ground. Others say God accepted Abel's offering because Abel brought the firstborn of the flocks, thus bringing a superior offering to God. But remember that God had not required an offering. When He described the offerings later (Lev. 2:1), a grain offering (called a "meat offering" in the King James Version) was included.

> "By faith Abel offered God a better sacrifice than Cain did."
> —Hebrews 11:4

> "Do not be like Cain, who belonged to the evil one and murdered his brother. And why did he murder him? Because his own actions were evil and his brother's were righteous."
> —1 John 3:12

Did you note in the sequence of words that God looked first at the man and then at the gift? God accepted Abel's offering because Abel's heart was right with God; Cain's was not. The condition of the *gift giver* not the nature of the gift determined its acceptability. This interpretation is supported by the text of Genesis 4.

Cain showed the kind of man he was by the way he treated his brother. His anger overcame him and he killed his brother Abel.

▶ **Read about Cain's punishment in Genesis 4:11-18. Check the statements that best describe his punishment.[8]**
- ☐ 1. Cain could not father children.
- ☐ 2. The ground would no longer yield its crops for Cain.
- ☐ 3. Cain faced capital punishment.
- ☐ 4. Cain was cursed from the ground.
- ☐ 5. God sent Cain out to become a wanderer on the earth.
- ☐ 6. God allowed anyone to take vengeance on Cain.
- ☐ 7. Cain suffered the loss of the presence of the Lord.
- ☐ 8. Cain could not live among other people in cities.

When God said that the blood of righteous Abel cried out to Him from the ground, He was saying that the blood of every person is precious in His sight. God created life, and He wants life preserved.

Cain's punishment contained three points:

[7]Answers: 1-D; 2-E; 3-F; 4-C; 5-A; 6-B.
[8]Answers: 2, 4, 5, 7.

- A literal translation of Genesis 4:11 reads: "Now cursed are you from the ground which has opened its mouth to take the blood of your brother from your hand." Cain was now cut off from the ground he had tilled. It would no longer yield him a bountiful harvest. This is an *in-kind* punishment. Cain used the ground to conceal his crime. God cut Cain off from the ground. Notice that this is much like the punishment of Adam his father.
- Cain was to become a nomad (a wanderer).
- Cain's greatest punishment was being sent out from the presence of the Lord. A person left to his or her own devices faces untold suffering.

God shows mercy even to those who are suffering the consequences of their sin.

Note the three-fold mercy God showed Cain. First, Cain was afraid that he would suffer his brother's fate--that whoever found him would kill him. God protected him. Second, Cain was given new relationships. God blessed him with a wife and children. Third, Cain prospered. He was no longer a tiller of the soil; he became a builder of cities.

▶ **In Cain we see a great lesson about the sorrow that sin produces. We also see a great lesson about the way God tempers judgment with mercy. Check each statement that identifies something we learn about God's mercy from Cain's experience.[9]**
- ☐ 1. Sin pays in the final analysis.
- ☐ 2. God loves and is concerned about a person who has failed.
- ☐ 3. Failure need not be the end.
- ☐ 4. God is willing to cancel the consequences of a person's sin.
- ☐ 5. God will bless even those who are suffering the consequences of sin.

Sin's Sorrow for Society (Gen. 4:19-24)

In the fourth chapter of Genesis sin appeared to triumph. Cain killed Abel. Lamech became a polygamist, marrying Adah and Zillah. Lamech lived by his own law. For this man, the law of an eye for an eye and a tooth for a tooth would have been a significant ethical advance. He boasted that he had killed a man who only had wounded him. Lamech lived on the selfish side of life. He thought only of himself and his needs. He refused to look at the needs and feelings of others. Sin always produces that kind of response toward other people.

▶ **List some modern day sins that result in "sorrow for society." I have given you one as an example.**

Child abuse — _____

_____ _____

_____ _____

You could have included in your list things like illegal drug traffic, alcohol abuse, pornography, terrorism, prostitution, and so forth.

Sin's Sorrow for the World (Gen. 5)

Genesis 5 is a structured account of the descendants of Adam and Eve. This chapter tells of humanity's multiplying on the earth. Each family had sons and daughters. Sadly, with one exception (v. 24), all of the people mentioned in chapter 5 died as God had said (2:17).

How did people live so long in the time period before the flood? How should we understand these long lives? A number of possible answers have been given to these questions. My own personal view is that declining lifespans show the progressive tragedy of sin. God created Adam and Eve to live, not to die. Tragically,

---

[9]Answers: 2, 3, 5.

sin brought death. Thus, before the flood individuals lived from 300-700 years or longer. After Noah's time (during the patriarchal period) people lived 100-200 years. Since then the normal life span is less than 100 years. Sin thus took its toll on the human race. What God intended for His people was destroyed by their own rebellion. Genesis 5 teaches that sin harms people. When we sin, we rebel against God and lose the good things God intended for us to have.

Three Lessons for Life

Genesis 5 gives three lessons for life:
(1) Sin brings death.
(2) Individuals and their families are important to God (the chapter is a record of individuals and their families).
(3) Even in the worst of times, fellowship with God is still possible. Though everyone else around him appeared to reject the ways of God, Enoch walked with God and did His will. Enoch did not suffer death. God took Enoch to be with Him.

RESPONDING TO GOD'S WORD

★ Take a walk with God. As you walk, do the following.
  ● Meditate on God and renew your fellowship with Him.
  ● Meditate on a time of failure in your life and thank God for the way He blended mercy with the consequences of your sin.
  ● Call to mind some person who is struggling with the consequences of sin. Determine ways you can communicate God's mercy and hope to that person.

DAY 5   Beginning Again (Gen. 6—11)

UNIT 2

GENESIS

1. The Beginnings
  Creation
  The Fall

_____

_____

Evidences of Sinfulness

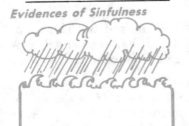

▶ Today's study includes the last two key events in the first part of Genesis: "The Flood" and "The Tower of Babel." Write those events on the overview chart in the margin.

Sin always yields sad consequences. In this study we will see how sin prompted God to bring judgment on the world He created. We also will see how His mercy prompted Him to spare Noah and his family so that they might repopulate the earth.

The Flood (Gen. 6—9)

The first 13 verses of Genesis 6 recount the increasing violence and corruption in the land. This rebellion against God showed the continuing effects of the sin of Adam and Eve. The world became filled with unrighteousness and lawlessness.

▶ Read Genesis 6:1-13 to identify words or phrases that refer to the people's sinfulness. List these in the box in the margin.

Righteous Noah. Only Noah found favor before God. He walked with God and sought to do His will. Again, even when people all around neglect God at every turn, a person can serve God and live a righteous life.

▶ **Read Genesis 6:5-9 and answer the following questions. Answers are at the bottom of the column.**[10]

1. What did God see? (v. 5) _____

_____

2. What did God feel? (v. 6) _____

_____

3. What did God decide? (v. 7) _____

_____

4. Why did God make an exception of Noah? (vv.8-9) _____

_____

God emphasized preservation and restoration in the midst of rebellion and judgment.

Noah's Qualities

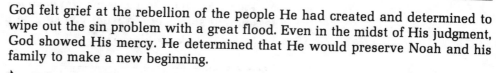

God felt grief at the rebellion of the people He had created and determined to wipe out the sin problem with a great flood. Even in the midst of His judgment, God showed His mercy. He determined that He would preserve Noah and his family to make a new beginning.

▶ **Take time now to find in Genesis 6:8-9 Noah's qualities that caused God to exempt him from the destruction of the flood. List these in the chart in the margin.**

The Peoples of the World (Gen. 10)

Genesis 10 describes the peoples of the world after the flood. This is an important chapter for four reasons.

> **GENESIS 10**
>
> - Details the beginning of the second humanity.
> - Shows the unity of human beings.
> - Prepares for recurrence of sin and separation of humanity.
> - Introduces Abraham's family line.

The Tower of Babel (Gen. 11:1-9)

▶ **In 11:1-9, what evidence do you find that the people were depending on God for their protection and security?**

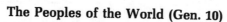

The account of the tower of Babel climaxes the story of rebellion against God. God had commanded the flood survivors to "fill the earth" (Gen. 9:1). Instead, they chose to gather in one place to build a city with a tower that would reach to the heavens and serve as a symbol of their common identity.

Beginning with Adam and Eve, the common denominator in sin is rebellion against God's will. The result of rebellion against God is always the same: we lose what we are trying to gain and destroy what we are trying to keep.

The point of 11:1-9 is that human arrogance breeds sin which divides people. The people were united, but they were united primarily in their language and in their rebellion against God. God rebuked their arrogance by confusing their language. Thus a people who sought to establish their identity, unity, and security around a great goal instead of the great God were scattered to "fill the earth."

---

[10]Your answers could have been something like these: (1) How evil humanity had become. (2) Grief. (3) To destroy the human race and animal life. (4) Noah was righteous, blameless, and walked with God.

▶ At this point you have covered the key events of "The Beginnings." See if you can complete the overview chart. If you need to jog your memory, check the overview chart at the beginning of Day 5's study.

GENESIS

The B_____

C_____

The F_____

The F_____

The T_____ of _____

The remainder of Genesis 11 introduces the descendants of Noah's son, Shem, and introduces Abraham. These verses serve as a bridge to the second major division of the book of Genesis.

▶ Now look back at the key lessons you have learned. In your own words state a lesson that stands out in what you studied about:

1. God's act of creation: _____

_____

2. The Fall: _____

_____

3. The Flood: _____

_____

4. The tower of Babel: _____

_____

Be ready to share your answers in the next group session.

▶

SUMMARY REVIEW

To review this week's study of the Old Testament, see if you can mentally answer the following questions. You may want to write the answers on a separate sheet of paper. Mark your level of performance on the left: circle "C" if you can answer correctly and circle "R" if you need to review.

C   R   1. What are two names by which the first five books of the Bible are known?

C   R   2. What are the two different focuses of creation in Genesis 1 and Genesis 2?

C   R   3. What are three key teachings about human beings in Genesis 2?

C   R   4. What was God's most serious punishment to Adam and Eve? What was their greatest loss because of their sin?

C   R   5. Give two possible reasons why God rejected Cain's offering.

C   R   6. Why did God spare Noah when He sent the flood?

C   R   7. What was the basic sin of people who tried to build what we call the "tower of Babel"?

RESPONDING TO GOD'S WORD

★ Of the lessons that to you stand out from the material you studied this week, which one do you most need to take to heart? _____

Spend time praying about how you will act on that lesson in the coming week.

UNIT 3 — God and the Patriarchs (Genesis 12—50)

When God began to proclaim His love for the world, He began with people. All of God's work revolves around people. God chose Abraham and his descendants to carry out His work in the world. As you study, consider how God uses people to do His work today. Specifically, think about how God wants to use you to do His work.

Theme

Outline

Genesis:

   I. Beginnings (Gen. 1—11)

 II. The Patriarchs (Gen. 12—50)
    A. Abraham
    B. Isaac
    C. Jacob
    D. Joseph

WordWatch

Watch for these words as you study this unit.

Covenant—describes a formal, solemn, and binding contract between two or more persons. In the Bible, some covenants place requirements on all parties involved and extend benefits to all parties involved. Other covenants are unilateral in that one covenanting party pledges to be faithful to the covenant unconditionally.

Birthright—a privilege that belonged to the oldest son. This right entitled the oldest son to the position of leadership of the family and a double portion of the inheritance left by the father.

DAY 1   Abraham (Gen. 12:1-9)

UNIT 3

GENESIS

The B *eginnings*

The *Creation*

The *Fall*

The *Flood*

The *tower of Babalon*

The Patriarchs

Abraham
Isaac
Jacob
Joseph

▶ The Book of Genesis covers two periods of Old Testament history. Last week you studied the first period. Can you complete the overview chart in the margin?

In this week's study we will focus on the activity of God during the period of the patriarchs. The first patriarch is Abraham.

Abram's name was changed to Abraham (Gen. 17:5) and Sarai's name, to Sarah (17:15). In our study, *Abraham* and *Sarah* will be used throughout for clarity's sake.

▶ **Write the names of the patriarchs below:**

A *braham*

I *saac*

Ja *cob*

Jo *seph*

Abraham, Isaac, Jacob, and Joseph commonly are called the patriarchs of Israel. God chose to work through them and their descendants to make for Himself a people of faith. The nation of Israel began with the patriarchs. Apart from God's leadership, Israel would not have existed. Though Genesis 1—11 speaks of several ancient nations, Israel was not among them. God brought Israel into existence by calling men and women of faith. As they responded to His call, God molded them into a people whom He used to call the world to Him.

The Call of Abraham (Gen. 12:1-5). God called Abraham to leave Ur of the Chaldees (an area near the Persian Gulf) and to go to the land of Canaan. This would have been an extremely dangerous journey of around 1,500 miles. In every age, God's call demands devoted service and a spirit of adventure. Abraham left familiar surroundings for the insecure life of a nomad—a nomad on mission for God.

▶ **1. On the map on the inside front cover, locate Ur near the head of the Persian Gulf. Now locate Haran, where Abraham's father settled after leaving Ur. Find Shechem and Bethel. Also notice the desert between Ur and Canaan. This desert prevented direct travel between the two places. Normal travel followed the "fertile crescent," the route taken by Abraham from Ur to Haran to Canaan.**

2. As you examine the map, consider the hardships of travel almost 4,000 years ago. On the following lines write your ideas of the fears and difficulties Abraham faced in leaving Ur of the Chaldees to journey to the land of Canaan.

_____

_____

Abraham left his homeland, his family, his security, and his family's religion to follow the call of God. Abraham's father worshiped other gods (Josh. 24:2-3). Ur of the Chaldees was located on the Euphrates River. Abraham evidently had lived on the east side of the river; he had crossed the Euphrates ("lived beyond

Following God's call may lead us into danger and difficulty-- not away from it.

the River," NIV; "the other side of the flood," KJV, Josh. 24:2) to travel to Canaan. He faced the fear of the unknown in traveling to a place he had never seen. By faith, Abraham received the call of the true God and began his journey.

The Bible does not tell us *how* God called Abraham. The call could have come as an inner compulsion within the heart and mind of Abraham, or God could have spoken with audible words. The important thing is that God did call Abraham and Abraham responded obediently.

Recently, I participated in Vacation Bible School at our church. One fifth grade girl asked me how God leads us today. She wanted to know how she could understand God's leading. Does God have to speak in certain ways? Hebrews 1:1 says: "In the past God spoke to our forefathers through the prophets at many times and in various ways." The different ways God spoke throughout the Bible seem to indicate that God can and does communicate to us in various ways. God is not limited to certain methods by which He can speak; He only allows Himself to be limited by our willingness to respond in faith.

▶ **How do you think God called Abraham? Was it by an audible voice or an inner conviction? Give reasons for your answer.**

_____

_____

How does God lead you?

_____

_____

Be prepared to discuss your responses in this week's group session.

The important thing is not the way God calls you but the fact that He does.

Blessings and difficulties. Blessings and difficulties always come when we serve God. For Abraham, the difficulties involved breaking ties with the past and moving to a foreign land. God's blessings more than offset the difficulties involved.

▶ **Read Genesis 12:1-9 to find specific blessings God promised to Abraham. Match the following words on the left with the correct Scripture on the right. Write the correct letters in the blanks. Answers are at the bottom of this column.[1]**

___ 1. Benefactor to all	A. I will make you into a great nation (v. 2).
___ 2. Power, prosperity	B. I will make your name great (v. 2).
___ 3. Property	C. I will bless those who bless you (v. 3).
___ 4. Protection	D. Whoever curses you I will curse (v. 3).
___ 5. Reputation	E. All peoples on earth will be blessed through you (v. 3).
___ 6. Support	F. To your offspring I will give this land (v. 7).

Abraham served God and obeyed His commands. The greatest words about Abraham are found in Genesis 12:4: "So Abram left, as the Lord had told him." Abraham's faith led him to obey the command of God. He left homeland and familiar surroundings in response to God's call.

Abraham journeyed with Sarah his wife and his nephew Lot through the land of Canaan, heading toward the Negev, a desert-like area in the southern part of Canaan. At each stop along the way Abraham made an earthen altar to the Lord who called him. Abraham followed God's leading.

One of my students is struggling with the call of God for his life. He feels led to serve as pastor in a situation that will be extremely difficult for him and his family both socially and economically. Can he go to this heavily populated area that has

---

[1] Answers: 1-E; 2-A; 3-F; 4-D; 5-B; 6-C.

no evangelical churches? How will his family live? Will his wife have to work outside the home? Will he have to take extra jobs?

The call of Abraham continues to be played out in the modern world. God calls people to obey Him. He calls us to leave the comfortable and affordable in order to serve Him.

RESPONDING TO GOD'S WORD

★ **Prayerfully check any of the following to which God may possibly be calling you:**
☐ 1. **To volunteer for a job in a church organization**
☐ 2. **To prepare for vocational Christian service**
☐ 3. **To tithe or increase your giving beyond a tithe**
☐ 4. **To witness to a particular lost person**
☐ 5. **To participate regularly in church visitation**
☐ 6. **To begin a daily Bible reading and prayer time**
☐ 7. **To seek reconciliation with a specific person**
☐ 8. **To focus on meeting specific needs of a friend, mate, child**
☐ 9. **Other** _____

★ **Pray for God to enable you to do what He is leading you to do.**

★ **Set a definite time to begin what you have checked. Write the date and time of day here:** _____

★ **Remember: Faith means trusting God *and* doing what He leads you to do.**

DAY 2 Abraham (Gen. 12:10—14; 16)

UNIT 3

GENESIS

The _____

_____

_____

Jacob
Joseph

▶ **You are studying the second major section of what Bible book? G_____**

Fill in the blanks on the overview chart in the margin.

Abraham and Pharaoh (Gen. 12:10-20). At this point Abraham did not follow God's guidance.

▶ **First, complete this pretest to see how much you already know about this incident in Abraham's life. Check your response.**
1. To find food Abraham traveled to

☐ a. the Negev.   ☐ b. Egypt.   ☐ c. Shechem.

2. Abraham said Sarah was his sister because

☐ a. he hoped her suitors would give him wealth.
☐ b. he was angry with her.
☐ c. he feared for his life.

3. Sarah's greatest admirer was
☐ a. Pharaoh.
☐ b. a prince of Egypt.
☐ c. an Egyptian merchant.

4. The Lord protected Sarah by
☐ a. sending adverse weather on Egypt.
☐ b. sending sickness on Pharaoh and his household.
☐ c. sending a drought on the land.

5. When Pharaoh learned Sarah was Abraham's wife, he
☐ a. had Abraham imprisoned.
☐ b. confiscated Abraham's possessions and sent him away.
☐ c. sent Abraham away with his possessions.

Now study Genesis 12:10-20 to check and correct your answers.

In the activity you just completed you discovered that Abraham went into Egypt to find food during a time of famine. This may seem to be a natural response, but there is no record of God's telling Abraham to go to Egypt.

God loves us even when we are not at our best.

In Egypt Abraham reached the lowest known point of his life. He faced many hardships and sad experiences. Sometimes he failed to act his best. Yet God led him all the way of his journey. When Abraham followed God, he found guidance and strength for daily living.

▶ **Probably you have faced difficulties, hardships, sad experiences. Check items in the following list that express your honest response to such occasions:**

☐ 1. I questioned God's love, wisdom, or justice.
☐ 2. My faith was strengthened as I trusted God to get me through.
☐ 3. I wondered if God had forgotten about me.
☐ 4. I felt as though God did not hear my prayers.
☐ 5. I was angry.
☐ 6. I just toughed it out.
☐ 7. I committed the situation to God and experienced His peace.
☐ 8. I usually go through a process that involves all the above.

Abraham and Lot (Gen. 13—14)

▶ **Read Genesis 13:1-7. Mark the following statements as T (true) or F (false). Answers are at the bottom of the column.[2]**
_____ 1. Abraham and Lot had a personality clash.
_____ 2. Both Abraham and Lot were wealthy in livestock.
_____ 3. Canaanite rustlers created problems between Abraham and Lot.
_____ 4. Bad feelings grew between Abraham and Lot.
_____ 5. The herdsmen of Abraham and Lot clashed.
_____ 6. Abraham and Lot owned much land.
_____ 7. Abraham and Lot parted because of their great wealth.

Both Abraham and Lot received abundant material blessings. Sometimes material blessings create problems in human relationships. Lot's herdsmen could not get along with Abraham's herdsmen. Each had so much livestock that the herdsmen found themselves competing for water and pasture. To solve the problem, Abraham graciously allowed Lot to choose an area in which to live and to graze his flocks.

Read Lot's response to Abraham's proposal in Genesis 13:10-13. Lot based his choice solely on material values. He looked toward the plain of the Jordan in

---

[2]Answers to true/false exercise: 1-F; 2-T; 3-F; 4-F; 5-T; 6-F; 7-T.

which the wicked cities of Sodom and Gomorrah were located. He chose that area for its prosperity. Lot did not seek God's guidance; he did not make his decision according to spiritual or family values. The decision proved to be the worst of Lot's life. From that point forward, Lot faced sorrow and sadness.

The most beneficial or profitable decisions may be the worst decisions of all.

Abraham never rejected his nephew. When Lot fell into the hands of four kings who fought the kings of Sodom and Gomorrah (14:8-12), Abraham rescued his nephew. Lot's later association with the people of Sodom resulted in the loss of his wife and future sons-in-law and in the degradation of his daughters (chap. 19). Lot's poor choices took their toll in human relationships.

► **Write A for Agree and D for Disagree in front of the statements below:**

_____ 1. The best business decision may not be the best decision.

_____ 2. The measure of a person's success is usually one's income.

_____ 3. The moral character of one's associates does not matter.

_____ 4. Anyone who wants to achieve great success must compromise on some issues.

Take another look at these statements. With which do you think Lot would have agreed? Circle your responses: 1   2   3   4

Possibly Lot would have agreed with all but the first statement.

Abraham and Hagar (Gen. 16)

► **Read Genesis 16 to find the answers to the following questions. Then use the following discussion to check and correct your answers.**

1. Whose idea was it for Abraham to bear a child by Hagar? _____

2. How did Sarah feel about Hagar's pregnancy? _____

_____

3. What did God promise Hagar? _____

_____

4. What was the name of Hagar's son? _____

5. Do you think Abraham and Sarah sinned in having a child by Hagar?

Was Abraham's having a child by Hagar sin? The answer probably is yes and no. Legally, what Abraham and Sarah did was acceptable practice in their day. However, they apparently acted because they did not believe God. God had promised Abraham and Sarah that their descendants would be as numerous as the stars or as grains of sand. Since they were childless and in advanced years, they decided to make God's promise come true by their own devices. The sin involved in this experience was the sin of unbelief.

Sarah plotted to have a child by her handmaid. When Hagar conceived, she felt superior to Sarah and showed it. As a result, Sarah treated her maid harshly and Hagar ran away. God spoke to Hagar and told her to return to Sarah. He promised that Hagar's seed would be too numerous to count. She was to name her son Ishmael. His life would be marked by hostility toward his brothers (Ishmael is the father of the Arabs, who have conflict with Israel even today). Hagar obeyed God.

RESPONDING TO GOD'S WORD

★ Have you ever found yourself doubting some of God's promises? Have you ever felt that God has forgotten about you? After committing a matter to God in prayer, have you ever decided to take that matter back into your own hands and deal with it?

★ Meditate on the following verses of Scripture and determine what God may be saying to you through these verses today.

"Wait for the Lord; be strong and take heart and wait for the LORD" (Ps. 27:14).

"I wait for the Lord, my soul waits, and in his word I put my hope" (Ps. 130:5).

★ Write a brief summary of what you feel God is saying to you through these verses:

_____

_____

_____

On the basis of what God seems to be saying to you, what should you pray to Him?

_____

_____

_____

Take a few moments actually to pray this prayer to God. Seek His guidance for today.

DAY 3   Abraham and Isaac (Gen. 15; 17—22)

UNIT 3

GENESIS

The Beginnings

The Creation
The Fall
The Flood
The Tower of Babel

The Patriarchs

_____

_____

Jacob
Joseph

▶ Complete the overview chart in the margin by writing in the names of the two patriarchs you will study in this session.

God's Covenant with Abraham (Gen. 15; 17). God promised to bless Abraham and sealed the promise by making a covenant. Covenants played an important part in the world of Abraham's day. They were as widely known and used as contracts are today. God used the form of the covenant to communicate His faithfulness to Abraham. God filled the *covenant* concept with new meaning.

CHARACTERISTICS OF GOD'S COVENANT WITH ABRAHAM

1. God's grace established the covenant.
2. The stipulations of the covenant vary in Genesis 15 and 17.
3. God gave signs of the covenant which would reassure Abraham and encourage him in his faithfulness to God.
4. God's covenant provided blessings.
5. God's covenant is everlasting (17:13,19)

covenant 1: a usually formal, solemn, and binding agreement: COMPACT 2 a : a written agreement or promise usually under seal between two or more parties especially for the performance of some action*

(1) God's grace established the covenant. Abraham did not initiate a covenant with God; rather God initiated and established the covenant with Abraham.

▶ **1. Read 15:18-21 to see what God covenanted to do?** _____

_____

2. Now compare the stipulations of the covenant in chapter 15 with those recorded in chapter 17. How are they different? _____

_____

_____

(2) The stipulations of the covenant vary from Genesis 15 and 17. In Genesis 15 the only requirement for Abraham appears to be his belief and trust in God (15:6). Paul in Galatians 3:6 picked up this emphasis on belief. Paul reminded his readers that the people of God are those who come to Him in faith. In Genesis 17, the stipulations are for Abraham to walk before God and for the males to be circumcised as a sign of the covenant (17:1,10-14). Yet the commands again have to do with following God. God commanded Abraham to live a life completely dedicated to Him. While Abraham could not live a sinless life, He could live committed to God.

▶ **Read Genesis 15:1-6.**

Notice Abraham's question and God's answer. God could have been angry or impatient because He had already answered the question (12:2, 7; 13:15-16). However, God dealt gently and patiently with Abraham. God's response should encourage us to bring our questions and doubts to God!

Abraham was not perfect, but God accepted him as a righteous person because Abraham believed God would do what He said.

(3) God gave signs of the covenant. These signs would reassure Abraham and encourage him in his faithfulness to God. In Genesis 15 God formalized the covenant by an apparently well-known and widely practiced ritual. Read Jeremiah 34:18-20 for more information about this ritual.

▶ **Read Genesis 15:8-21 and describe that ritual in your own words.**

_____

_____

_____

_____

We can learn these lessons from this study:
● The slain animals indicate the serious nature of the covenant.
● Only the smoking firepot with a blazing torch, symbolizing God, passing between the pieces of the slain animals indicates that God's covenant was unconditional; it depended only on Him, not on Abraham.

▶ **Check the following statements that reflect what Abraham learned from this experience. Answers are at the bottom of the column.[3]**

☐ 1. The promise of possessing the land would not be fulfilled in his lifetime.
☐ 2. God's plan for him and his descendants was a long-range plan.
☐ 3. God was willing to use customs familiar to Abraham to communicate His truth to him.
☐ 4. Abraham's descendants would not have smooth sailing.
☐ 5. One part of God's purpose in giving the land to Abraham's descendants would be to execute judgment on the sinful tribes that would then be occupying that land.

Webster's Ninth New Collegiate Dictionary [Springfield, Merriam-Webster, Inc., Publishers, 1984], 300.

[3]Answers: All of these statements are true. To check this, compare the numbered statements with the verses cited: 1-verses 13-15; 2—verse 13; 3-verses 9-10; 4-verse 13; 5-verse 16.

In Genesis 17, God confirmed and expanded His covenant with Abraham. Circumcision was the sign of the covenant. Since other peoples also practiced circumcision, this act received new meaning. Since circumcision marked the body, circumcision constantly reminded the Hebrews of God's faithfulness, Abraham's obedience, and that they belonged to God.

Circumcision served both as a sign of acceptance of the covenant and as a witness to the revelation of God's salvation. The covenant with Noah had been an unconditional covenant made with all the people of the earth, as well as with the animals and the earth itself. The covenant of Genesis 17 was for a definite group of people and demanded their obedience.

(4) God's covenant provided blessings. God does not leave His people without blessings. He gives far beyond our capacity to give to Him.

▶ **Draw lines to match the category of blessing on the left with the biblical promises of blessing on the right:**[4]

1. Descendants	A. 15:5, offspring as numerous as the stars
2. Property	B. 15:7, possession of the land
3. Long life	C. 15:15, buried in peace at a good old age
	D. 17:4, be father of many nations
	E. 17:6, kings will come from you
	F. 17:8, Canaan an everlasting possession

At this point God changed Abram's name to Abraham, a change that foreshadowed the birth of his son. Abram (which means *exalted father*) would become Abraham (father of a multitude, 17:5). God promised to give Abraham a long life and an heir and to give him and his descendants the land of Canaan. God promised to multiply the descendants of Abraham—all these promises to a man without a son born to him!

(5) God's covenant is everlasting (17:13,19). It has timeless validity.
Eventually, God did what He promised and Isaac was born (21:1-5). The greatest crisis of Abraham's life occurred when God called him to give up his son. Except for obscure groups, the western world does not see or hear of human sacrifice. In Abraham's day sacrifice played a major role in all religions. Unfortunately, most of Abraham's neighbors practiced infant sacrifice. God neither commanded nor accepted human sacrifice (see Jer. 7:30-34). God abhors human sacrifice and the loss of human life. He loves people and desires them to yield themselves to Him.

▶ **Read Genesis 22:1-18 and place a check beside each statement you can verify by what you find in that passage.**
☐ When Abraham received the command to sacrifice Isaac, he began immediately to obey.
☐ Abraham's willingness to take Isaac to Moriah shows that his commitment to God was complete.
☐ God's command for Abraham to sacrifice Isaac indicates that God desires primary allegiance from His people.
☐ On the three day trip to Moriah, Abraham refused to doubt God and his promises.
☐ When Abraham took up the knife, he was preparing to kill Isaac.
☐ God said that Abraham's willingness to sacrifice his son proved that he truly feared God.

God calls us to sacrifice ourselves and for that sacrifice to be a living sacrifice (Rom. 12:1-2)

You should have decided that Genesis 22:1-18 verified all the statements above. God had no intention for Abraham to sacrifice Isaac. Rather, He was testing Abraham's commitment to Him as Lord. Abraham yielded himself to God. He passed the test of obedience.

---
[4]Answers: 1-A,D,E; 2-B,F; 3-C.

> **RESPONDING TO GOD'S WORD**
>
> ★ Read Genesis 22:16 and John 3:16.
>
> 1. How do you think Abraham felt about the prospect of sacrificing his only son?
>
> 2. How do you think God felt about the prospect of sacrificing His only Son?
>
> ★ Read Romans 12:1-2, meditating especially on the words in verse 1: "in view of God's mercy." What should you be doing in light of Romans 12:1-2?

DAY 4   Isaac and Jacob (Gen. 24—27)

U N I T   3

The Patriarchs

Abraham

_____

_____

Joseph

▶ **Complete the overview chart in the margin. Use the chart on page 41 to check your answers.**

Isaac apparently did not have the initiative of either his father or his son. He dug again the wells of his father and yielded authority to his wife Rebekah. The record of Isaac seems to serve as an interlude between that of the two great men, Abraham and Jacob.

A Wife for Isaac (Gen. 24)

Genesis 24 reveals the beautiful and heartwarming record of Abraham sending his servant to find a wife for Isaac. The obedience of the servant and the strength of Rebekah are the highlights of the chapter. The servant prayed to know and to do God's will. He prayed for God to lead him, asking for a sign to indicate the wife he should choose for Isaac (24:12-14). When Rebekah came on the scene, she fulfilled the requirements for which Abraham's servant had prayed. She accepted difficult tasks with enthusiasm. She did more than she was asked to do. Rebekah showed that she was deserving of Isaac and of the family of Abraham. God answered the servant's prayers and provided a wife for Isaac.

▶ **How has God given guidance to you in a specific situation?**

_____

_____

The Death of Abraham (Gen. 25:1-11)

After Sarah's death, Abraham married Keturah. Genesis 25:8 shows the ideal life of an Old Testament individual: "Then Abraham breathed his last and died at a good old age, an old man and full of years; and he was gathered to his people."

Jacob

Isaac, Rebekah, Esau, Jacob. Jacob's history is filled with deceit and trickery. Jacob used people and events to his own advantage.

"Oh, what a tangled web we weave when first we practice to deceive."
    —Sir Walter Scott

▶ Do this pretest to see how much you already know about Jacob and Esau. Read Genesis 25:19-34. Beside the following words or phrases, write "J" for those that apply to Jacob and "E" for those that apply to Esau. Answers are at the bottom of the column.[5]

_____ 1. Isaac's firstborn son.

_____ 2. Would serve his brother.

_____ 3. Descendants would be stronger.

_____ 4. Red and hairy.

_____ 5. Quiet homebody.

_____ 6. Outdoorsman.

_____ 7. Mama's boy.

_____ 8. Manipulator.

_____ 9. Nicknamed Edom.

_____10. Shortsighted.

The birth and the birthright (25:19-34). From the beginning Jacob and Esau seemed to be at odds with each other. Esau, the firstborn son, was to receive his father's birthright, which bestowed the future leadership of the family plus a double share of the inheritance (Deut. 21:17). According to archaeological discoveries, the birthright could be sold or transferred. At his mother's suggestion and with her help, Jacob was able to make this exchange with Esau.

"Bread of deceit is sweet to a man; but afterward his mouth shall be filled with gravel."
—Proverbs 20:17(KJV)

▶ Read Genesis 25:27-34 to see how Jacob persuaded Esau to give up the birthright. What Jacob did was legally right, but do you think it was morally right? Explain your answer here.

_____

_____

The trickery practiced by Jacob and his mother knew no end. After Jacob took advantage of his brother Esau, Jacob and his mother Rebekah tricked Isaac. As the end of his life approached, Isaac called for Esau to confer his blessing on him. In Hebrew thought the formal blessing by the father held monumental significance. So Jacob and Rebekah conspired to trick Isaac into giving blessing to Jacob instead.

▶ Read Genesis 27:1-13 and check all responses that are correct for each statement.[6]
1. Isaac intended to give Esau his formal blessing because
   ☐ a. Esau was his firstborn son.
   ☐ b. Esau was his favorite son.
   ☐ c. Esau prepared his favorite foods.

2. In deceiving Isaac, Rebekah played
   ☐ a. a small part.
   ☐ b. a major part.
   ☐ c. the major role and directed the whole affair.

3. Without Rebekah's leadership,
   ☐ a. Jacob would have received the blessing by more subtle means.
   ☐ b. Jacob would not have been a manipulative person.
   ☐ c. Jacob may have missed Isaac's blessing.

4. Isaac was suspicious of Jacob's disguise because
   ☐ a. Jacob's voice gave him away.
   ☐ b. the goat meat did not have the flavor of wild game.
   ☐ c. the goat hair did not feel like Esau's hair.

---

[5]Answers: 1-E, 2-E, 3-J, 4-E, 5-J, 6-E, 7-J, 8-J, 9-E, 10-E.

5. Isaac finally was convinced that Jacob was Esau by
   ☐ a. Jacob's claim that God had helped him get the meat.
   ☐ b. Jacob's effort to talk like Esau.
   ☐ c. the smell of Esau's clothing on Jacob.

6. Isaac's blessing included
   ☐ a. material blessings.
   ☐ b. political power.
   ☐ c. rule over the family.

7. Esau responded to Jacob's deceit with
   ☐ a. grief.
   ☐ b. anger.
   ☐ c. a plot to kill Jacob.

8. Rebekah's plan to save Jacob from Esau was
   ☐ a. to send him away for a while.
   ☐ b. to send Esau away.
   ☐ c. to placate Esau's anger.

You might wonder why Isaac simply did not take back the words. In ancient times people believed that the spoken word could never be retracted. In reality, this is still the case. You may ask forgiveness for your words, you may confess your wrong speech, but words can never be taken back. Once they leave our lips and are registered on the brain of another person, they are there forever. The Hebrews viewed the spoken words of blessing in this way as well.

▶ **1. Can you recall an experience in your own life in which someone's words caused you great joy or pain? or greatly encouraged or discouraged you? Jot a note to remind you of that experience.**

_____

_____

2. Can you recall a time when *your* words caused great joy or pain, encouraged or discouraged someone else? Do you perhaps need to apologize or otherwise make amends for those words? Jot a note below to remind you of what you need to do. Spend a moment in prayer confessing your wrong use of words, thanking God for His forgiveness, and asking His guidance in seeking any needed reconciliation. Ask God to help you bless others with your words.

_____

_____

Rebekah felt that she had to do something to protect Jacob because Esau wanted to kill him. She sent him to Haran to live with her brother, Laban; and he stayed there 20 years.

Do people like Jacob always turn out to have the good things of life? Do they enjoy the fruits of their trickery without the sorrows of their sin? No. Punishment always follows sin. Jacob became the victim of Laban's deceit and we do not know that he ever saw his mother again.

How does God use someone like Jacob? Perhaps the answer is something like this: God used Jacob in the same way He can use you and me. Jacob certainly was not perfect; neither are we. He needed to grow in his spiritual life. So do we.

The latter experiences in Jacob's life helped him come to God, recognize his sin, and seek God's guidance. I am thankful that God does not judge us simply by how

---

[6]Answers: 1-a or b or both; 2-b is OK, but c is more accurate; 3-c; 4-a; 5-c; 6-a,b,c; 7-a,b,c; 8-a.

we begin life or by how we begin our adult years. I am also thankful that He allows us to grow and helps us to change so that we can become what He wants us to be.

RESPONDING TO GOD'S WORD

★ Take a few moments right now to thank God for His patient work in your heart and life. Renew your commitment to find and follow His will for your life.

DAY 5 Jacob and Joseph (Gen. 28—50)

UNIT 3

The Patriarchs

_____

_____

_____

_____

▶ Fill in the blanks on the overview chart in the margin.

Jacob's High Spiritual Experiences (Gen. 28—32)

Genesis 28—32 describes Jacob's journey to the land of Haran, his 20-year stay there, and his return to the land of Canaan. As Jacob left Canaan and as he returned to Canaan, he had encounters with God that helped change his life.

Jacob's dream (28:10-22). As Jacob left the land of Canaan, he stopped for the night. Being in internal torment, he dreamed a remarkable dream.

▶ **1. Read Genesis 28:10-22. List the promises God made to Jacob:**

_____

_____

_____

_____

2. What was Jacob's response to God's revelation of Himself and to His promises?

_____

_____

_____

_____

How wonderful that God works in our lives, changing us from who we are and what we have been! God focuses on who we can be by His grace. This experience might have been Jacob's first personal encounter with God. All his life Jacob had heard of the promises to Abraham and to his father, Isaac. In some way he may have understood that those promises applied to him as well. But as far as we know, this was the first time that Jacob ever came into the presence of God. For the first time, he knew God as his God, not just the God of his father.

Jacob had his personal encounter with God as he left the land of Canaan. This experience helped him recognize God as the Lord of his life.

► **Reflect back to the time when you first had a personal encounter with God. What were the circumstances? What means did God use to speak to your heart? What was your response? Would you thank Him for taking the initiative to draw you to faith in Him? Note: If you have never had a personal experience with God, ask your group leader or pastor to help you understand what this involves.**

After more than 20 years Jacob left Haran to return to Canaan. He was filled with fear because Esau's threat to kill him still haunted Jacob. Jacob prayed for God's guidance and deliverance. Genesis 32:6-12 shows four ways in which Jacob acknowledged God and grew in service and devotion to Him.

► **Read and think about your response to the questions below.**

- Do you need to acknowledge some sin to God right now?
- What promises in God's Word have helped you in your praying to God?
- Recall four or five of the greatest of God's blessings you have received.
- Do you need God's deliverance from some circumstance, habit, or influence?

Jacob Responded to God

- Jacob recognized his sin (32:6-8).
- Jacob prayed a spontaneous prayer based on God's promises (32:9,12).
- Jacob confessed his unworthiness before God (32:10).
- Jacob prayed a sincere prayer for deliverance (32:11).

Later that night, Jacob had a most unusual encounter with God (32:24-32). Bible scholars do not agree on the exact interpretation of these verses. That Jacob limped after the struggle, strongly implies a physical struggle. Whether the angel of the Lord wrestled with Jacob physically or the struggle was spiritual, all agree that Jacob encountered God during that long night. God spoke to Jacob and blessed him. Jacob (the deceiver) became Israel (the prince of God). So the Lord blessed Jacob and preserved his life from the threat of Esau.

In spite of—not because of—Jacob's sin, immaturity, and shortcomings, God used him to continue His covenant and to make from him a great nation.

Joseph

Genesis 37—50 relates the history of Jacob's family, emphasizing the life of Joseph. These chapters also show that sin always brings punishment. Just as Jacob had dealt treacherously with his father, Jacob's sons deceived and took advantage of him.

God blessed Jacob with twelve sons, but he loved Joseph more than the others. Joseph was spoiled by Jacob and hated by his brothers who were primarily the sons of Jacob's concubines. Because of their jealousy, Joseph's brothers carried out a horrible act of revenge. This act of revenge started a chain of events that would determine the future of God's people for hundreds of years.

Key events in Joseph's life include:

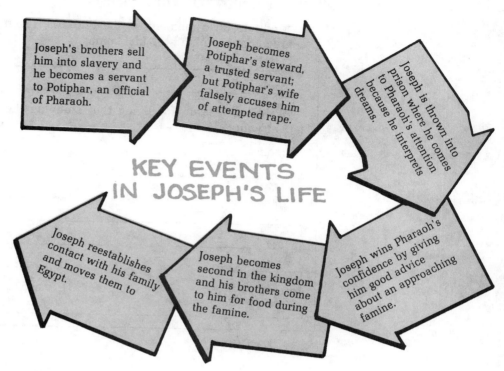

Joseph's brothers sell him into slavery and he becomes a servant to Potiphar, an official of Pharaoh.

Joseph becomes Potiphar's steward, a trusted servant; but Potiphar's wife falsely accuses him of attempted rape.

Joseph is thrown into prison where he comes to Pharaoh's attention because he interprets dreams.

KEY EVENTS IN JOSEPH'S LIFE

Joseph reestablishes contact with his family and moves them to Egypt.

Joseph becomes second in the kingdom and his brothers come to him for food during the famine.

Joseph wins Pharaoh's confidence by giving him good advice about an approaching famine.

The story of Joseph reminds us that God is the sovereign Lord of the universe. He can work all things together for good (Rom. 8:28). When we allow God to work in our lives, He can perform wonderful works we could never imagine.

GENESIS

1. The _____

The _____
The _____
The _____
The _____

2. The Patriarchs

_____

_____

_____

_____

▶ **SUMMARY REVIEW**

1. You have completed your study of the Book of Genesis with its two periods of Old Testament history. Can you complete the full Genesis overview chart in the margin? Turn back to pages 26, 41 to check your chart.

To review this week's study of the Old Testament, see if you can mentally answer the following questions. You may want to write the answers on a separate sheet of paper. Mark your level of performance on the left: circle "C" if you can answer correctly and circle "R" if you need to review.

C R 1. What are three promises God said He would perform for Abraham if he would go to the land God would show him?

C R 2. What did Abraham and Sarah do that showed they doubted God's promise to give them a child?

C R 3. Name three characteristics of the covenant God made with Abraham (Gen. 15; 17).

C R 4. What did Abraham's willingness to sacrifice his only son reveal?

C R 5. In one word, characterize Rebekah and her brother Laban.

C R 6. Under what circumstances did Jacob receive the name *Israel*?

C R 7. Which of the patriarchs had the most godly character?

RESPONDING TO GOD'S WORD

★ Meditate for a moment on the Patriarch Joseph. Do you find Christlike characteristics in his life? List some:

_____

_____

★ Write one lesson for living that studying the following patriarchs has taught you:

Abraham:_____

_____

Isaac: _____

_____

Jacob: _____

_____

Joseph: _____

_____

God and the Exodus (Exodus 1—19:2)

In this unit you will study only through the first outline point: Deliverance from Egypt. The remaining sections of the Book of Exodus as well as the Books of Leviticus and Numbers will be covered in the next unit.

Without the Book of Exodus we would know little or nothing about the Old Testament law or the early history of Israel. In this book, we have the Ten Commandments, the making of the covenant, the crossing of the Red Sea, the tabernacle, and many other important teachings.

Exodus reveals God's work of redemption and His call to obedience. Though Jesus did not refer directly to the Book of Exodus, it obviously played an important part in the history of Israel and in God's great work of redemption. From this great biblical book, we learn much about God.

Exodus:

   I. Deliverance from Egypt (Ex. 1:1—19:2)
  II. Making the covenant (Ex. 19:3—24:18)
 III. Instructions to Moses concerning the tabernacle (Ex. 25:1—31:18)
 IV. Breaking and renewal of the covenant (Ex. 32:1—34:35)
  V. Instructions from Moses concerning the tabernacle (Ex. 35:1—40:38)

DAY 1   The Book of Exodus (Ex. 1—2:10)

U N I T   4

THE LAW

▶ **The first five books of the Bible are described as the Pentateuch (the five books), the Torah (the law), and the books of the law. Complete the book titles in the margin.**

The Book of Exodus continues the story of God's people in Egypt and of God's making for Himself a people who would follow Him in obedience and faith. The Book of Exodus shows how the people of Israel became the people of God. It shows how Israel became a nation. The book further indicates how the people of Israel learned to follow the direction of God who delivered them from Egypt.

The date and authorship of Exodus are basically the same as the other books in the Pentateuch (also referred to as The Law or Torah). Please refer to the discussion of the Old Testament canon in Unit 1, Session 4 and the timeline in Unit 1, Session 5.

Israel in Egypt (Ex. 1)

Israel went into Egypt as a small family clan. Israel came out of Egypt as a great nation. Exodus 1:7 describes how God led the people of Israel and made them into a great nation that would one day possess the land of Canaan. This people truly would be God's own people.

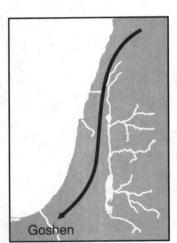

Goshen

The Book of Exodus emphasizes that Israel existed because of God. It also shows that God's blessing made the people a numerous and mighty people. Exodus 1:7 uses four phrases to describe God's blessing: "the Israelites were fruitful and multiplied greatly and became exceedingly numerous, so that the land was filled with them."

In Egypt, the people of Israel lived in the northeastern corner of the country near the Nile delta. The land was known for its cattle farming. At one time in its history, Egypt's capital was within the same area. Since Moses and Pharaoh spoke often, Egypt's capital must have been in the same region during the time of the Exodus.

After a long period of time, the Egyptians' attitude toward the family of Joseph changed. Instead of looking at the people of Israel and thinking what great things Joseph and his descendants had done, the people of Egypt became fearful. A new king, who recognized the dangers involved with a subject people living in Egypt's most vulnerable area, arose over Egypt (any attacking force from the north would have to come through the area inhabited by the Israelites and could conceivably enlist their support against the Egyptians). The people of Israel were strong and numerous. The Pharaoh decided to enslave and oppress the people.

▶ **Read Exodus 1:11-22 to find three means Pharaoh used to oppress the people of Israel. Write a one-sentence description of each of those means:**

1. (v. 11) _____

2. (v. 16) _____

3. (v. 22) _____

The Birth of Moses (Ex. 2:1-10)

Exodus 2 is a wonderful example of how God works in history and through people to accomplish His purpose. In the birth of Moses we see how God acted by raising a leader to release the people of Israel from Egypt. God worked and humans worked. God's providential care brought the Hebrews to the land of Canaan.

▶ **Read Exodus 2:1-10. Note the simple and direct way the account of Moses' birth is written. Mark the following statements as T (true) or F (false). Answers are at the bottom of the column.[1]**

_____ 1. Moses' parents were of the tribe of Levi.

_____ 2. When Moses' mother hid him among the reeds, she could have known that the daughter of Pharaoh bathed at that place.

_____ 3. Scripture indicates that Pharaoh's daughter knew that the girl who offered to find a nurse for the baby was Moses' sister and that the nurse was his mother.

_____ 4. Moses' mother went to live in Pharaoh's palace and nursed Moses.

_____ 5. Though Pharaoh's daughter knew that Moses was a Hebrew, she adopted him.

_____ 6. Moses' education was the best available in his day.

The story of the birth of Moses is simple but beautiful. A man and a woman were married. They had a family. Notice that neither mother nor father are named. Only in Chapter 6 do we learn that their names were Amram and Jochebed. The biblical writer wanted us to know that God is at work. The name of Pharaoh is never given. Biblical scholars certainly would like to know who the Pharaoh was. Knowing his name would help settle the issue of when the Exodus occurred.

The biblical writer wanted to communicate about God. He emphasized that God is at work doing His will in the world. While human beings are tremendously important, they go unnamed in the Book of Exodus. The writer wanted us to know that God is at work in human history.

▶ **Why do you think many historical details are not included in the biblical record? Briefly write your response:** _____

_____

Be prepared to discuss this question in your group session this week.

The account of Moses' birth and protection is captivating. His mother hid him for three months. No healthy child can stay hidden long. The baby's cry and the joy of the parents would make concealing the child almost impossible.

The mother conceived a beautiful plan. She decided to take the child to the Nile River. How ironic that the Nile served as the place of the child's deliverance (see 1:22). God works to protect His own.

Moses' mother placed the child in a basket, stationed the boy's sister along the Nile, and watched her plan and God's providence come together to protect her son. Moses' mother probably knew the habits of Pharaoh's daughter. She may have known that this daughter had a compassionate spirit, caring even for the Hebrews. Moses' mother evidently planned for the child to be found. She instructed Moses' sister to go immediately to the daughter of Pharaoh and suggest a nurse for the child—his own mother.

If this was the plan, it worked beautifully. God worked and humans worked to spare the life of Moses.

_____

[1]Answers: 1-T, 2-T, 3-F, 4-F (she raised him through infancy at home), 5-T, 6-T (he had the early foundation of Hebrew education, and the best that Egypt could offer).

DAY 2 Moses (Ex. 2:11—3:5)

UNIT 4

By divine providence Moses received the best of Hebrew and Egyptian tradition and education. Nursed by his Hebrew mother, Moses lived his early years in the home of his parents. As the son of Pharaoh's daughter, he received the best instruction that Egypt could give. This training prepared Moses for the future. At his mother's knee, Moses learned about God. He must have learned the wonderful stories of Abraham, Isaac, Jacob, and Joseph. From his mother he learned of God's promise to give the Hebrews the land of Canaan. From this experience he began to identify with his own people, the Hebrews. In all these ways God prepared Moses for the great day when Moses would lead the people from Egypt.

About 40 years passed between verses 10 and 11.

Between Exodus 2:10 and 2:11, Moses grew up. As a man, he identified with the people of Israel. He saw that the Hebrews suffered cruel oppression. He determined to deliver his people. However, Moses ran ahead of God's plan. The following exercise leads you to study that incident and its consequences.

▶ **Read Exodus 2:11-22. Check the correct answer for each of the following questions. Answers are at the bottom of the column.[2]**

1. When Moses saw an Egyptian beating a Hebrew,
☐ a. he was embarrassed.
☐ b. he was irritated.
☐ c. he was enraged.

2. After Moses killed the Egyptian,
☐ a. he felt guilty.
☐ b. he was sure no one knew what he had done.
☐ c. he was sick at heart.

3. When Moses stopped two Hebrews from fighting,
☐ a. they thanked him for his help.
☐ b. they threatened to tell what he had done to the Egyptian.
☐ c. they rejected his effort to rule over them and asked if he would kill them as he had the Egyptian.

4. When word of what Moses had done came to Pharaoh
☐ a. he tried to kill Moses.
☐ b. he exiled Moses.
☐ c. he was inclined to be merciful for his daughter's sake.

5. Moses left Egypt and traveled to
☐ a. Moab.
☐ b. Mithria.
☐ c. Midian.

6. Moses' good deed of defending Reuel's daughters from some shepherds resulted in
☐ a. his being given a free meal.
☐ b. his marrying into Reuel's family.
☐ c. his gaining a reputation for being tough.

7. "Gershom"
☐ a. sounds like the Hebrew phrase for "an alien there."
☐ b. means "a new start."
☐ c. is the place where Moses settled.

You saw that Moses' rash action caused nothing but trouble. The Hebrews apparently did not appreciate what Moses had done. When the murder became known to Pharaoh, Moses was forced to flee for his life to Midian.

"We know that in all things God works for the good of those who love him, who have been called according to his purpose."
—Romans 8:28, NIV

Even in Midian God worked to prepare Moses for what he would do later in life. There Moses learned the ways of the wilderness. He married Zipporah and received valuable help from Jethro, his father-in-law. If Jethro was a worshiper of God, as he seems to have been, Moses might have learned greater things about God while in Midian.

The Call of Moses (Ex. 2:23—6:1)

a. Jacob
b. concern
c. Isaac
d. slavery
e. God
f. Abraham
g. covenant

▶ **Read Exodus 2:23-25 and fill in the blanks in the following statements from the list of words on the left.**[3]

1. The Israelites were distressed because of their _____ .

2. They cried for help to _____ .

3. God remembered His _____ with _____ , _____ and _____ .

4. God felt _____ for the Israelites.

We see in Exodus 2:23-25 that God acted to deliver the Israelites because He loved them and cared about their suffering. In love God called the people of Israel out of Egypt. Verses 24 and 25 particularly speak of God in terms of a human being. Notice the words that are used: "God heard their groaning and he remembered his covenant. . . . So God looked on the Israelites and was concerned about them." Human terms never can describe God accurately. Yet these terms show that God really cares for His people and that He intends to work on their behalf.

God has a right time and a right method for doing His will.

Moses at Mount Horeb (Ex. 3:1-10)

The following materials will lead you to study the call of Moses recorded in Exodus 3—5. You will see that Moses was a real person with difficult problems. He proved to be a person much like we find ourselves to be on occasion—fearful and lacking confidence.

[2]Answers: 1-c, 2-b, 3-c, 4-a, 5-c, 6-b, 7-a.
[3]Answers: 1-d, 2-e, 3-g,f,c,a, 4-b.

Our lives are full of burning bushes. We just need the sensitivity to see them.

A FRIEND IN NEED

A COMMITTEE VACANCY

A PROBLEM IN YOUR OFFICE

A DISCUSSION IN YOUR CAR POOL

A COMMUNITY SERVICE NEED

A SICK NEIGHBOR

God spoke to Moses at Mount Horeb (the Semitic name for Mount Sinai). This mountain was identified with the presence of God. Notice that the passage describes the mountain as the mountain of God. Could it be that Moses had learned of this mountain from Jethro, his father-in-law? Later the Bible describes Jethro as a worshiper of the Lord. Some scholars think that Moses also learned of the Lord through Jethro and that God used these years with Jethro to reveal Himself to Moses.

Moses' call occurred during a normal work day while he kept the sheep of his father-in-law. Moses worked on this day as he had every other day. He cared for the needs of the sheep. How amazing that God often speaks to us through the ordinary experiences of life! As Moses experienced one more ordinary day, God called him to lead the Hebrews out of Egypt.

▶ **How has God spoken to you in the ordinary affairs of your life? Be prepared to share your personal experience in the group session this week. Make notes here to remind you of what you will share:**

_____

_____

In this ordinary daily task, God used an extraordinary event. He caught Moses attention with a bush that burned but was not consumed. Moses turned to see the bush and had an encounter with the living God.

▶ **Read Exodus 3:1-5.**

To be holy means to be set apart for God's purpose, or to be set apart from that which is profane. Any time you are in God's presence, you are on holy ground. Moses was standing on holy ground because God was there. Removing his shoes (Ex. 3:5) showed the reverence Moses had for God. In the ancient world, taking the shoes off indicated reverence. This was Moses' way of showing his reverence for God.

▶ **Mark the following statements as T (true) or F (false).[4]**
_____ 1. Only certain places on earth truly can be called holy places.
_____ 2. Removing shoes in a holy place was a sign of reverence.
_____ 3. Mount Horeb was holy only because God appeared to Moses there.
_____ 4. To be holy means to be set apart from what is profane or unclean.
_____ 5. To be holy means to be set apart for God's purpose.

RESPONDING TO GOD'S WORD

★ **Would you agree that God not only has a purpose, but also a time for that purpose to be carried out? Also, do you agree that God has clearly defined methods to use in carrying out that purpose?**

★ **Could it be that some early effort of yours to serve God proved so ineffective or fruitless that you gave up the idea of ever serving in that way? Ask God to show you the ministry or ministries in which He wants to use you. Ask Him for wisdom in knowing when and how to begin. Trust and obey and enter into the exciting realm of serving God in His time, His way, and His strength!**

---

[4]**Answers:** 1 is false because the presence of God makes a place holy; 2-T; 3-T; 4 and 5 both are technically false because each statement expresses only half the meaning of holiness; however, T or F could be correct answers for 4 and 5.

DAY 3 Moses' Call and Excuses (Ex. 3:6—9:35)

U N I T 4

When we put our life in the hands of God, we have the same kind of protection, guidance, and care that Abraham, Isaac, Jacob, and Moses had. We worship and serve the same God. He is as faithful to us as He was to them.

In the previous session you studied God's call to Moses. Today you will study Moses' response. When Moses was running ahead of God's will, he was willing to commit murder to free his people from their bondage. But when God wanted to send him and promised him success, Moses could hardly be persuaded.

Exodus 2:24-25 and 3:7-8 show us that God is a personal and loving God who cares for the individual needs of human beings.

▶ **Read Exodus 2:24-25 and 3:7-8. Pause a moment to meditate on how the truth of those verses applies to your own life.**

Moses gave five excuses to God concerning why he should not go back to Egypt and deliver the people of Israel. When you read through this passage, you may think you are listening to someone in your local church. These excuses sound contemporary. Today we will study the first three of these excuses.

Moses' Excuses

1. I am not worthy.
2. I don't know enough about God.
3. The people will not believe me.
4. I cannot speak in public.
5. Send somebody else.

Excuse 1: I am not worthy (3:11-12). Moses questioned his own ability to lead the people out of Egypt. After all, he had tried once and failed. Besides that he was a wanted man in Egypt.

▶ **Have you found yourself giving reasons for not serving God in some particular way? Some reasons are valid; some are excuses. God's answers to Moses' excuses show that his excuses were empty. Consider what these answers indicate about the reasons you have given for not serving God in some specific ways.**

God has an answer for every excuse. Moses asked, "Who am I?" or "Why should I be the one?" or "How can I go?" God said, "I will be with you." The word for "I will be with you" in Exodus 3:12 is the same word that is used in 3:14 where God said, "I AM WHO I AM." The answer to Moses' unworthiness is the presence of God. Moses by himself would be unworthy, but with God he would be able to accomplish what God wanted accomplished.

▶ **God also promised Moses a sign that would confirm to him that he was the one to go. Read Exodus 3:12.**

What was the sign Moses would receive? _____

_____

When would Moses receive that sign? _____

_____

Have you ever been a bit uncertain about what God wanted you to do? In that uncertainty, did you act in what you felt was probably God's will for you? After your obedience, were you confirmed as obeying God or rebuked in your heart as acting on your own? Be prepared to share your experience in the group session this week.

Do not let that get by you! Moses did not receive the sign until *after* he had obeyed! Three months after Moses led the people out of Egypt, he arrived with the people at Mount Horeb. Then he *knew* that God indeed had called him and had been with him. Often we cannot be absolutely certain about God's will until after we have done what we believed God wanted us to do.

Wanting to know for certain before we act is a normal human tendency. Sometimes God may give us that certainty. Most of the time, however, God wants us to be people of faith, following His leading and doing what we understand to be His will for us. When we have completed the task and are able to look back over it, we can see that God was leading us all the way. He gives direction to His people.

Excuse 2: I don't know enough about God (3:13-23). Moses said, "What is your name?" In Old Testament times a person's name indicated that person's character. Moses was actually complaining that he did not know enough about God. He probably felt that others could do a better job of telling the Hebrews and the Egyptians about the God of the Patriarchs.

Whatever Moses might have meant by his excuse, God made one of the most profound statements ever made about His character. God said, "I AM WHO I AM" (Ex. 3:14). In that statement He used two words, both of which are exactly the same in Hebrew. One of my seminary professors suggested that the first word may be pointing forward and the second word may be pointing backward. Both words in Hebrew indicate continuous activity. God's answer to Moses may have meant this: "The faithful God that I have been in the past, I always will be in the future."

God identified Himself as the God of Abraham, Isaac, and Jacob. God showed Moses that He was the God who had made a covenant with his fathers. God had led Abraham from Ur of the Chaldees and ultimately brought him to the land of Canaan. The same God who led and protected Abraham would lead and protect Moses. He was the God of the miracle child Isaac, born to parents past the time of childbearing. He was the God who wrestled with Jacob and changed his name to Israel. The message in God's name seems to be: "You can depend on Me."

▶ **Take time now to list things you know God has done in the past to guide, protect, and bless you and people you know.**

_____

_____

_____

On the basis of the list you have made, what can you believe God will do for you in the future? _____

_____

_____

What if we do our very best and others still refuse to believe and follow?

Excuse 3: Nobody will believe me (4:1-9). This excuse, like the previous one, may have stemmed from Moses' failed attempt to lead the people out of Egypt. The people had already refused to follow him once. Why should they follow him now? God responded to this third excuse by giving Moses three tangible signs.

▶ **Read Exodus 4:2-9 and list the three signs God gave Moses to prove that God had sent him.**

1. _____

2. _____

3. _____

Believers should not expect that God automatically will give a visible sign of His leadership which others cannot or will not deny. Moses would have been more faithful had he simply obeyed God without offering this excuse. God wants us to have enough faith to move out, believing that He will bless our efforts and convince the hearts and minds of others.

Moses' third excuse is understandable to modern day readers. In modern terms he said: "I don't have a dynamic testimony; people will not believe that I have a message from God."

In reality, God has not given us the job of forcing others to believe. He has called us to follow Him and to obey His leadership. The people of Israel had to believe for themselves just as Moses had to believe and obey for himself. You and I will face times when people will not believe. Even when others refuse to believe, we must obey God by doing what He calls us to do.

▶ **In light of the preceding paragraph, what will you do the next time you have an opportunity to witness or speak a word for the Lord? Write your response here:**

_____

_____

All of these signs had a purpose. God gave these signs in order that the people might believe Moses' message that the Lord God of Abraham, the God of Isaac, and the God of Jacob had appeared to Moses. The signs would validate his message from God.

The primary purpose of God's signs and miracles in the Bible is to lead people to believe in Him. God never gave signs merely to impress people or for the selfish use of the individual to whom they were given. God granted those extraordinary events in order that others might know Him and that they might believe that He indeed is God.

RESPONDING TO GOD'S WORD

★ **Meditate for a moment on what God may be leading you to do. If you have been making excuses for not acting on His leadership, evaluate the validity of your reasoning. Are you willing for God to make you willing? Tell Him that in prayer. Claim the answers that God gave to Moses that are appropriate to your situation. Write what you will do within two weeks about the matter:**

_____

_____

_____

DAY 4

Moses' Excuses and the Plagues
(Ex. 4:10—12:51)

U N I T   4

In the previous session you studied the first three of five excuses Moses offered when God called him. Today you will study the final excuses and you will see how God acted through Moses to secure the release of the Israelite slaves.

Moses' Excuses, continued (Ex. 4:10-20)

EXCUSES! EXCUSES!

1. _____
_____
2. _____
_____
3. _____
_____
4. _____
_____
5. _____
_____

▶ **As a review, list Moses first three excuses in the margin. Look at yesterday's session to check your work. Add the last two to the list as you study.**

Excuse 4: I can't speak before people (4:10-12). No one knows the exact nature of Moses' speech problem. The original language simply says that Moses was *heavy of mouth*, a way of describing inability to speak eloquently. Whatever the problem with his speech, Moses thought it would keep him from gaining a hearing.

God's answer should be enough for any person to believe. God said to Moses: "Now go; I will help you speak and will teach you what to say" (Ex. 4:12).

God gives His people the gifts they need to serve Him. This does not mean that we will be preachers of great renown. It does not mean that we will have the theological insights of Paul. It does mean that God will give us whatever we need in order to do what He wants us to do.

▶ **What evidence can you cite from your experience or observation that God equips people to do what He leads them to do?** _____
_____
_____

Be prepared to share this in your group session this week.

Excuse 5: I don't want to go (4:13-17). We are not sure why, but Moses did not want to go. He begged God to send someone else. In response God sent Aaron, Moses' brother, to help Moses.

▶ **Check the following statements with which you agree. Answers are at the bottom of this column.[5]**
   ☐ 1. God showed great patience and mercy in dealing with Moses.
   ☐ 2. In view of Moses' reluctance, God should have used someone else.
   ☐ 3. Moses had lost all confidence since being in Midian.
   ☐ 4. Moses was in a comfortable rut in which he could not realize his full potential as a person or as a servant of God.
   ☐ 5. Moses blamed God for not intervening 40 years earlier when he had to flee Egypt.

After God answered all Moses' excuses, Moses agreed to obey. Exodus 4:19 may record a turning point in Moses' life. God told him that all those who sought his life in Egypt were dead. Moses could go in peace, and God would take care of him.

---

[5]Answers: (1) I agree. Even though God grew angry with Moses, He dealt graciously with him. (2) I disagree. I am glad God uses us in spite of our failings and lack of faith in Him. (3) I agree. Moses' excuses seem to indicate a total lack of confidence. (4 and 5) The Bible does not support either statement. However, I agree that both could be true, based on my own personal experience.

▶ **Match Moses' excuses with God's response.**[6]

_____ 1. I am not worthy.
_____ 2. I don't know enough about God.
_____ 3. The people will not believe me.
_____ 4. I cannot speak in public.
_____ 5. Send somebody else.

a. I will help you speak.
b. I will be with you.
c. I will send Aaron with you.
d. You can count on me.
e. Three signs.

The Plagues (Ex. 6—12)

The plagues had their background in the Egyptian Pharaoh's stubborn refusal to let the people of Israel return to Canaan. In Exodus 3:19, God had said that He knew that Pharaoh would not let the people of Israel go except by a strong hand (God's). Pharaoh's hardness of heart kept the people of Israel in Egypt.

Hardening Pharaoh's Heart (Ex. 6:28—7:5). What does the Bible mean when it says that God hardened Pharaoh's heart? Does God determine how people think? Does He determine that people will act in opposition to His plans?

English translations differ, but the Hebrew text clearly indicates that God did not harden Pharaoh's heart until the conclusion of the sixth plague. Prior to that time, the Hebrew text either does not specify how Pharaoh's heart was hardened, or it indicates that Pharaoh hardened his own heart.

We know from the Hebrew text that Pharaoh started with a heart already hardened. God did not do anything to harden the heart of Pharaoh. He had done that for himself.

At the conclusion of the sixth plague, we finally see the specific language which states that God hardened the heart of Pharaoh: "The Lord hardened Pharaoh's heart" (Ex. 9:12). This statement probably means that God allowed Pharaoh to have his own way. He continued to harden his heart and rebel against God. At the conclusion of the sixth plague, after repeated warnings, God let him continue on in his hardness of heart. God did not use Pharaoh as a puppet. We know that the nature of God is to love people rather than to use them. Pharaoh made his own choices to rebel and to follow in his own stubborn ways. The consequence of his own choice was disaster for the people of Egypt.

▶ **How would you explain the statement that God hardened Pharaoh's heart? Write your own explanation of the statement that God hardened Pharaoh's heart. Be prepared to share the statement with your group.**

_____

_____

_____

_____

What We Learn from the Plagues:

Power and sovereignty are God's.

Laws of nature are subject to God.

All creation belongs to God.

God is in control.

Ultimate victory is God's.

Eventually, God gives us our way.

Stubbornness breeds stubbornness.

See Romans 1:18-32 for a New Testament statement of God's response to hardened hearts.

The Nature of the Plagues. The plagues were real events God used to free His people from oppression in Egypt. Several questions usually are asked about the plagues. For example, How long did the plagues last? Did these plagues occur one after the other and last no more than two weeks or a month? Or did they happen over several months? Many Bible scholars believe that they occurred over a period of time ranging from nine months to one year.

Some plagues have both a natural and a supernatural element. The "natural element" in some is that they were events that could have occurred in nature. The frogs, the locusts, the stinging gnats, the boils, the death of the livestock are examples. At the same time, note the "supernatural element" in each of these. There can be no doubt that they were the work of God.

---

[6]Answers: 1-b, 2-d, 3-e, 4-a, 5-c.

> **Factors that Declare the
> Supernatural in the Plagues**
>
> - Their timing
> - Their intensity
> - Moses' foreknowledge of each one
> - The Hebrews immunity from them all

Some of the plagues naturally could be expected to follow the others. For example, when animals die, we expect insects to gather. However, those pests afflicting the Egyptians and not the Israelites can in no sense be considered natural. The death of the firstborn might result from a plague, but it would not account for the fact that only the firstborn died.

RESPONDING TO GOD'S WORD

★ Are you aware of some of your acquaintances, or perhaps family or friends, who seem to be hardening their hearts against God? Write their initials below and covenant to pray for them each day for the next week. Offer yourself to God as an instrument He may use to touch their hearts.

_____

_____

DAY 5   The Plagues and Leaving Egypt (Ex. 14:5-22)

U N I T   4

The Purposes of the Plagues

The plagues against Egypt had two purposes. First, they were to show the people of Israel and the people of Egypt that the Lord is God. Second, the plagues were to bring about the release of the Hebrews. In this session you will see how the plagues accomplished each of those purposes.

The Lord is God. Each plague struck at the very fabric of the Egyptian religion. Here are four basic principles of the Egyptian religious system.
- Pharaoh was a god.
- The Nile made life possible.
- The sun was viewed as a god.
- Animals possessed religious significance.

The plagues attacked the Egyptian religion in all four of these areas. By bringing destruction or defeat in these areas, God showed both Hebrews and Egyptians that He is the Lord of the universe and that He is a greater God than the false gods of Egypt.

▶ **Draw a line from the plague to the Egyptian religious belief discredited by that plague. Answers are at the bottom of the column.[7]**

1. Pharaoh was a god.

2. The Nile made life possible.

3. The sun was viewed as a god.

4. Animals possessed religious significance.

A. Blood
B. Frogs
C. Gnats
D. Flies
E. Plague on livestock
F. Boils
G. Hail
H. Locusts
I. Darkness
J. Death of firstborn

When Moses and Aaron first appeared to Pharaoh to demand the release of the Israelites, they were rebuffed with arrogance and ridicule. The oppression of the people was increased (Ex. 5:1-10). What a change the plagues effected! Pharaoh called Moses in the middle of the night and told Moses, "Go! Get out of Egypt! Take all the people and everything they own." The Egyptian people urged the Israelites to get out immediately (Ex. 12:31-33).

Leaving Egypt. When Pharaoh finally allowed the people of Israel to leave Egypt, they headed toward the wilderness of Sinai. However, we do not know the exact date they left or the route they took. We are going to look at these alternate views, and you should not let that bother you. Remember: If having exact and precise knowledge of these things were important, God would have made that knowledge plain in His inspired Word.

▶ **Read about the confrontation at the Red sea in Exodus 14:5-22.**

As you read the following find on the adjoining map the three possible places where the Israelites could have crossed the "sea" in leaving Egypt.

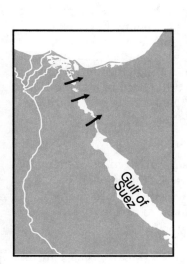

Bible scholars identify three different places the Israelites could have crossed the sea.

1. The traditional view is that they crossed the Red Sea. However, the Hebrew word in 13:18 means *Sea of Reeds*. Since the Red Sea does not have reeds, many people assume the Hebrews did not cross the Red Sea. Notice on the map that crossing the Red Sea would have brought Israel to what is now the Arabian Peninsula.

2. A second view is that the people of Israel crossed the Gulf of Suez. This is an arm of the Red Sea and would call for a miraculous work of God to provide for the people's crossing into the wilderness of Sinai. If they crossed the Gulf of Suez, they would have done so at its northern end.

3. A third view sees the Hebrews crossing a series of shallow lakes, which were drained when the Suez Canal was created.

Any one of these routes would have been impossible apart from God's divine intervention. Without God's miracle, any of these routes would have left Israel trapped facing certain capture or death (Ex. 14:21).

▶ **On the map, mark and number the three possible routes across the sea.**

---

[7]Answers: 1-you may have chosen any or all since together the plagues brought him to obey God in releasing the Israelites; 2-A; 3-I; 4-B,C,D,E.

From the sea the people went to Mount Sinai. Little is known concerning the exact route the people of Israel took to enter the wilderness of Sinai and finally the wilderness of Judea. In fact, we cannot be absolutely certain of Mount Sinai's location. Bible scholars offer two possible locations.

1. The traditional view puts Mount Sinai at Jebel Musa. The mountain is a rugged place which fits the description given in the Book of Exodus.

2. Another view places Mount Sinai to the south of the Dead Sea. Some biblical evidence points to a site closer to the land of Canaan. Also, the Midianites traveled in this area. Exodus 3 indicates that the mountain of God (Mount Horeb) was located in the Midianite area of travel.

The Time of the Exodus. Biblical scholars give two views for the time of the Exodus. Both views have considerable biblical and archaeological evidence to support them. Either date could fit the biblical evidence.

1. The first view dates the Exodus at about 1450 B.C. The strongest evidence for this date is the reference in 1 Kings 6:1. Adding the 480 years mentioned in 1 Kings 6:1 to the date of Solomon's reign (about 970 B.C.) gives a date of about 1450 B.C. for the Exodus.

2. The second view places the Exodus about 1200 B.C. The evidence for this view includes the cities of Ramses and Pithom which the Hebrews helped to build in the Nile Delta. These cities were not built until about 1200 B.C. Biblical and archaeological evidence of the conquest of the land of Canaan under the leadership of Joshua also supports this view.

Are essential facts missing? We would like to be able to be definite about the dates and places in Old Testament history. Since we know the names of many Egyptian pharaohs, God could have solved our problem by simply giving us the name of one of the pharaohs. Then, with the knowledge we now have, we could date closely the time of the Exodus. True, some of the facts we would like to have are missing. But not one of the *essential* facts is missing. We have all the information we need to learn the lesson God wants to teach us through the deliverance of Israel: He alone is God. He is the Lord of creation and the Lord of history. He is the great God who cares for His people and leads them through the dark and difficult times of life.

▶ **SUMMARY REVIEW**

To review this week's study of the Old Testament, see if you can mentally answer the following questions. You may want to write the answers on a separate sheet of paper. Mark your level of performance on the left: circle "C" if you can answer correctly and circle "R" if you need to review.

C R **1. What is the purpose of the Book of Exodus?**

C R **2. What was happening to the Hebrews at the time of Moses' birth?**

C R **3. Why did Moses flee Egypt?**

C R **4. What was Moses' profession when God called him?**

C R **5. Who did God provide to help Moses?**

C R **6. Why did God send plagues on Egypt?**

C R **7. How did the Hebrews finally escape the Egyptians?**

RESPONDING TO GOD'S WORD

★ Why do you think information about which we are naturally curious is sometimes not in the Bible record?

_____

_____

_____

2. What should be our primary purpose in studying a Bible passage?

_____

_____

5

God and His Law *(Exodus 19—Numbers)*

In this unit you will study many important events in the life of Israel that also have great significance for us as Christians. You will study the covenant, the giving of the law, the tabernacle, instructions in worship, and the experiences in the wilderness.

This unit begins with Exodus 19 and continues through Leviticus and Numbers.

Leviticus sets forth basic principles about how to approach God and how to live holy lives that are as applicable today as when they were first given.

Numbers begins with the people of Israel encamped at Sinai. The book is the story of their wilderness wanderings and of how God prepared them for their future.

Theme

Outline

Exodus:

   I. Deliverance from Egypt (Ex. 1:1—19:2)
  II. Making the covenant (Ex. 19:3—24:18)
 III. Instructions to Moses concerning the tabernacle (Ex. 25:1—31:18)
 IV. Breaking and renewal of the covenant (Ex. 32:1—34:35)
  V. Instructions from Moses concerning the tabernacle (Ex. 35:1—40:38)

Leviticus:

   I. Directions for offering sacrifices (Lev. 1—7)
  II. Establishing the priesthood (Lev. 8—10)
 III. Laws about cleanness and uncleanness (Lev. 11—15)
 IV. The Day of Atonement (Lev. 16)
  V. Laws about holiness (Lev. 17—27)

Numbers:

   I. Preparation for leaving Sinai (Num. 1:1—10:10)
  II. Journey from Sinai to Moab (Num. 10:11—22:1)
 III. Prophecies of Balaam (Num. 22:2—25:18)
 IV. Instructions and preparation for entering the promised land (Num. 26:1—36:13)

WordWatch

Watch for these words as you study this unit.

Priest/priesthood—These words describe a privilege/responsibility more than an office or position. It is a dynamic relationship positioned uniquely between God and people. In such a relationship "to priest" is to be the conduit through which each is taken to the other.

DAY 1 The Covenant

UNIT 5

This unit begins with Exodus 19 and continues through the Book of Numbers. In this unit you will study many important events in the life of Israel that also have great significance for us as Christians. You will study the covenant, the giving of the law, the tabernacle, instructions in worship, and the experiences in the wilderness.

The Covenant with the Nation (Ex. 19:3-7)

Chapter 19 records God's making the covenant with Israel and is the central chapter of the Book of Exodus.

Exodus 19:3 is the sign God promised Moses in Exodus 3:12

▶ **Complete this pretest to see how much you already know about this important event. Check and correct your answers as you study the following material.**

1. In verses 4-6, the speaker is _____ .

2. The greatest act of God witnessed by the Israelites was _____ .

3. Two conditions God required of the Israelites were:

A. _____

B. _____

4. If the Israelites would do those two things, God said they could be described by three terms:

A. _____

B. _____

C. _____

When we follow God in faith, the time always comes when we can look back and know that it was right to obey.

Covenant:
Contract...
Commitment...
or Relationship...

Nature of the covenant. Scholars define the term *covenant* differently. Some people think of it as a contract, while others think of the covenant as a commitment. I prefer to think of the covenant as a relationship.

At Sinai God established a new relationship between His people and Himself with a covenant, as He earlier had established a relationship with Abraham and his descendants. By the covenant, God bound Himself to His people and showed His love and grace for them. God emphasized the concept of relationship in what He said about the covenant in Jeremiah 31:33: "I will be their God, and they will be my people."

God's love (the Hebrew word is *chesed*) is difficult to define. To get at the meaning of the word, many biblical scholars describe God's *chesed* as His covenant love, a steadfast love that binds God to His people. Because of His love, He initiated the covenant and pledged Himself to be faithful in His relationships with the people of Israel.

Elements of the covenant. The covenant made at Mount Sinai contains three essential elements:

Covenant: Based on what God has already done.

FIRST, God based His covenant on His acts in history. In Exodus 19:4 God reminded the people that He had brought them out of the land of Egypt. Like a protective, powerful mother eagle, God had carried the people of Israel. He had borne them on "eagles' wings." The goal of His carrying the people out of Egypt and leading them to Sinai was to bring them to Himself.

SECOND, God gave conditions for the covenant. Unlike the covenant with Noah recorded in Genesis 9 God conditioned this covenant on two requirements. He required the people (1) to obey His voice and (2) to keep His covenant.

THIRD, the covenant contains the promises of God. God promised three wonderful blessings to His people. The blessings are found in Exodus 19:5-6.

A. God promised to make the people His own "treasured possession." The Hebrew word is a beautiful description of a special treasure. Out of the vast possessions of a king who owned everything in his domain, there would be a chest containing his very special possessions. These possessions were his in a way that was separate and unique from all else he owned. God affirmed that Israel would be His own treasured possession. The whole earth belongs to God, but Israel would be His people in a unique way.

B. God promised to make the people of Israel a kingdom of priests. The doctrine of the priesthood of believers came into being in Exodus 19:6. But priesthood is far more than the privilege of going to God directly in prayer. It is responsibility. Priests bring God and people together. As a kingdom of priests, the whole nation would serve God by bringing people to Him. This promise implies both blessings and responsibilities.

C. God promised to make the people of Israel a holy nation. To be holy means to be set apart for a specific purpose. God wanted to set apart this people for His purposes. He wanted the people to turn from sin and its harmful consequences and to turn toward Him.

God called the people to obedience and faith. They promised to serve and follow Him. Unfortunately they did not serve God for long. The only covenant Israel had was a broken covenant. The people immediately disobeyed God.

▶ **Check the best response concerning the first element of the covenant. Answers are at the bottom of the column.[1]**

1. God based His covenant on
   □ a. His promise to Abraham.
   □ b. the Israelites' needs.
   □ c. His acts in history.

2. *Chesed* may best be defined as
   □ a. God's covenant love.
   □ b. God's caring love.
   □ c. God's compassionate love.

3. The major difference in God's covenant with Noah and His covenant with the Israelites in Exodus 19 is that
   □ a. the earlier covenant involved a flood.
   □ b. the latter covenant involved conditions.
   □ c. the earlier covenant involved conditions.

4. Check the two requirements God made of the Israelites:
   □ a. To follow Moses faithfully.
   □ b. To obey God's voice.
   □ c. To make regular sacrifices to God.
   □ d. To observe the Passover every year.
   □ e. To keep God's covenant.

Covenant: Conditioned upon two requirements.

Covenant: God promised three blessings.

5. Read what was promised in Exodus 19:5-6; also read 1 Peter 2:9. Check the correct terms that are used of God's people in both passages of Scripture.
☐ a. Kingdom of priests.
☐ b. Treasured possession.
☐ c. Holy nation.

The Ten Commandments (Ex. 20)

The Ten Commandments are central both to Judaism and Christianity. While Christians believe the teaching of the New Testament supersedes Jewish dietary laws, we believe the Ten Commandments contain high ethical requirements that believers ought to obey. For this reason, we begin a study of the commandments here and continue through the next two sessions.

The Numbering of the Commandments. Read Exodus 20:1-17, and keep your Bible open before you as you study the following material. Jews and various Christian groups number the commandments differently. Jews believe that the first commandment is "I am the Lord your God." Catholics and Lutherans believe that the first commandment is verses three through six comprising what Baptists would call commandments 1 and 2. In this arrangement, Catholics and Lutherans form commandment 10 by dividing verse 17 into two commandments.

No group denies any part of the biblical text. However, the way the interpreter numbers the commandments reflects the way the interpreter understands the Scripture.

The traditional Baptist way of numbering the commandments seems more appropriate to me for several reasons. First, verse two does not read like a commandment. It does not contain a "you shall" or "you shall not" saying. This verse appears to be the basis for the commandments rather than the first of the commandments. While verses three through six could be only one commandment, verse three easily stands alone. Dividing verse seventeen into two commandments seems arbitrary and unnecessary. For these reasons, I hold to the traditional Baptist and Protestant way of dividing the commandments.

▶ **Write the answers to the following questions in your own words:**
1. What reasons argue against Exodus 20:2 being the first commandment?

_____

_____

2. Why is considering verse 3 as a separate commandment reasonable?

_____

_____

3. Why should verse 17 not be divided into two commandments?

_____

_____

Answers are in the preceding paragraph.

---

[1]Answers to multiple choice: 1-c; 2-a; 3-b; 4-b,e; 5-You could have checked all three. "A chosen people" or "a people belonging to God" correspond to "treasured possession"; "a royal priesthood" corresponds to "kingdom of priests."

RESPONDING TO GOD'S WORD

★ Meditate for a few moments on what it means to be God's "treasured possession."

★ In prayer, renew your commitment to obey Him and to live as one who is in covenant with Him.

DAY 2   The Ten Commandments (continued)

U N I T   5

Form of the Ten Commandments

Understanding the form of certain sections of the Bible helps our interpretation of it. For instance, in Bible days, the numbers three, seven, and ten indicated completion. Does this mean that the Ten Commandments are ideal and give the believer a correct view of life? That could be part of the message.

Did the commandments originally come in short statements beginning "you shall" or "you shall not?" We really do not know. Already, though, we have seen how a presumed answer to that question guides in understanding whether the Commandments are ten in number.

▶ **Read again Exodus 20:1-17. Decide which commands relate primarily to our relationship with God and which relate primarily to our relationship with other people.**

You should have discovered that the first four commandments pertain to our relationship with God--how we worship God and how we carry out our religious duties. The last six commandments relate to how we get along with other people. Properly understood, the first four commandments prepare us for the second six commandments. As we relate correctly to God, we are able to relate better to human beings. Commandments six through ten do not tell us simply how to get along with other people. They instruct us in how to get along with other people as we are influenced by our relationship with God.

By looking at the Ten Commandments in this way, we realize that those commandments are not simply rules that ensure a high quality of human relationships. The commandments provide a high quality of human relationships because God is involved with us.

In the diagram in the margin, A represents God; B represents another person. What happens as the two people draw closer to God? A person's relationship to another person becomes closer as each draws nearer to God.

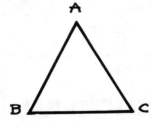

A. God
B. Others
C. You

Another way of looking at the Commandments is to view them in pairs. Although it is impossible to work out this design with complete satisfaction, they can be paired under the following five categories:

1. God (v. 3 and vv. 4-6)
2. Religion and Sabbath (v. 7 and vv. 8-11)
3. Family (v. 12 and v. 14)
4. Humanness (v. 13 and v. 15)
5. Social Life (v. 16 and v. 17)

▶ Read the pairs of verses above and decide why the five different categories were chosen to describe each pair. Make notes below and be prepared to discuss your insights at the group session this week.

1. _____
2. _____
3. _____
4. _____
5. _____

The Ten Commandments and Their Meaning for Today (Ex. 20:1-17)

The Ten Commandments are valid guidelines for people today. To be guided by them, we must find the true meaning of the Ten Commandments for today.

Verse 2 is not a command, but a preface and the basis for all the commandments. The Lord is God. He brought the people of Israel out of Egypt by His wonderful acts of redemption. On this basis He gave the Israelites commandments they were to hear and obey.

Commandment 1: No other gods (20:3). The first Commandment calls us to an exclusive worship and devotion to the Lord. No other god exists. The Israelites were to worship and obey Jehovah God, and so are we today.

▶ A. What other religions are represented in your community or your county?

_____

B. How should you relate to people who worship other gods? _____

_____

Be ready to discuss your answers to these questions in the small-group session this week.

Commandment 2: No images (20:4-6). God prohibited the making of any kind of image that would represent Him or that could be worshiped by human beings. To what can God be compared? What image could we use to represent God? God is Spirit. He cannot be represented by anything in the material world. To make an engraved image is to create God in our image. We control what we create; but God created us. Therefore, no image we could make would really represent God.

Commandment 3: Reverence God's name (20:7). Most of us who have known Christ for a long time do not use profanity because we know that crude language is offensive to God. However, the Third Commandment goes much deeper than profanity. To take the name of the Lord our God in vain is to make His name insignificant. It is to use the name of God in ways that do not fit His character.

In the Old Testament the name indicated the character of the individual. To take God's name in vain means to understand Him in ways that are inappropriate. To

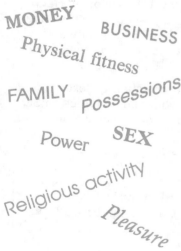

"No other gods" includes:

MONEY
BUSINESS
Physical fitness
FAMILY
Possessions
Power   SEX
Religious activity
Pleasure

Jealous: The Hebrew word means to have an intense desire for.

take the name of the Lord our God in vain means to defame His character. We break this Commandment when our deeds, as well as our words, fail to reflect God's character.

▶ **A. Is it a new idea to you that deeds as well as words take God's name in vain when they misrepresent, or defame God's character? With that idea in mind, list ways you may have been consciously or unconsciously taking God's name in vain.**

_____

_____

_____

"On the first day of the week we came together to break bread."
—Acts 20:7, NIV

"Upon the first day of the week let everyone of you lay by him in store, as God hath prospered him."
—1 Corinthians 16:2, KJV

Commandment 4: Keep the Sabbath (20:8-11). The Jewish Sabbath begins Friday at sunset and continues until sunset on Saturday. Christians do not worship on the Sabbath. For a while Jewish Christians worshiped in the synagogue on the Sabbath. Then they gathered on Sunday to worship again and celebrate Christ's resurrection. When Jewish Christians were later excluded from the synagogue, their worship moved exclusively to Sunday.

The Bible lacks specific instructions concerning how believers should observe the Lord's day. Therefore, we try to be guided by a careful study of the Sabbath Day in the Old Testament and by looking at how Jesus used the Sabbath Day to do good.

In the Old Testament, the Sabbath Day was the day to remember that God had created the heavens and the earth. This is the major emphasis in verses 8-11. In six days God created the heavens and the earth. The seventh day is a day of rest to celebrate His creative acts.

In the New Testament, we find that Jesus is the Lord of the Sabbath (Matt. 12:8). Jesus healed on the Sabbath Day. He noted that on the Sabbath the Father works and that He also works (John 5:1-17). On the Sabbath Day, He went out of His way to do good works. We should take Christ's teaching and practice as our example in observing the Lord's Day. As Jesus worshiped on the Sabbath, so we should worship God regularly. As Jesus cared for the needs of people, so we should make our day of rest and worship a day of caring for the needs of people.

The Lord's Day is special. On it we celebrate the resurrection of Jesus Christ. Each Sunday is a mini-Easter celebration. All of our work and activities on Sunday and every day should be pleasing to the One who is Lord of the whole world.

RESPONDING TO GOD'S WORD

★ Not all Christians agree on how to observe the Lord's Day. List some ways that you feel Christians can please and honor the Lord on the Lord's Day.

1. _____

2. _____

3. _____

4. _____

5. _____

★ Be prepared to discuss your answers in the small-group session this week.

DAY 3   The Ten Commandments (continued)

U N I T   5

▶ **Can you recall the first four of the Ten Commandments? Write a key word for each commandment. Look at the previous lesson if you need help.**

1. _____

2. _____

3. _____

4. _____

Commandment 5: Honor parents (20:12). This commandment bridges the gap between those that relate to God and those that relate to human beings. When we correctly or appropriately worship God, we show true care for our earthly parents. When we show proper concern for parents, we have begun the process of showing the concern that God has for all human beings.

Note two important facts about this commandment. It was given to adults, and it contains a promise. This promise probably is understood best as a promise to society, not as a promise to individuals. This commandment's promise is that a society that honors its aged people will receive the blessings of God. The unspoken warning in this command is that a society without concern for human beings cannot endure.

▶ **What is your response to this statement: Since the fifth commandment was spoken to adults, young children and adolsecents are relieved of the responsibility to obey their parents.**

_____

_____

_____

_____

"My son, keep your father's commands and do not forsake your mother's teaching."
—Proverbs 6:20, NIV

Although the fifth commandment is not a command for young children and adolescents to be obedient, numerous other Old Testament passages make it clear that they are expected to do so. The New Testament plainly says, "Children, obey your parents in the Lord, for this is right" (Eph. 6:1, NIV).

Commandment 6: **No deliberate taking of life *(20:13).*** Human life is sacred to God. No individual should take the life of another person. The most precise translation of this Commandment may be; "You shall not murder."

▶ **Read Matthew 5:21-26. In light of Jesus' comments on the sixth commandment, in your own words explain the meaning of that commandment for today.**

_____

_____

_____

_____

Commandment 7: No adultery (20:14). Committing adultery destroys family life. God placed human beings within families for nurturing, attention, and fellowship. Adultery destroys the vital elements of trust and respect in family life. Modern society has seen the tragedy associated with failure to take this commandment seriously. Sexual immorality destroys human society.

▶ **Read Matthew 5:27-28. Mark the following statements as T (true) or F (false). Answers are at the bottom of the column.[2]**

____ 1. The Commandment against adultery does not apply in our modern day with its changed values.

____ 2. Like many sins, adultery begins in the heart.

____ 3. Since the sex drive is so strong, we should overlook violations of the Sixth Commandment.

____ 4. Adultery is the unpardonable sin.

____ 5. A person can be guilty of adultery without touching a member of the opposite sex.

____ 6. Since Jesus spoke of a man lusting after a woman, women are excluded from His warning about lust.

____ 7. Sexual purity in our day is impossible.

Commandment 8: No stealing (20:15). In the ancient world, property and human life were bound inseparably. The loss of crops or clothing could produce hardship that ultimately resulted in death. This commandment does not place property above people. Rather, it protects persons' rights to have the things that are rightfully theirs. It also protects persons' rights to possess the things they have labored for and which are a part of their daily existence.

▶ **Check the box by each statement with which you agree:**

☐ 1. Goofing off on the job is stealing from the employer.

☐ 2. Taking office supplies for personal use is stealing.

☐ 3. Having a doctor write an illness on an insurance form to cover a routine checkup is stealing.

☐ 4. Not paying a legitimate bill is stealing.

☐ 5. Borrowing something and not returning it is stealing.

☐ 6. Not leaving a tip in a restaurant is stealing.

☐ 7. Not correcting a clerk's error in your favor is stealing.

☐ 8. Refusing to pay fair market wages is stealing.

Be prepared to discuss your answers in this week's group session.

Commandment 9: No false testimony (v. 16). We should care for other people's reputations as we care for our own. Hints, rumors, and insinuations have no place among believers. We should protect the reputation of other people as we wish our own to be protected.

The law called for two true witnesses before a person could be convicted of a crime. In "the gate" (where legal matters were decided) the word of a witness received high creditability. If two people decided to bear false witness, they could destroy a person's reputation and the person's life. Apart from honesty and integrity, justice cannot prevail.

We must remember, also, that perjury in a court of law is only one form of false witness. Gossip, slander, lies, and half-truths are just as much a false witness as perjury and are just as destructive.

---

[2]Answers to true-false exercise: 1-F; 2-T; 3-F; 4-F; 5-T; 6-F; 7-F (see Gal. 5:16,19,22-25).

➤ **Think of a time you or someone you love has been the victim of false witness. What was the effect of the false witness?**

_____

_____

_____

When is the last time you gave a false witness about another person?

_____

_____

Commandment 10: No coveting (v. 17). The Tenth Commandment has been called the most inward of the commandments. If you do not desire your neighbor's property, you most likely will not steal it. If you do not covet your neighbor's wife, you most likely will not commit adultery with her. When we meditate on taking what belongs to another, we have begun the process of committing sin. Refusing to covet is the first step in keeping the other commandments.

➤ **Do a final review. Try to recall the commandments in order and write a key word for each. Review your study if necessary.**

1. _____   6. _____

2. _____   7. _____

3. _____   8. _____

4. _____   9. _____

5. _____   10. _____

These Commandments are given by God to guide us in righteous living. When we take these Commandments seriously and seek to live as God would have us live, we begin the process of experiencing the best life available.

The Book of the Covenant (Ex. 20:22—23:33)

Exodus 20:22—23:33 commonly is called the Book of the Covenant. This name is taken from Exodus 24:7. While the Ten Commandments are found in "you shall-you shall not" style, the laws in the Book of the Covenant refer primarily to "if or when" situations. If or when a certain circumstance occurs, the law prescribed what action should or should not be taken.

The Book of the Covenant applies the Ten Commandments to particular situations. Some of the laws found in the Book of the Covenant have been superseded. For example, the laws concerning slavery no longer affect modern society. Yet, these laws provide principles on which to base our care and concern for people.

> **Principles Reflected in the Book of the Covenant**
> - Religious and civil laws come from the Lord.
> - Human life is of supreme value.
> - Gross retaliation is prohibited.
> - Class distinction is prohibited.
> - Weaker members of society should be protected.

RESPONDING TO GOD'S WORD

★ 1. What are some new insights you have gained regarding the commandments you have studied?

_____

_____

_____

★ 2. What differences should these new insights make in your life? ____

_____

_____

★ 3. Pray now and make a covenant with God about bringing those differences about in your life beginning right now.

DAY 4   The Tabernacle (Exodus 25—31; 35—40)

UNIT   5

How significant that one of the first things God did for the new nation was to give them instructions for constructing the tabernacle. The tabernacle was the symbol of God's presence in their midst and the place where they met with God to worship Him. If the number of chapters devoted to the tabernacle is any indication of its importance, then we need to consider it carefully. Exodus 25—31 contains God's instructions to Moses about the tabernacle. Exodus 35—40 contains Moses' instructions to the people about the building of the tabernacle.

The following diagram condenses these 13 chapters. Study the arrangement and furnishings. Note the rich symbolism of every part of the tabernacle.

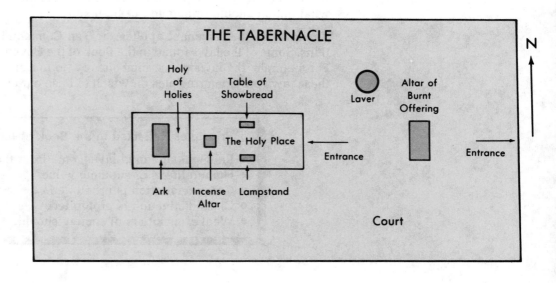

The tabernacle was a tent divided into two chambers: the holy of holies and the holy place. The tabernacle stood in an open court that was bounded by bronze posts and silver rods from which hung linen curtains.

The holy of holies (25:10-22; 26:1-37). The holy of holies contained the ark of the covenant, a box approximately 45 x 27 x 27 inches (25:10-22) which came to be regarded as the throne of God. Once a year on the day of atonement the high priest would enter the most holy place to make atonement for the sins of the people.

The holy place (26:1-37). The holy place was the second chamber of the tabernacle and contained the table, the lampstand, and the altar of incense. Only the priests were permitted to enter the holy place, which they did each morning.

The table (25:23-30). The table for the bread of the Presence (25:23-30) also held the utensils for drink and incense offerings. The bread reminded the people that God was present with them and that He gave them the necessities of life.

The lampstand (25:31-40). The lampstand stood in the holy place (25:31-40). The lampstand reminded the people that the way to God always is lighted. The New Testament describes Jesus as the light of the world. All those who come to Him leave darkness and enter the light. Some scholars also think that the light and the lampstand's resemblance to a tree presented the concept of life.

Altar of incense (30:1-10). Smoke from the burning incense represented the eternal presence of God with His people.

The court. The court was the enclosed outer area which the people could enter. This area contained the bronze basin and the altar for burned offerings.

Bronze basin (30:17-21). This basin contained water the priest used for washing and signified the need for purity on the part of the person who comes to meet God.

Altar for burned offerings (27:1-8). This was used for burning animal sacrifices and signified the people's need for forgiveness.

God provided the tabernacle as a sign of His continuous presence. He wanted to be known. He wanted the people to come to Him in obedience and faith. In the New Testament, Jesus Himself and the abiding presence of the Holy Spirit remind us that God is with us always. God's purpose has not changed. The tabernacle signifies the kindness, care, and faithfulness of God.

▶ **Meditate on the symbolism of the tabernacle. Then write a brief statement describing how the the concept embodied in each symbol is important in your life.**

1. The presence of God _____

2. Access to God _____

3. The need for forgiveness _____

4. The need for personal purity _____

Breaking and Renewal of the Covenant (Ex. 32—34)

Exodus 32—34 records a sordid, tragic event. While Moses was away from the people, they showed their instability and lack of faithfulness by rebelling against God and making an idol to worship. The following activity will guide you to study this terrible hour in the life of Israel.

▶ Read Exodus 32—34. Mark the following statements as T (true) or F (false). Answers are at the bottom of the column.[3]

_____ 1. Aaron opposed the idea of making a god.
_____ 2. Joshua told Moses about the people's idolatry.
_____ 3. God said He would destroy the nation and raise up another nation through Moses.
_____ 4. Moses prayed for the people, reminding God of His promises to their ancestors.
_____ 5. God ignored Moses' prayer.
_____ 6. Moses had stone tablets on which he had written God's laws.
_____ 7. Moses accidentally broke the tablets.

Even within such sad chapters, we see the grace and love of a forgiving God. Moses interceded for the people and God allowed them to live. Exodus 34:6 is a powerful revelation of God. God revealed Himself as merciful and kind, forgiving sin and bringing judgment against those who rebel against Him.

The Book of Leviticus

The Book of Leviticus may appear to contain little of value for us today. What can we possibly learn from animal and grain sacrifices, priestly wardrobes, and clean and unclean animals? The basic principles behind those laws answer the basic question of how sinful people can come into the presence of a Holy God. Those principles are just as relevant today as they were then.

Principles from Leviticus

- We should take our sin problem to God because He is willing to forgive and accept the sinner into His presence (chaps. 1—7).
- Leaders among God's people are to live holy and devoted lives (chaps. 8—9).
- God wants to be known to His people and He wants them to live in fellowship with Him (chaps. 11—15).
- God is a God of grace (chap. 16).
- All of life is significant to God. No area lies beyond His care and concern (chaps. 17—27).
- Our gratitude to God should lead us to worship and seek forgiveness and cleansing (chaps. 21—25).

---

[3]Answers to true/false exercise: 1-F; 2-F; 3-T; 4-T; 5-F; 6-F; 7-F.

RESPONDING TO GOD'S WORD

★ 1. Two formal ceremonies observed in most Baptist churches regularly are the ordinances of baptism and the Lord's Supper. As the Old Testament ceremonies were designed to remind God's people of certain basic truths, so are our New Testament ceremonies. As you meditate on the truths behind baptism and the Lord's Supper, rededicate yourself to the Lord's service.

★ 2. What elements in your church's worship reflect the principles that underlie the various laws in Leviticus?

_____

_____

_____

_____

DAY 5 The Book of Numbers

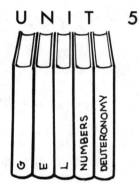

U N I T 5

Another tragic failure of faith in the life of Israel

▶ Do you recall the first division of the Old Testament? Complete the diagram in the margin. Answers are at the bottom of the column.[4]

Numbers begins with the people of Israel encamped at Sinai. God had given instructions for wholesome living and worship. Now the people faced a future with new experiences and challenges. God prepared the people for that future. He directed Moses to take a census. Then He had Moses organize the nation to assign duties to different tribes and groups; and He gave regulations to improve their lives. Giving such detailed instructions and guidance showed His continual protection. In the pillars of cloud and fire He was continually present to guide them on their journey.

How Israel's fear and stubborn disobedience prevented the people from entering the land immediately is a familiar story. Since leaving Egypt, they had continually complained about their existence in the wilderness. In preparation for giving the people the land, God instructed Moses to send spies into the land. However, the people rejected the counsel of the faithful spies and listened only to those spies who were fearful and unbelieving. God brought judgment on the people for their lack of faith. Except for Joshua and Caleb, no person over 20 years of age would enter the land God had promised. The whole nation would wander in the wilderness 40 years, the time required for that generation to die (Num. 14:10-45).

▶ Recall a time when you failed to follow God's leadership because of fear or lack of faith. Briefly describe the experience and its consequences in your life.

_____

_____

_____

---

[4]Answers to review: LAW, 1-Genesis, 2-Exodus, 3-Leviticus.

Even while we suffer the consequences of our failure, God prepares us for success.

What we have been in the past, to some extent, determines what we will be in the future. We are not bound by our past, but we are influenced and guided by past experiences. By structuring the present correctly, we exert a positive influence on our future. When God instructed the people of Israel about life in the wilderness, He also helped prepare them for their life in the land of promise.

Life often takes unexpected twists and turns. For example, when you were a teenager did you expect to live where you presently live? Did you expect to make your living the way you do? Most of us have found that life is not like we expected. In fact, the twists of life often make life more interesting.

If this observation is true, the people of Israel certainly lived exciting lives. Life took a turn when they left Egypt. Another turn came with the formalizing of the covenant and the giving of the Law. A radical turn came when they refused to act in faith and go into the land God had promised. Now their 40 years of wandering were nearly at an end, and life was about to take another turn for the nation Israel.

Once again, God turned the people toward the land He had promised. After defeating two kings who sought to block their way, they came to the territory of Moab. Though the journey from Moab to Jericho covered only a short distance, Israel faced significant obstacles.

Balak, the king of Moab, hired the prophet Balaam to curse Israel. God, in His sovereignty and grace, turned the curses of Balaam into blessings. What humans intended for evil, God used for good for His chosen people (22—24). However, at Moab these same people whom God had blessed turned to worship other gods (25).

▶ **Match the following Scripture references on the left with the correct topics on the right. Write the correct letters in the blanks.**[5]

____ 1. Numbers 22:5-6	A. Balak's second offer to Balaam
____ 2. Numbers 22:12	B. Balaam's first blessing of Israel
____ 3. Numbers 22:15-17	C. Balak's message to Balaam
____ 4. Numbers 22:35	D. The Israelite's seduced by immorality to idolatry
____ 5. Numbers 23:7-12	E. God's command to Balaam to say only what God told him to say
____ 6. Numbers 25:1-3	F. God's command to Balaam not to curse His people
____ 7. Numbers 25:4	G. God's judgment on sin among His people

Different directions produce changing circumstances.

Changing circumstances produce different obstacles and challenges.

New obstacles and challenges require new strategies.

In Moab, Israel faced new circumstances. New circumstances required renewed efforts to meet the needs of the people. Moses commanded that a second census be taken in preparation for entering the land (chap. 26). The daughters of Zelophehad demonstrated that new laws were needed to deal with the problems associated with inheritance. Moses handled these problems well (27:1-11).

▶ **A. Read Numbers 27:1-11. Remember that this passage concerns a matter of civil law. Put a check by any of the following statements that you feel are valid inferences to draw from that Scripture.**[6]

☐ 1. General rules will not cover every specific situation.
☐ 2. You can't fight city hall.
☐ 3. Changing circumstances may call for civil laws to be revised.
☐ 4. When treated unfairly, God's people should suffer in silence.
☐ 5. People should call unfair rules to their leaders' attention.

[5]Answers: 1-C; 2-F; 3-A; 4-E; 5-B; 6-D; 7-G.

B. Now read 36:1-12 about a further development concerning the case of Ze-lophehad's daughters. Check the correct answer for each of the following questions.
1. The leaders of Zelophehad's clan feared
  ☐ a. the loss of Zelophehad's lands to another tribe.
  ☐ b. that Zelophehad's daughters would not marry.
  ☐ c. the Year of Jubilee.

2. The Lord commanded Moses to affirm the following principle:
  ☐ a. Israelites should never intermarry with heathen tribes.
  ☐ b. People are free to marry whom they please.
  ☐ c. No inheritance in Israel is to pass from tribe to tribe.

Before Israel crossed the Jordan, God gave final instructions to the people concerning their days ahead. God reminded them of His presence and power and encouraged them for the future. The following activity will help you discover several important things that happened during these final days in the wilderness[4].

▶ **From the Book of Numbers answer the following questions.[7]**
1. Find in chapter 27 two things God revealed to Moses on Mt. Abarim.

  a. _____

  b. _____

2. The land to be occupied was assigned by tribes. Find in chapter 32 the two tribes that asked to settle on the east side of the Jordan.

  _____ and _____

3. What did these two tribes agree to do in return for having their request granted?

  _____

  _____

  _____

4. Since the tribe of Levi was the priestly tribe, they received no inheritance of land. Find in chapter 35 the provisions made for them. _____

  _____

  _____

The tribes of Reuben and Gad and half the tribe of Manasseh settled east of the Jordan but promised to help the other tribes take the more difficult territory west of the Jordan (28—36).

---

[6]Answers to multiple choice: A: Did you check 1, 3, and 5? B: 1-a, 2-c.
[7]Answers to study exercise: 1-Moses would not be permitted to enter the Promised Land, Joshua was to be his successor; 2-Reuben and Gad; 3-They agreed to help the other tribes take their land; 4-The other tribes were to provide cities and land for them.

▶ **SUMMARY REVIEW**

To review this week's study of the Old Testament, see if you can mentally answer the following questions. You may want to write the answers on a separate sheet of paper. Mark your level of performance on the left: circle "C" if you can answer correctly and circle "R" if you need to review.

C R 1. Briefly summarize the covenant God made with His people at Sinai.

C R 2. List seven of the Ten Commandments.

C R 3. How many of the Ten Commandments relate to our relationship with God and how many relate to our relationship with other people?

C R 4. List the three main parts of the tabernacle.

C R 5. List four of the six items of furniture associated with the tabernacle.

C R 6. What was the primary significance of the ark of the covenant?

C R 7. In one sentence describe the Book of Leviticus.

C R 8. Why did the Israelites wander in the wilderness 40 years?

RESPONDING TO GOD'S WORD

★ Are you aware of some injustices or inequities that exist because of present ordinances in your community? If so, pray for God's guidance about action that you could take to help people who are being adversely affected.

God and the Land of Promise

(Deuteronomy—Judges)

When God called Abraham, He promised to make him a great nation, to make his name great, and to give him and his descendants a land (Gen. 12:1-3). This unit is a study of how God gave Israel the land He had promised and how He helped them keep it.

Theme

In this unit you will study the books of Deuteronomy, Joshua, and Judges.

Deuteronomy is the account of Moses' preparing the people to enter the promised land.

Joshua is the account of military conquest. The primary message is that God led the people and gave them the land of Canaan.

Judges covers the difficult period when the people were trying to consolidate their holdings and establish themselves in the land of Canaan.

Outline

Deuteronomy:

    I. Moses' first address: Lessons from History (Deut. 1—4)
    II. Moses' second address: Lessons from the Law (Deut. 5—26)
    III. Moses' third address: The Way of Blessings and The Way of Curses (Deut. 29—30)
    IV. Miscellaneous materials (Deut. 27—32)

Joshua:

    I. Taking the land (Josh. 1—12)
    II. Division of the land (Josh. 12—23)
    III. Joshua's charge (Josh. 24)

Judges:

    I. Final battles and death of Joshua (Judg. 1—2)
    II. Work of the judges (Judg. 3—16)
    III. Life without leadership (Judg. 17—21)

WordWatch

Watch for these words as you study this unit.

Shema—refers to Deuteronomy 6:4-9. The word comes from the first Hebrew word in the paragraph; the word means "hear."

Judge—used in Judges is entirely different from judges in our society. In this context, judges were persons raised up by God during times of political or military oppression. Their function was to lead the people and deliver them from the oppression.

DAY 1 The Book of Deuteronomy—Moses' First Address (Deut. 1—4)

U N I T 6

THE LAW

▶ **The first five books of the Bible are described as the Pentateuch (the five books), the torah (the law), and the books of the Law. Complete the book titles in the margin.**

The Hebrew title for the Book of Deuteronomy is "and these are the words." This title comes from the opening words of the Book of Deuteronomy and points to the book's main emphasis. Deuteronomy contains mainly three addresses Moses spoke to the people of Israel in the land of Moab. The book concludes with the death and burial of Moses. Take time now to look at the outline on page 89.

Moses could not enter the promised land, but he could prepare the people to enter. In his three addresses Moses reminded them of what God had done in the past and encouraged them to be faithful by keeping God's law.

In this session you will study the first address in which Moses reminded Israel's people of their history. Moses looked on history as an opportunity to remember the past and learn from it. By remembering their past, the people of Israel learned that the same God who took care of them in earlier times also would care for them in the difficult times to come.

▶ **Read Deuteronomy 2:7. Meditate a moment on whether that verse applies to your life. Conclude your meditation with a prayer of thanksgiving for God's watching over you.**

As you look back over your own life's history, you can be reminded of how God has shown His care for you. If you can testify to God's wonderful blessings in the past, you can have hope for the future. The same God who took care of Moses and the people of Israel cares for you. The same God who carried you in earlier days will guide you in the difficult days ahead. You can count on God.

Let's look now at the things Moses called to the people's remembrance to see what we can learn from them.

What happens when leaders get too busy?

Who should receive special favors and preferred treatment?

Fair and equitable judgments. In 1:9-18, Moses reminded the people how they had been divided into groups with judges to make decisions over those groups.

▶ **Read Deuteronomy 1:9-18. Mark the following statements as T (true) or (F) false. Answers are at the bottom of the column.[1]**
____ 1. The number of Israelites was to Moses both a problem and a cause for praise.
____ 2. Moses chose the leaders who were to have authority as judges over the people.
____ 3. The judges were to use a different standard of judgment when disputes were between Israelites and non-Israelites.
____ 4. Judges generally were expected to rule in favor of the poor and powerless.
____ 5. Moses was to hear any case too difficult for the appointed judges.
____ 6. The larger a group's membership becomes, the more complex the organization and administration of the group's affairs become.

---
[1]Answers: 1-T; 2-F; 3-F; 4-F; 5-T; 6-T.

What happens when fear outweighs faith?

_____

_____

_____

_____

What happens when you decide to obey after it is too late?

The Tragedy of Lack of Faith. In a previous session you studied how the people did not have enough faith to follow God and claim the promise He had made to them. You also saw the tragic consequences of their decision born out of fear.

➤ **What circumstances of life today does Satan use to try to fill us with enough fear to outweigh our faith? Write these below the balance scale in the margin.**

Now meditate on these Scriptures that encourage faith:

- 2 Corinthians 4:7-11
- Psalm 32
- Luke 12:22-32
- 1 Corinthians 10:13

Moses called on the Israelites to remember another bitter lesson they had learned. God's people must do *what* He tells them to do. And they must do it *when* He says. The following activity will guide you as you study what the people learned about deciding to obey after it is too late.

➤ **Read 1:41-46 and mark the correct answer or answers. Answers are at the bottom of the column.[2]**

1. The people decided to change their minds and enter the promised land
☐ a. because they remembered what God already had done in their behalf.
☐ b. because Moses convinced them they were wrong.
☐ c. because of God's pronounced punishment.

2. When the people decided to enter the promised land, the Lord
☐ a. warned them not to go in.
☐ b. was pleased.
☐ c. said He would not be with them.

3. When the people were defeated by the Amorites, God
☐ a. ignored their cries.
☐ b. told them to try again.
☐ c. told them to try later.

The second chapter of Deuteronomy describes the 38 years Israel spent in the wilderness after the people came to Kadesh-Barnea. Moses recalled how that entire generation passed away and missed the wonderful opportunity of taking the land of promise.

➤ **Read Deuteronomy 2:14-15. What do these verses teach about God's words of warning and judgment?**

_____

_____

Your answer should have included the idea that God means what He says, that He does what He says He will do.

In chapter 3, Moses described the difficulties of entering the land. He told how Og, the king of Bashan, battled against the people of Israel.

➤ **Read Deuteronomy 3:3-4 and fill in the blank: The key to victory was . . .**

_____

The people of Israel prevailed because God gave Og into their hands. God was the key to their victory. He reminded the people of what He had done for them in the past. Speaking through Moses, He called on them to serve Him diligently and to do His will.

---

[2]Answers: 1-c; 2-a,c; 3-a.

The fourth chapter of Deuteronomy instructed the people to obey God so they might receive the full blessings which God intended for them. Moses cautioned the people against forgetting that God had led them to this place and encouraged them to keep the Ten Commandments.

▶ **Read Deuteronomy 4:1-2. Answer the following questions:**
1. How do people add to God's commandments today? _____

_____

2. How do people subtract from God's commandments today? _____

_____

Your answers may have indicated that people add to God's commandments when they insist that God's people keep non-biblical rules and regulations (see Mark 7:1-23 for a biblical example). People subtract from God's commandments by declaring them out of date or irrelevant for today. In a sense, any disobedience is subtracting from God's commandments.

Deuteronomy chapter four also describes the God whom the people of Israel worshiped.

▶ **Read Deuteronomy 4:32-40. Then match the following statements on the left with the correct references on the right. Write the correct letters in the blanks.[3]**

_____ 1. God reveals Himself to people.   A. Deut. 4:32
_____ 2. God redeems His people.   B. Deut. 4:33
_____ 3. God offers security for the days ahead. C. Deut. 4:35, 39
_____ 4. God is incomparable.   D. Deut. 4:37
_____ 5. God is the only God.   E. Deut. 4:38
_____ 6. God is the God of providential mercy. F. Deut. 4:39-40

RESPONDING TO GOD'S WORD

★ Meditate on the following statements about God:
- He is incomparable (Deut. 4:32).
- He reveals Himself to people (Deut. 4:33).
- The Lord is the only God (Deut. 4:35, 39).
- He redeems His people (Deut. 4:37).
- He is the God of providential mercy (Deut. 4:38).
- He offers security for the days ahead (Deut. 4:39-40).

★ In prayer, praise Him for Who He is. Rejoice that you can count on Him!

---

[3]Answers to matching exercise: 1-B, 2-D; 3-F; 4-A; 5-C; 6-E.

DAY 2 Moses' Second Address (Deut. 5—26)

U N I T   6

The Law

Moses began the second speech by restating the law and calling on the Israelites to obey the law of God. Notice in Deuteronomy 5:5-21 a review of the Ten Commandments. While the commandments are the same as those found in Exodus 20, some of the accompanying remarks are different.

▶ **A. Compare Exodus 20:8-11 with Deuteronomy 5:12-15. Briefly explain what Exodus includes that Deuteronomy omits:**

_____

_____

B. Briefly explain what Deuteronomy includes that Exodus omits:

_____

_____

Your answers should indicate that Exodus emphasizes not working on the Sabbath because God completed His work in six days and rested on the seventh. This is not in Deuteronomy.

Deuteronomy emphasizes that keeping the Sabbath involves remembering that the people were servants in the land of Egypt and that the Lord brought them out with His mighty hand. Moses reminded the people that they had been slaves in Egypt and therefore should allow their slaves to rest on the Sabbath Day. This is not in Exodus.

Deuteronomy 6:4-9 is often called the Shema. This title comes from the first Hebrew word in the paragraph. The word means "hear," but carries the weight of:
- Listen to me!
- Pay attention!
- Now hear this!

▶ **What is so important for us to hear? Read 6:4-9 and list in the box in the margin the four things God wants to be sure we hear.**

In the preceding exercise you should have expressed these ideas in your own words: The Lord is one God; we must love Him with all our being; we must pass this knowledge along to our children; and we are to cultivate a constant awareness of God's law.

Three Key Ideas

Chapters 7—11 present three key ideas that are essential to the relationship between God and His children. Complete the following pretest to see how well you understand those concepts. Then check and correct your work as you study the material that follows.

Compare Ephesians 2:8-9. →

▶ **1. On what basis had God chosen Israel (chap. 7)?** _____

_____

LISTEN TO ME!

PAY ATTENTION!

1.

2.

3.

4.

NOW HEAR THIS!

Compare Luke 12:17-21. →

2. Why are periods of prosperity dangerous times for God's people (chap. 8)?

_____

Compare Matthew 24:14-30. →

3. What factor determines whether God's people receive the blessing He wants them to have (chap. 11)? _____

_____

Moses explained why God chose the people of Israel to be His own people. His reason was not Israel's greatness or genius for religion or size. God chose Israel because He loved Israel. In His love He honored His promise to Abraham, Isaac, and Jacob. God was faithful to the covenant relationship. The people of Israel could depend on Him.

Isn't it interesting that the best times are sometimes the worst times? Most of us can accept difficult times and make the most of it. In fact, difficult times often draw us closer to the Lord. We have difficulty with good times. When life seems easy, we may tend to drift away from God rather than giving thanks for the good things He has given. Moses warned the people of Israel to be faithful and obedient in the good times.

God provided a way that would result in blessings; He warned against a way that would lead to being cursed. Obedience would bring the blessing of God. Disobedience would remove the blessing and leave only a curse.

Focus on God

Chapters 12 and 13 record two actions God took in order to focus the people's worship on Himself:

- **First**, He established one central sanctuary for worship and commanded the destruction of pagan idols and shrines.

▶ **In your own words, why was it essential for this to be done?** _____

_____

_____

Check your answer against 12:29-30.

- **Second**, He established three feast days:

1. *The Passover* occurred in March or April each year. During the feast of Passover, the people of Israel celebrated the death angel's passing over their homes on the night that the firstborn of the Egyptians were killed.

2. *The Feast of Pentecost* was celebrated fifty days or seven weeks after the Passover in May or June, so it also was known as the Feast of Weeks. Another name was the Feast of First Fruits, for it came after the first barley harvest.

3. *The Feast of Tabernacles or Booths* reenacted the Israelites' journey in the wilderness. The people made booths or shelters to commemorate their ancestors' living in tents during their wilderness wanderings. The people observed this feast later in the year during October. This feast also was known as Ingathering because it came at the end of the great harvest.

The Book of Deuteronomy emphasizes faithfulness and obedience. God gave Israel the land of Canaan. He made clear that for them to live there in security, they would have to obey Him. On the Plains of Moab, Moses encouraged the people to obey God all their lives. There Moses spoke his last words to the people. He died at the age of 120, before the people of Israel entered into the promised land.

THE LAW

▶ You have completed your study of the books of the Pentateuch. These five books also are known by two other names. They are:

The T _____ and The L _____.

Write in the names of all five books in the margin. Answers are at the bottom of this column.[4]

RESPONDING TO GOD'S WORD

★ What annual religious celebrations or seasons does your church observe?

_____

★ What value do you see in such annual celebrations? _____

_____

★ Which is most meaningful to you? _____

★ What makes it most meaningful to you? _____

_____

★ Take a moment to thank God for this observance.

★ Consider the intensity and quality of your singular focus on God and commitment to Him. What can you do to remove the distractions and foster your focus and commitment?

_____

_____

_____

DAY 3 The Book of Joshua

U N I T 6

The second division of the Old Testament is history. Joshua is the first book in that division. Look at the bookcase on the back of this book to see what other books are in this division.

The Book of Joshua

The Book of Joshua begins a new era in Israel's history. For the first time as a nation, Israel did not have Moses as leader. Moses' faithful assistant Joshua led the people from this point forward. Joshua proved to be a capable and effective leader. His method for taking the land of Canaan was that of divide and conquer. He led the people to establish themselves within the land.

---

[4]Answers: Torah, Law, Genesis, Exodus, Leviticus, Numbers, Deuteronomy.

▶ The introduction to this unit told you that Joshua has three main divisions and what those divisions are. Can you recall them and write them here? If not, look back at page 89.

1. Chapters 1—12 _____

2. Chapters 12—24 _____

3. Chapter 24 _____

As with many other books of the Old Testament, the authorship of the Book of Joshua is anonymous. Some chapters contain the preaching of Joshua. Joshua charged the people to serve God and to remain loyal to the covenant relationship. Joshua preached and promised that if the people were obedient to God, God would allow them to live forever in the land He had given to them.

The Conquest of the Land (Josh. 1—12)

The first 12 chapters of the Book of Joshua tell how the people of Israel captured the land of Canaan. Although the book is an account of military conquest, the primary message is that God led the people and gave them the land of Canaan. God required the people of Israel to demonstrate faith and courage, but God gave them the land. The Israelites could not claim that superior military techniques enabled them to conquer the land of Canaan. God led them all the way and gave them the land He had promised.

Joshua's Commission (Josh. 1). The great leader Moses had died. No longer could Israel turn to Moses in times of trouble and distress. The Lord commissioned Joshua to continue the work Moses had begun. Now, Joshua would be the leader of the people of Israel.

▶ Read Joshua 1:1-5. In this part of God's commission to Joshua, which words do you think were most helpful to Joshua? In the space below, write the words, phrases, or sentences and explain how you think Joshua was helped.

_____

_____

_____

Read Joshua 1:6-9. Answer the following questions. Answers are at the bottom of the column.[5]

1. How many times did God tell Joshua in verses 6-9 to be strong and courageous? _____

2. Why do you think God repeated that charge? _____

_____

3. List God's instructions to Joshua concerning the law: _____

_____

_____

Crossing the Jordan (Josh. 1:10-18). Before Joshua led the people of Israel across the Jordan River, he allotted the east bank of the Jordan to the tribes of Reuben, Gad, and to half the tribe of Manasseh. These tribes raised cattle. The area east of the Jordan was well suited to their needs.

----

[5]Answers: 1-3; 2-God was calling him to a fearful task that at times would seem impossible; 3-your answer should have included the ideas of speaking of the law, meditating on the law, and doing all that the law said.

Joshua placed one stipulation on the men of these tribes. Since the land east of the Jordan would not have to be conquered, Joshua commanded that the men of Reuben, Gad, and the half-tribe of Manasseh leave their wives, children, and belongings behind and help the other tribes take the land of Canaan. The leaders of these tribes quickly agreed to Joshua's request. After the Israelites settled in the land of Canaan, the men of these tribes could return to their new land east of the Jordan and live in peace.

▶ **Mark the following statements as T (true) or F (false):[6]**

_____ 1. Some tribes were given territory east of the Jordan.

_____ 2. Three tribes did not have to fight for the land they received.

_____ 3. The tribes that settled east of Jordan were Reuben, Gad, and Manasseh.

_____ 4. The land east of the Jordan was well suited for raising grain.

Spies in Jericho (Josh. 2:1-24). Joshua sent two men to cross the Jordan and spy out Jericho. As these men entered the city, they were hidden by Rahab, a prostitute. She protected the men and gave valuable information concerning the fortification of Jericho. When Israel captured Jericho, Rahab received protection from them. She was remembered as a heroine in Israel's history.

▶ **Read Joshua 2:8-14 and answer the following questions:[7]**

1. To whom did Rahab credit the Israelites' victories? _____

2. How would you describe the morale of the Canaanites? _____

3. What deal did Rahab make with the spies? _____

4. How do Hebrews 11:31 and James 2:23-26 help us understand Rahab's reason for helping the Israelites?

_____

God's Leadership and Israel's Obedience (Josh. 3:1—5:15). Before Israel crossed the Jordan, the people consecrated themselves anew to the Lord. They recognized God's leadership and indicated their own obedience by worshiping God and following the ark of the covenant.

God allowed the people to cross the Jordan on dry land. The priests carrying the ark of the covenant first entered the waters. The ark symbolized the presence of God among His people. In a real sense, when the people followed the ark of the covenant, they followed God.

▶ **Read Joshua 4:4-9 and fill in the blanks.[8]**

1. Joshua appointed a man from each of Israel's _____ .

2. Each man picked up a stone from _____ .

3. The stones were used to build a _____ .

4. The stones were to remind the people of following generations that

_____ .

---

[6]Answers: 1-T; 2-F, but this is a tricky statement—the Israelites had earlier defeated the tribes in that area, and the tribes receiving the land had to agree to fight to help win the land for the other tribes; 3-F, Reuben, Gad, and half the tribe of Manasseh; 4-F, it was good for raising livestock.

[7]Answers: 1-God; 2-Their courage had failed; morale was at rock bottom; 3-She and her family would be spared in return for helping the Israelites; 4-She was acting on her faith in God.

[8]Answers: 1-tribes; 2-the middle of the dry riverbed; 3-memorial; 4-the river stopped flowing before the ark of the covenant when it crossed the river.

Israel memorialized the crossing of the river and the entering of the land of Canaan by making a monument of 12 stones. The men of Israel took 12 stones from the dry bed of the Jordan River and stacked them as a memorial of the miraculous crossing. In later years people would ask what these stones meant. The response would remind the people of God's power, protection, and guidance. These stones memorialized God's leading the people across the Jordan River.

Chapter 5 recounts Joshua's circumcising all the men of Israel and the people's keeping the Passover in the plain of Jericho. At this time, the people ate unleavened cakes and the manna ceased. From that day forth, the people of Israel would eat from the bounty of the land of Canaan.

RESPONDING TO GOD'S WORD

★ Think of the most significant blessings God has given you on your Christian pilgrimage. Imagine each blessing to be a stone. Label the stones in the memorial in the margin so that it becomes *your* memorial, built of *your* stones-of-blessing. Draw additional stones if they are needed.

★ Praise God for the significant blessing.

★ Before tomorrow ends, tell another person about the significant blessing.

DAY 4   Conquest of the Land (continued)

U N I T   6

In yesterday's session you began studying the conquest of the land. At the end of that session, the Israelites were on the west side of the Jordan River. Everything was ready for the beginning of the conquest. Three basic campaigns made up the conquest: the central campaign, the southern campaign, and the northern campaign. In this session you will study those campaigns; you will review the division of the land; and you will see Joshua's final address to the people.

The central campaign (6:1—9:27). The attack on Jericho marked the start of the central campaign. Jericho symbolized the strength of Canaan. The city is one of the oldest in the world. It was fortified well and strategically located. By taking Jericho, Joshua divided Canaan in half.

The account of Jericho's conquest by Israel stirs the heart and the imagination. Simply by looking at the people of Israel, the impartial observer would never have imagined that the people of Israel could take Jericho. Only as the Israelites obeyed the Lord and looked to Him in faith could they take the ancient city of Jericho. God led the people and gave them the city just as He had promised. The Lord went before them and fought for them.

By all reason, Israel should never have been able to conquer Jericho. But God kept His promise. Israel won an unbelievable victory.

▶ **Read Joshua 6:1-19 to discover how this happened. Mark the following statements as T (true) or F (false). Answers are at the bottom of the column.[9]**

_____ 1. Joshua devised the unusual strategy to defeat Jericho.

_____ 2. The Israelites used the first six days to convince the people of Jericho that they were fierce soldiers.

_____ 3. The ark of the covenant was prominent in the marches around Jericho.

_____ 4. On the seventh day, the people marched around Jericho three times.

_____ 5. No one was to take any personal loot from Jericho.

_____ 6. No person in Jericho was to be spared.

The unbelievable victory was followed by an unbelievable defeat. Ai should have fallen easily. Israel attacked with a relatively small force of 3,000 men. The people of Ai fought bravely and repelled the invaders. Israel's confidence was shattered.

▶ **Read the cause of Israel's defeat in 7:10-12,19-23.**

God had commanded that all silver, gold, and bronze be set aside for His treasury. All other spoils were to be destroyed (6:17-19,24). Achan disregarded the command of God and hid some of the spoils of Jericho under his tent. Achan presumed on God, seeking to use for his own purposes what God had set apart for Himself. Achan's sin resulted in God's removing His protection from the people of Israel.

▶ **Some people defend their sinful actions by saying that they are harming only themselves. Do you agree or disagree? Explain your answer:**

_____

_____

When the sin was removed from among the people, God directed Joshua to take Ai and Bethel. Afterwards, Joshua built an altar to the Lord at Mount Ebal. The people worshiped the Lord by offering burnt offerings as Moses had commanded.

Joshua was not a perfect leader. He was human, and he did make mistakes. Joshua 9 is the story of an occasion when Joshua made a mistake and allowed Israel to be tricked into forming an alliance.

▶ **Read Joshua 9 and decide how Joshua could have avoided falling for the Gibeonite's trickery.**

_____

What decision are you now facing for which you must seek the counsel of the Lord?

_____

The southern campaign (Josh. 10:1-43). The southern campaign began when Adoni-Zedek, the king of Jerusalem, called four other kings to join him in attacking Gibeon. Gibeon appealed to Joshua for help and Israel defended them because of the covenant they had been tricked into making.

Joshua defeated these kings with the Lord's help. Notice in Joshua 10:10 that the Lord threw Israel's opponents into a panic. This victory did not result in the conquest of all the land in the southern part of Canaan, but it did give Israel superiority in that region. However, Israel was unable to conquer Jerusalem until the time of David.

---

[9]Answers: 1-F, God did; 2-F, their march was almost reverent; 3-T; 4-F; 5-T, all was devoted to the Lord's treasury; 6-F, Rahab and her family were spared.

▶ **Label Joshua's three campaigns on the map in the margin.**

The northern campaign (Josh. 11:1—12:24). Though the Bible tells us little about the northern campaign, this was a strategic campaign. Jabin, the king of Hazor, gathered other kings and a huge army. The Lord gave them into the hand of the people of Israel, and Joshua's army pursued them as far as Sidon to destroy them.

This victory enabled Joshua to control the northern part of Canaan as well as the central and southern areas. The people of Israel did not take the entire land of Canaan. In the northern part, for example, the only fortified city taken was the city of Hazor (11:13).

The Bible records that Joshua did not take the other cities which were built on mounds. Archaeologists call these mounds *tells*. These cities were built on high places and over the centuries they continued to be elevated further by building on the rubble of former generations. Finally, the inhabitants built walls around these cities. Thus these cities were virtually impossible to conquer. During the northern campaign, Hazor was the only strongly fortified city taken.

Joshua 11:16—13:7 gives summary statements of areas conquered and those not conquered by the children of Israel. The Lord said to Joshua, "You are very old, and there are still very large areas of land to be taken over" (13:1). Though Joshua and the people of Israel took much land, much area remained for future generations to take.

The Division of the Land (Josh. 13:8—23:16)

Last week in session 5 you saw how God directed the division of the land among the tribes. You also saw the provisions that were made for the Levites who were to own no land because they were priests. Joshua 13:8—23:16 describes the actual division of the land of Canaan.

During this early period in Israelite history, the whole congregation of the people of Israel gathered at Shiloh and set up the Tent of Meeting. From other Old Testament passages, as well as from Joshua 18:1, Shiloh appears to have been an early and important worship center.

Joshua 20 describes cities of refuge. These cities were set apart to protect the person who killed another accidentally. Three cities of refuge were located west of the Jordan River, and three east of the Jordan. These cities were set up so that one who had harmed another without malicious intent would be able to have a place of sanctuary.

▶ **Check the correct answer for each of the following statements:**[10]
1. An ancient religious center for Israel was
☐ a. Jerusalem.
☐ b. Shiloh.
☐ c. Hebron.

2. The "Tent of Meeting" was
☐ a. the tabernacle.
☐ b. Joshua's headquarters.
☐ c. the seat of justice.

3. A tribe that received no allotment of territory was
☐ a. Gad.
☐ b. half the tribe of Manasseh.
☐ c. Levi.

4. The two tribes descended from Joseph's sons who received an allotment of land were
☐ a. Reuben and Asher.
☐ b. Ephraim and Manasseh.
☐ c. Dan and Asher.

5. The cities of refuge were provided to protect
☐ a. murderers.
☐ b. those who had unintentionally caused a person's death.
☐ c. thieves.

Joshua's Charge (Josh. 24)

One of Joshua's last acts was to challenge the Israelites to be faithful to God. Joshua's charge is divided into three parts:
• The basis of his charge: What the Lord had done for Israel (vv. 1-13).
• The charge: Fear God and serve Him (vv. 14-23).
• The renewal of the covenant (vv. 24-28).

▶ **Read the specified verses and write the answers to the following questions:**[11]

1. What was the source of Joshua's message? (24:2) _____

_____

2. Was there a time when Abraham worshiped other gods? (24:2) _____

3. How could you summarize what God did for Israel? (24:13)

_____

4. Why did Joshua charge the people to be faithful to God? (24:23)

_____

5. What was the large stone's significance? (24:26-27) _____

_____

RESPONDING TO GOD'S WORD

★ **What objects symbolize or bear witness to your commitment to be faithful to God?**

_____

★ **What witness could those objects bear today to your faithfulness?**

_____

★ **In a time of prayer right now renew your allegiance to Christ as Lord of your life.**

---

[10]Answers: 1-b, 2-a, 3-c, 4-b, 5-b.
[11]Answers: 1-the Lord; 2-yes; 3-God gave them a settled and productive homeland; 4-some of them still held to their idols and had not yielded their hearts to God; 5-the stone "heard" the message from God that day and would "witness" against them if they were untrue to God.

DAY 5   The Book of Judges

U N I T   6

BOOKS OF HISTORY

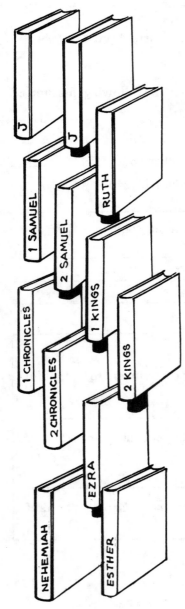

▶ **In this session you will study the Book of Judges. Begin by writing in the two book titles in the margin and by reviewing the information on the unit page for this unit.**

Let's begin by answering some important questions about the Book of Judges.

1. First, dating the writing is difficult. We know the setting took place between the conquest of Canaan (1400-1200 B.C.) and the destruction of Shiloh (about 1050 B.C.).
2. Were the judges national leaders? Probably not. Most of the judges were regional deliverers. They served a certain tribe or in specific regions of the country.
3. Is the record of the judges in chronological order? We can't be sure. Most biblical scholars believe that many of the judges may have served Israel at or about the same time. Since the judges usually were regional military leaders, this certainly could have been the case.

The Judges

The judges who appear in the book are classified as either major or minor judges. The classification does not describe their significance. Rather, it indicates the amount of biblical material devoted to their roles.

▶ **Use the references from Judges given below to identify the six minor and six major judges. Answers are at the bottom of the column.[12]**

MAJOR JUDGES

1. 3:7-11 _____
2. 3:12-30 _____
3. 4:1-5:31 _____
4. 6:1-8:28 _____
5. 10:6-12:7 _____
6. 13:1-16:31 _____

MINOR JUDGES

1. 3:31 _____
2. 10:1-2 _____
3. 10:3-5 _____
4. 12:8-10 _____
5. 12:11-12 _____
6. 12:13-15 _____

[12]Answers: Major Judges: 1-Othniel; 2-Ehud; 3-Deborah; 4-Gideon; 5-Jephthah; 6-Samson. Minor Judges: 1-Shamgar; 2-Tola; 3-Jair; 4-Ibzan; 5-Elon; 6-Abdon.

As you read through the Book of Judges, a recurring four-phase cycle becomes apparent. First, the people of Israel rebelled against the Lord. Second, God punished the people by delivering them into the hands of evil oppressors. This oppression usually involved domination by foreign nations or tribal groups. Third, the people of Israel cried out to the Lord for deliverance. This crying out to God implied repentance on their part. Fourth, God raised up a judge to deliver the people of Israel from their oppressors.

A Four-Phase Cycle

▶ **Use the account of Jephthah (3:1-11) to identify one cycle. Write the references that show the four phases.**[13]

A. Reference that shows REBELLION: _____

B. Reference that shows OPPRESSION: _____

C. Reference that shows REPENTANCE: _____

D. Reference that shows DELIVERANCE: _____

Othniel (3:7-11). Othniel delivered the people of Israel from the hand of the king of Mesopotamia. Othniel was Caleb's younger brother. He typifies the strength and calling of the judges. He delivered the people of Israel when the Spirit of the Lord came on him. Because God was with him, Othniel gave rest to the people of Israel.

Ehud (3:12-30). Ehud, a Benjaminite, delivered the people of Israel from Eglon, the king of Moab, who had dominated them for 18 years. Judges 3:12 is a typical reference showing the people's rebellion and God's punishment for their sins: "Once again the Israelites did evil in the eyes of the Lord, and because they did this evil the Lord gave Eglon king of Moab power over Israel."

Repentance is the only hope of deliverance.

Deborah (4:1—5:31). Deborah and her army commander Barak delivered the people of Israel from Jabin, king of Canaan, and his army commander, Sisera. Deborah selected Barak from the tribe of Naphtali to lead the army of Israel against Sisera. This military action was the closest that any of the judges came to a national movement of the tribes. God used Deborah herself to defeat Sisera. Judges 5 is poetry. It contains a beautiful song of Deborah and Barak concerning the defeat of Sisera and the deliverance of Israel.

Gideon (6:1—8:28). Gideon delivered the people of Israel from the hand of the Midianites. When God chose him, Gideon protested his inability to lead the people of Israel. God gave Gideon a sign to counteract his weakness. Possibly because of Gideon's weakness and lack of faith, God told Gideon to release most of the troops to go home. God used a small army of 300 men to defeat the Midianites. The story of Gideon illustrates the power of God and the importance of faithfulness.

The people of Israel wanted Gideon to be their king, but Gideon refused. His reply was that only the Lord is king. In Judges 8:23, Gideon responded to their request by saying; "I will not rule over you, nor will my son rule over you. The Lord will rule over you."

Compare Romans 12:1.

Jephthah (10:6—12:7). Jephthah, a Gileadite, is best known for having delivered the people of Israel from the power of the Ammonites. He also is known for the foolish, unnecessary vow he made. He vowed to the Lord that if He would grant him victory over the Ammonites, he would offer whatever would come forth first from his house to the Lord. Sadly, Jephthah's daughter rushed out to greet him at his victory. Later, Jephthah sacrificed his daughter because of his vow.

---

[13]Answers: A-3:1 or 6; B-3:8; C-3:9a; D-3:9b-11.

The Scripture is clear. God does not want human sacrifice. God wants human beings to yield themselves in commitment to Him.

Potential apart from responsibility and service is useless.

Samson (13:1—16:31). Once you have read Judges 13—16, you may find it hard to think of Samson as a hero. Certainly he judged Israel and saved the nation from the oppression of the Philistines. But he was a man of little character and few principles. Samson possessed enormous potential, but he used his opportunities unwisely. God gave Samson the responsibility to lead the nation, but Samson failed.

Lack of Sound Leadership (Judg. 17—21)

Judges 17—21 describes how people lived when they had little leadership or when they had poor leadership. The end of the Book of Judges may be describing how Samson had failed as a judge. Or, it may be an attempt to justify the need for a king. References to the lack of a king appear three times (Judg. 18:1; 19:1; 21:25). Whatever the purpose of these chapters, they record some of the most sordid events found anywhere in the Bible.

▶ **SUMMARY REVIEW**

To review this week's study of the Old Testament, see if you can mentally answer the following questions. You may want to write the answers on a separate sheet of paper. Mark your level of performance on the left: circle "C" if you can answer correctly and circle "R" if you need to review.

C R 1. What one word could describe the contents of Moses' first speech in Deuteronomy 1—4?

C R 2. What one word could describe the contents of Moses' second speech in Deuteronomy 5—26.

C R 3. What is emphasized in the part of Deuteronomy called the *shema*?

C R 4. Why was an emphasis placed on worshiping God at one central place in the promised land?

C R 5. Name two of three great feasts to be observed by the Hebrews.

C R 6. What major subject is covered in each of the two main divisions of Joshua?

C R 7. Explain the term *judge* as used in the Book of Judges.

C R 8. How many major and how many minor judges are mentioned in the Book of Judges?

C R 9. What four events recur again and again in Judges?

RESPONDING TO GOD'S WORD

★ Thank God for His commandments and that He has given them to us for our good.

God and the Beginning of the Monarchy *(Ruth—2 Samuel)*

The people of Israel faced serious questions. Did they need a king? Should they become like the surrounding nations? Should they continue to find the Lord's leadership in temporary leaders? What would the years ahead hold for the people of Israel? In this unit you will see how the people became a monarchy.

In this unit you will study the books of Ruth, 1 Samuel, and 2 Samuel.

Ruth is the story of Naomi and her daughter-in-law, Ruth, and the tragedy that befell them. The purpose of the Book of Ruth is to show that God is present in times of deep tragedy, that He can be trusted in our darkest hours, and that all persons are persons of worth.

1 Samuel and 2 Samuel describe how Israel acquired a king. The books begin with the story of Samuel and end with David's family trying to determine who would follow David as king. The books tell us of the beginning of the monarchy and how God continued to make a people for Himself.

Ruth:

   I. Naomi and Ruth (Ruth 1)
  II. Ruth and Boaz (Ruth 2:1—4:12)
 III. Genealogy of David (Ruth 4:13-22)

1 and 2 Samuel:

    I. Samuel (1 Sam. 1—8)
   II. Samuel and Saul (1 Sam. 9—15)
  III. Saul and David (1 Sam. 16—2 Sam. 1)
  IV. David as King of Judah and Israel (2 Sam. 2—8)
   V. The Events of David's Court (2 Sam. 9—20)
 VI. Various Incidents in David's Life (2 Sam. 21—24)

WordWatch

Watch for these words as you study this unit.

Anoint—to set apart for special service. Anointing did not convey power or the ability to obey God perfectly, since Saul himself had been anointed. Anointing designated a person as having been chosen of God for special service. God chose Saul and David to serve responsibly as kings over Israel. For most of his life David served God obediently. Saul disobeyed God though he had been anointed to be king over Israel.

Urim and Thummim—small objects used to discern God's will in matters that might be doubtful or uncertain. Questions with which urim and thummim were used almost always called for a yes or no answer; and they were always questions related to national matters, never personal or individual matters. The urim and thummim were carried in a small pouch over the priest's heart. They were probably cubes made of precious metal or stones and engraved with characters on each surface.

DAY 1   The Book of Ruth

U N I T   7

BOOKS OF HISTORY

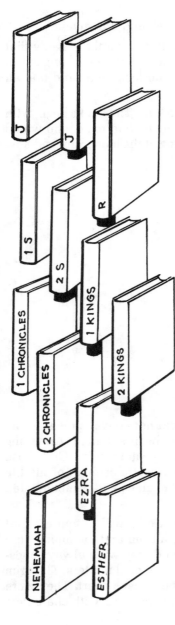

▶ **In this session you will study the Book of Ruth. Begin by writing in the five book titles in the margin and by reviewing the information on the unit page for this unit.**

Why was the Book of Ruth written? Ruth may have been written to show that God is in control of history. God, the Ruler over the universe, works in people's lives to bring about His will. He can work in even the worst circumstances to accomplish His purposes. He worked through the terrible famine Naomi and her family endured to bring them to Moab. Here Ruth married into the family. God worked through Ruth's faith and her loyalty to her impoverished mother-in-law to bring Ruth and Boaz together. He worked through that union eventually to provide David as the finest king Israel had. In God's ultimate plan, He worked through Ruth's descendants to provide an earthly stepfather for His Son, the Lord Jesus Christ (Matt. 1:1,5,16).

▶ **Briefly explain how the Book of Ruth shows that God is in control of history.**

_____

_____

_____

Compare your explanation to information in the previous paragraph.

The Book of Ruth also may have been written to show David's Moabite blood. The author obviously wanted to reveal that Ruth was David's ancestor. The Book of Ruth shows that God loves and cares for all people, even non-Israelites.

Finally, the book may have been used in later times to teach that Israel could accept returning exiles from Babylon or foreigners who wished to come and worship with the people of Israel. The book further demonstrates that the people of Israel could live with non-Israelites in peace and joy as they all served the Lord God.

▶ **Check the statements with which you agree. Answers are at the bottom of the column.[1]**
  ☐ 1. The Book of Ruth encourages people to view people from other ethnic groups as people about whom God cares.
  ☐ 2. The Book of Ruth shows that Israelites could not live in Moab.
  ☐ 3. The Book of Ruth encourages people to trust God even in painful and difficult times.
  ☐ 4. The Book of Ruth reveals that Moabites were unreliable.
  ☐ 5. The Book of Ruth demonstrates that people who trust in the Lord can live together in peace and harmony, even when they are of quite different backgrounds.

When was the Book of Ruth written? The Book of Ruth contains some of the most ancient material in the Old Testament, though it probably was not written until after David's lifetime (4:13-22). The setting of the Book of Ruth is the time of the judges. All we know about the date of the book comes from references in the fourth chapter. The date of the writing was much later than the events described in the book.

[1]Answers: You should have agreed with 1, 3, and 5.

Chapter 4 contains two references that indicate that the date of the writing was much later than the events described in the book. Notice that Ruth 4:7 describes the ancient practice of exchanging or redeeming a piece of property. The practice involved removing a sandal and giving it to the other party in the transaction. Notice that Ruth 4:7 says that this custom was practiced in former times. This phrase obviously meant that this custom no longer was practiced in Israel at the time Ruth was written. The one who wrote the story had to explain it to readers of a later day.

Ruth 4:17 refers to the birth of David. We would expect that the Book of Ruth would not have been written until David's true significance was apparent. The book probably was written after Israel realized David's importance as its greatest king.

Who wrote the Book of Ruth? We cannot identify the author of Ruth. Many generations had told and retold the story before the author recorded it.

▶ **Let the following exercises guide you in a brief overview of Ruth.[2]**

1. Read Ruth 1:1 and fill in the blank: The account of Ruth is set during the time that _____ ruled in Israel.

2. Read Ruth 4:7 and check your choice of a completion to the following sentence: A reasonable conclusion based on Ruth 4:7 is that
   ☐ a. Ruth was written in earlier times.
   ☐ b. People generally are ignorant of real estate law.
   ☐ c. The events of Ruth occurred long before Ruth was written.

3. Read Ruth 4:17 and check your choice or choices of a completion to the following sentences:
   A. The most well-known of Ruth's descendants listed in 4:17 is
   ☐ a. Obed.
   ☐ b. Jesse.
   ☐ c. David.

   B. The Book of Ruth obviously was written
   ☐ a. after David was born.
   ☐ b. after David achieved great success as king of Israel.
   ☐ c. before Jesse died.

4. Read Ruth 1:1-5, 8, 16-21; 2:2-3; 4:13-16 and match the following incomplete statements on the left with the correct completion on the right. Write the correct letters in the blanks.

   ____ 1. Naomi and her family moved
   ____ 2. Naomi lived in a foreign land for
   ____ 3. Naomi was bitter because she had
   ____ 4. Naomi encouraged her daughters-in-law
   ____ 5. Ruth insisted on
   ____ 6. Ruth gleaned in fields belonging to Boaz,
   ____ 7. After Ruth was married and bore a son,

   a. to stay in Moab.
   b. who was kin to Naomi's husband, Elimelech.
   c. Naomi's friends cited her blessings from God.
   d. suffered the loss of her husband and sons.
   e. 10 years.
   f. remaining with Naomi.
   g. from Judah to Moab.

---

[2]Answers: 1-judges; 2-c; 3A-c; 3B-a, b; 4: 1-g, 2-e, 3-d, 4-a, 5-f, 6-b, 7-c.

RESPONDING TO GOD'S WORD

★ Can you, like Ruth and Naomi, look back and see how God has used events, both good and bad, happy and sad, to guide your life into certain channels that have proven to be a blessing? Did your faith ever waver during the bad/sad times?

★ Pray a prayer of thanksgiving for God's patience and His lovingkindness that never faltered.

DAY 2 The Books of 1 Samuel and 2 Samuel

U N I T   7

Relationship of the two books. Although 1 and 2 Samuel are two books in our English Bibles, they really are one book. The division of the Book of Samuel into two books probably occurred when the Old Testament was translated from Hebrew into Greek around 200 B.C. That translation is known as the Septuagint. It was produced because Greek speaking Hebrews living outside Palestine needed the Old Testament in their own language.

▶ Read 1 Samuel 31:11-13; 2 Samuel 1:1. What conclusion can you draw concerning the relationship of 1 and 2 Samuel based on those verses? Write your answer here:

_____

_____

Did your answer indicate that the second takes up where the first leaves off? Further conclusions could be that the Book of Samuel was divided for ease of handling. Simply by reading 1 and 2 Samuel, you can see that the content is continuous. You also can see that no logical reason dictates the division between 1 and 2 Samuel.

The Date and Authorship. The author of 1 and 2 Samuel is unknown. The book itself makes no claim as who the author or authors might be. Hebrew tradition indicates that Samuel wrote the book. Since 1 Samuel 25:1 records Samuel's death, that he wrote 1 Samuel 25:2—2 Samuel is certainly unlikely.

The nature of the books indicates that the author lived during the time of the early monarchy and was well-acquainted with the characters and events recorded in 1 and 2 Samuel. Some material appears to have been taken from actual court records. Many biblical scholars believe that 2 Samuel 9—20 was written by a contemporary eye witness of the events.

The date of 1 and 2 Samuel cannot be pinpointed with certainty. One important clue concerns David. David is a central character of the book. Since his death is not mentioned in Samuel, many Bible students believe that the book was written late in David's reign or near the time of his death. If this view is correct, then the books would have been written near the time of the events which they describe.

▶ Review the outlines of 1 and 2 Samuel on page 105 and fill in the blanks in the following statements. Answers are at the bottom of the column.[3]

1. The main characters in 1 Samuel are _____, _____, and _____.

2. The main character in 2 Samuel is _____.

3. In 1 and 2 Samuel more chapters are devoted to _____ than to anyone else.

Samuel's life bridged the gap between the judges and the early kings of Israelite history. Samuel served as the last of the judges and paved the way for the coming of Saul as king. Since he served in such a pivotal time, Samuel rightly deserves recognition as one of Israel's great leaders.

The Life and Ministry of Samuel

The birth and dedication of Samuel (1 Sam. 1:1). Elkanah had two wives, Hannah and Peninnah. Hannah's inability to bear children created a serious problem.

▶ Find the answers to these questions in 1 Samuel 1.
1. How did Hannah's problem affect her relationship with Peninnah?

_____

2. How did Hannah deal with her problem? _____

_____

3. How was the problem resolved? _____

_____

_____

Elkanah and Hannah, along with Elkanah's other wife and children, went once a year to Shiloh, the place of worship. Hannah took her problem of childlessness to God. She prayed for a son and God promised to give her a son. She in turn promised to return the child to God to serve Him at the worship center at Shiloh. When God blessed her with the child, she kept her promise. She brought the child to serve with Eli the priest.

Eli's Sons (1 Sam. 2:11-36). Eli had two sons whom the Scripture called "worthless men." Literally, the Hebrew text says that they are sons of Belial, a phrase that describes their rebellious nature and disregard for the ways of God.

▶ A. The Scriptures describe three ways Eli's sons showed their rebellion against God. Read of those three ways in 1 Samuel 2:12,17,22 and fill in the blanks:[4]

First, they had no _____ for the Lord Himself (1 Sam. 2:12).

Second, they treated the _____ of the Lord with contempt, not handling it according to God's law (1 Sam. 2:17).

Third, they had slept with the women who served at the _____ _____, showing their immorality and their disregard for worship and worshipers alike (1 Sam. 2:22).

_____

[3]Answers: 1-Samuel, Saul, and David; 2-David; 3-David.

B. Read 1 Samuel 2:26 for a refreshing contrast to Eli's sons. List the three areas in which Samuel grew:

1. _____

2. _____

3. _____

The Call of Samuel (1 Sam. 3:1-21). God called Samuel, and Samuel responded. He obeyed the word of the Lord and sought to follow God all the days of his life.

▶ **Read 1 Samuel 3:7-18. Put a check by the following facts that seem especially significant to you.**
____ Eli helped Samuel understand that God was speaking to him.
____ Samuel identified himself as the Lord's servant.
____ Samuel's first assignment was to pronounce God's judgment on Eli and his family.
____ Eli accepted God's message.
____ Samuel was recognized throughout Israel as a prophet whose words proved true.
____ God continued to reveal himself to Samuel through His Word.

Be prepared to share your responses at this week's small-group session.

While the Bible says that God called Samuel by name, the Bible does not tell us exactly how He called Samuel. Was this an audible voice from heaven? Or, did God speak by means of an inner voice that only Samuel heard? Could Eli have heard the voice as well? All of these questions remain unanswered. We simply know that God spoke and that Samuel obeyed.

Often, one of the greatest things we can do is to help another person understand and respond to the call of God.

God's word to Samuel required decisive action for such a young person. God told Samuel to tell Eli that judgment would come upon his house. When Eli asked what God had said, Samuel told Eli. To Eli's credit, the priest helped Samuel understand the call of God. He also accepted God's word.

God blessed the ministry of Samuel (1 Sam. 3:19-21). Samuel grew and the Lord blessed him, bringing to pass all the words that Samuel spoke. All the people who heard Samuel recognized him as God's prophet because of God's blessing His message through Samuel.

Samuel was a prophet.

▶ **Read 1 Samuel 4:1-3,10-11,12-18 and answer the following questions:[5]**

1. Did the Israelites depend on God or on the ark as they went into battle against the Philistines?

_____

2. What happened to 30,000 of Israel's soldiers and Eli's wicked sons?

3. How old was Eli at the time of the battle? _____

4. What happened to Eli when he received word of the battle's outcome?

_____

Because of the wickedness of Eli's sons, God judged the house (family) of Eli. All Israel experienced judgment as well because of the sin and neglect of Eli and his sons. When Israel went out to fight against the Philistines,
● 30,000 of their soldiers died
● the ark of God fell into the Philistines' hands
● Eli's two sons were killed.

---

[4]Answers for A: First-regard; Second-offering; Third-Tent of Meeting or tabernacle. Answers for B: stature (physically), favor with the Lord (spiritually), favor with men (socially).
[5]Answers: 1-the ark—they treated it as a good luck charm; 2-they were killed; 3-98; 4-he fell off his chair, broke his neck, and died.

When word came to Eli that his sons were dead and the Philistines had captured the ark, he fell backwards in shock and died of a broken neck (1 Sam. 4:1-22). Since Eli's sons could not succeed him as priest, the way was opened for Samuel to serve as priest after Eli.

Samuel was a priest.

The Ministry of Samuel (1 Sam. 7—12). God afflicted the Philistines until they returned the ark to Israel (1 Sam. 5—6), but they still dominated Israel for the next 20 years. The people began to turn to Samuel saying they wanted to seek the Lord. Samuel performed his priestly duty by leading the people of Israel to turn away from other gods and to serve God alone.

▶ **Read 1 Samuel 7:1-13. Mark the following statements as T (true) or F (false).**[6]

_____ 1. The people of Israel tried to seek God while holding on to their false gods.

_____ 2. Samuel led the people to forsake their foreign gods.

_____ 3. At Hebron Samuel led the people to confess their sins.

_____ 4. The people had little confidence in Samuel's prayers when the Philistines moved to attack them.

_____ 5. The people depended on God when the Philistines attacked them.

_____ 6. Israel won the victory because of superior military strategy.

_____ 7. The stone "Ebenezer" was set up to mark the boundary beyond which Philistines could no longer come.

When the people repented of their sins and turned to the Lord, the Lord blessed them and gave them victory over the Philistines. After the victory over the Philistines, Samuel placed a stone near Mizpah and called the name of the stone Ebenezer, a word which literally means "stone of help." The stone reminded the people that God had been their help in defeating their enemy and would continue to help them in years to come.

Samuel was a judge.

Samuel also served as a judge. His work as a judge is closer to our idea of what a judge should do. The judges of the Old Testament primarily had been military deliverers, but Samuel helped the people settle disputes and solve their problems. Samuel rode a circuit in his service as judge. He went between four towns in Israel: Bethel, Gilgal, Mizpah, and Ramah, his home.

▶ **A. With a pencil, draw a line connecting the towns of Samuel's circuit: Mizpah, Bethel, Shiloh, Gilgal, and Ramah.**

Shiloh

Bethel Gilgal

Mizpah
Ramah

RESPONDING TO GOD'S WORD

★ Who helped you understand that God was speaking to your heart? Write that person's name here: _____

★ Circle the most accurate response to the following questions:

1. Can you identify yourself as God's servant? (usually, sometimes, never)

2. Do you accept God's Word to you? (usually, sometimes, never)

3. Do others recognize you as God's child? (usually, sometimes, never)

4. Are you growing in the Lord? (usually, sometimes, never)

★ What do you think God is saying to you? Talk with God right now about your responses to this activity.

---

[6]Answers: 1-T; 2-T; 3-F, it was at Mizpah (yes, that was a low blow; sorry); 4-F, they asked for his prayers; 5-T (though you may have answered "F" thinking that they were depending on Samuel; I marked "T" because they asked Samuel to pray "that he [God] may rescue us"); 6-F, God intervened; 7-F, it was a memorial to how God had helped them that day.

DAY 3 Saul and the Monarchy (1 Samuel 8—15)

UNIT 7

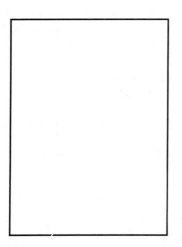

Draw something in the box that symbolizes a time when God blessed you in spite of a bad decision.

anoint—a symbolic act indicating that a person has been chosen and set apart for a special task.

The rise of a monarchy was one of the most important events in Israel's history. Saul became Israel's first king and for a while served effectively, but later failed to live up to God's high ideal for Israel's king.

The Beginning of the Monarchy (1 Sam. 8—12). The elders or leaders of Israel's tribes realized that Samuel's two sons likely would succeed him as judge when he died. They recognized that his sons lacked their father's integrity and devotion to God. Thus the two young men did not command the respect and following of the people like Samuel did. They approached Samuel and bluntly explained that they wanted a king because his sons were not fit to serve as judges.

Their second reason for requesting a king was that they wanted to be like the other nations around them. They wanted a king to lead them into battle. This request emphasized the need for a strong central authority (like a king) over the loose confederation of tribes. Israel faced real dangers from its neighbors. The tribal leaders felt they had to have a strong leader to unite them against outside threats.

Samuel saw the request for a king as a rejection of the Lord as king. To have a human king constituted rebellion against the Lord God. Samuel served as Israel's leader, but he did so knowing that the Lord was the true king over His people.

God brought Saul to Samuel and revealed to Samuel that He had chosen Saul to be king. While they were together Samuel told Saul that he was to be king and anointed him. Later, at a public gathering at Mizpah, Saul was chosen and proclaimed king.

The early experience of Saul demonstrated clearly that God does not forsake us when we make bad decisions. Rather, if we permit Him to do so, He continues to bless us in spite of bad decisions.

▶ Samuel plainly told the Israelites that by asking for a man to be king, they were rejecting God as their king. Study 1 Samuel 10—12 and note each indication that God was willing to bless Israel and their new king in spite of the bad decision they had made. List four indications.

1. _____

2. _____

3. _____

4. _____

These three chapters give numerous indications of God's intention to bless the nation in spite of their bad decision. The list includes: Saul's transforming experience with the prophets (10:6-7); his "heart experience" upon leaving Samuel (10:9); Saul's anointing by the Spirit of God (11:6); the victory over the Ammonites (11:11); the promise of God (12:14); God's faithfulness to His purpose (12:22).

The Fall of Saul (1 Sam. 13—31). Why did Saul fail when he started out as a God-anointed, good king? Saul failed because he refused to obey God. In the following ways, Saul proved himself unfit to lead the people of Israel.

Nothing should be so urgent that it keeps us from waiting on the Lord.

Psalm 40

"¹I waited patiently for the LORD; and he inclined unto me, and heard my cry.
²He brought me up also out of an horrible pit, out of the miry clay, and set my feet upon a rock, and established my goings.
³And he hath put a new song in my mouth, even praise unto our God: many shall see it, and fear, and shall trust in the LORD. Saul made his first serious mistake as he prepared to go into battle against the Philistines."

▶ **Read 1 Samuel 13:1-14. Explain in your own words why you think Saul's actions were such a serious mistake. Compare your answer with the paragraph that follows.**

_____

_____

_____

As Saul waited for Samuel to come and bless the army by offering a sacrifice, Saul's troops began to desert. Saul panicked. What should he do? Would Samuel arrive in time? Or should he go ahead and offer the sacrifice himself and then go into the battle? Saul behaved as many people behave. He decided to do something even though it was wrong. He offered the sacrifice himself in disobedience to God's command. Saul had performed a duty God had assigned only to His priests. Samuel told him that because of his disobedience his kingdom would not endure.

Saul's second mistake was in making a foolish vow (1 Sam. 14:24-45). In the heat of battle, Saul made a major mistake. Without all his men being able to hear the command, he vowed that anyone who ate before the battle was completed would be put to death. When Jonathan and his men came upon some wild honey, Jonathan did the natural thing after a day of battle. He dipped his staff into the honey and ate because he had not heard his father's command. According to the vow of Saul, Jonathan must die.

Saul's men knew they owed the victory to Jonathan. To put him to death would have been a great injustice. Fortunately, they were able to talk Saul out of the death of his own son who had fought so valiantly.

▶ **Read 1 Samuel 14:43-45. Ponder these two questions: (1) To what extent does God hold us responsible for foolish promises we have made? (2) To what extent does God hold us responsible for being controlled by foolish promises our leaders have made? Be prepared to share your ideas with your group.**

What does this experience reveal about Saul? Check the responses with which you agree:

☐ 1. Saul was prone to lose his perspective.
☐ 2. Saul was prone to use poor judgment under pressure.
☐ 3. Saul was indifferent to his men's needs.
☐ 4. Saul wanted to win at any price.
☐ 5. Saul was more concerned with saving face than doing right.

Be prepared to share your responses in this week's small-group session. You probably should have checked all responses except 3.

Saul made his third mistake after a victory over the Amalekites. Samuel gave Saul a command from the Lord to wipe out the Amalekites and to destroy totally all their livestock and belongings. Saul and his army crushed the Amalekites, but Saul spared the king, Agag, and some prize livestock. Other nations paraded captured generals and kings through the major cities of their countries. Saul might have wanted to do the same. So, Saul disobeyed God another time (1 Sam. 15). He showed poor judgment after the battle was completed.

At this point, the word of the Lord came to Samuel saying; "I am grieved that I have made Saul king" (1 Sam. 15:11). Saul had turned away from following God.

▶ **Read 1 Samuel 15:13-35. Match Saul's statements on the left with the corresponding question on the right. Write the correct letters in the blanks.[7]**

_____ 1. I have done all God has commanded (v. 13).

_____ 2. The soldiers brought them to be sacrificed to God (v. 15).

_____ 3. But I did obey (v. 20).

_____ 4. I have sinned because I was afraid of the people and gave into them (v. 24).

_____ 5. I have sinned, but honor me before the elders and before Israel by worshiping with me (v. 30).

A. Do we sometimes excuse our sins?

B. Do we sometimes accuse other people of being responsible for sins we have done?

C. Do we sometimes care more about appearances than about being right with God?

D. Do we sometimes remodel God's commandments to make them fit our behavior rather than guide our behavior?

E. Do we sometimes deny our sins?

When Samuel confronted Saul with his disobedience, Saul justified his actions by claiming the soldiers had taken the animals for a sacrifice to God. In response, Samuel affirmed that God wanted obedience, not sacrifice. Because Saul had rejected God's word by disobeying it, God had rejected Saul as king.

▶ **Before concluding today's session, take time to check your recall of the books you should have learned to this point. Write in the missing names on the books below.**

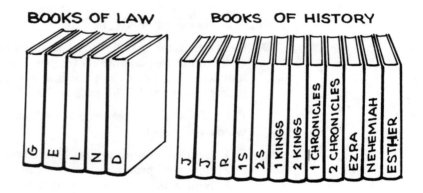

BOOKS OF LAW   BOOKS OF HISTORY

G E L N D   J J R 1S 2S 1 KINGS 2 KINGS 1 CHRONICLES 2 CHRONICLES EZRA NEHEMIAH ESTHER

RESPONDING TO GOD'S WORD

★ Ask yourself the questions in the previous learning activity related to 1 Samuel 15:13-35. Answer them as honestly as you can. Do your answers indicate that you should take some actions in order to be more consistent in obeying the Word? Write any actions you will take here: _____

_____

_____

★ Meditate on James 1:22: "Do not merely listen to the word, and so deceive yourselves. Do what it says." If you become an excellent student of the Word but fail to obey it, what are you doing?

---

[7]Answers: 1-D; 2-B; 3-E; 4-A; 5-C.

DAY 4 Saul and the Monarchy—continued (1 Sam. 16—31)

U N I T   7

In yesterday's study you saw three ways that Saul proved himself unfit to lead the people of Israel:
(1) Saul disobeyed Samuel and violated God's law (1 Sam. 13).
(2) Saul made a foolish vow (1 Sam. 14:24-45).
(3) Saul disobeyed God a second time (1 Sam. 15).

Today you will examine three more ways that Saul proved himself unfit to lead God's people.

anoint—a symbolic act indicating that a person has been chosen and set apart for a special task.

Saul allowed his jealousy to control him (1 Sam. 16—31). Because of Saul's spiritual rebellion, God led Samuel to anoint David to be king over Israel (1 Sam. 16). Although several years would pass before David began to reign, the person after God's own heart was destined to take the place of Saul as king of God's people.

First Samuel 17 tells how David defeated Goliath. David was indignant over the giant Philistine's scornful challenge. David saw that he was defying the army of the living God. Goliath taunted the people of Israel and acted as if the Lord did not exist. David felt compelled to go against the giant and to uphold the honor of Israel's God.

▶ **Read 1 Samuel 17:1-11,32-54. Check the statements with which you agree:**[8]

☐ 1. Goliath was an effective instrument of psychological warfare.
☐ 2. Goliath's "deal" (17:8-9) was not offered sincerely.
☐ 3. The Israelites made jokes about Goliath behind his back.
☐ 4. David was drafted to fight Goliath.
☐ 5. David's testimony of his experiences and his faith persuaded Saul to let him face Goliath.
☐ 6. Goliath was impressed by David's courage.
☐ 7. David depended on God more than on his sling.
☐ 8. David approached Goliath with great caution.
☐ 9. When the Philistines saw Goliath was dead, they surrendered to Israel.

David's heroism and attractive personality endeared him to the people of Israel. Saul grew jealous of David's increasing popularity. Saul's jealousy took control of him. The final chapters of 1 Samuel show that Saul thought more and more of himself and less and less of the kingdom of Israel.

▶ **Match the following references on the left with the correct descriptions on the right. Write the correct letters in the blanks.**[9]

_____ 1. 18:5-9	A. Hoped the Philistines would kill David
_____ 2. 18:17-25	B. Jealous of David's military victories
_____ 3. 19:9-10	C. Saul and his army pursued David
_____ 4. 19:11	D. Told Jonathan David had to die or else
_____ 5. 20:30	Jonathan would not be the next king
_____ 6. 23:25	E. Tried to spear David
	F. Sent men to David's house to kill him

---

[8]You should have checked: 1 (he had completely demoralized Israel's troops); 2 (the Philistines did not surrender to serve the Israelites when David won); 5; and 7 (see vv. 45-47).
[9]Answers: 1-B, 2-A, 3-E, 4-F, 5-D, 6-C.

Jealousy, envy, and hatred are born out of a heart whose eyes have lost sight of the Lord.

Saul began to fear David and many other people around him. On at least two occasions Saul tried to kill David, but he escaped. In sharp contrast to Saul's irresponsible behavior, David honored God with his actions. Although he could have killed Saul on several occasions he refused to do harm to God's anointed.

Saul often said, "I have sinned" or "I am sorry," but failed to do anything to indicate true repentance.

► **For Saul's confession after David had spared his life in a cave, read 1 Samuel 24:16-17. Also read 1 Samuel 26:21 for Saul's words after David spared his life a second time. In your opinion, how important is it for confession of wrong to be accompanied by changed attitudes or actions?**

_____

CONFESSION AND REPENTANCE   CHANGED ATTITUDES AND ACTIONS

In spite of Saul's confessions, little evidence of repentance showed in his life. Saul's jealousy and hatred of David became an obsession that dominated and ruined his life.

Saul violated his own law (1 Sam. 28). First Samuel 28:3 states how Saul removed the mediums and witches from the land of Israel. He banished these soothsayers, according to the law given in Deuteronomy 18:10-11. Later, Saul violated his own law by seeking the witch of Endor.

Saul desperately needed a word from the Lord. His personal rebellion against God had caused God to depart from him. Saul no longer could receive a word from God. In his desperation, Saul went to the medium at Endor. In what might have been a great hoax, the witch described to Saul a person who looked like Samuel. The point is that Saul had violated his own law and again had disobeyed the law of God. Saul proved himself unworthy to be the king of Israel.

This incident in Saul's life illustrates the hypocrisy of the leader whose actions are not consistent with what he requires of his followers. This is the person who says, "Do what I *say* do, not what I *do.*"

► **In your opinion what are the dangers of such an inconsistency in the lives of church leaders? Parents? Community leaders who are professing Christians?**

_____

_____

_____

_____

Saul took his own life while fighting with the Philistines (1 Sam. 31:1-6). In battle the enemy wounded Saul. Rather than fall into the hands of the Philistines, Saul fell on his own sword, taking his own life. Jonathan also died in the same battle. Second Samuel 1:1-10 relates a different account of Saul's death. Take time to read that account now.

How do you reconcile both passages? Are they contradictory? I think they are not. First Samuel 31 probably reflects the true story of what happened to Saul. He took his own life. Second Samuel 1 is the story of a young Amalekite who found Saul and Jonathan dead. Hoping to win David's favor and profit from their deaths, he probably made up the story of how he had killed Saul at Saul's request.

David mourned at the news of Saul's and Jonathan's deaths. Then he reacted in a way totally consistent with his character. David consistently had refused to lift his hand against the Lord's anointed, king Saul. Because the Amalekite claimed to have taken the life of the king, David had the man put to death.

▶ As a review of the ways in which Saul proved himself unfit to be king of Israel, fill in the blanks using the words below:[10]

a. life   b. disobeyed   c. vow   d. Samuel   e. jealousy   f. law

1. Saul disobeyed his _____ and violated God's law (1 Sam. 13).
2. Saul made a foolish _____ (1 Sam. 14:24-45).
3. Saul _____ God a second time (1 Sam. 15).
4. Saul allowed his _____ to control him (1 Sam. 16—31).
5. Saul violated his own _____ (1 Sam. 28).
6. Saul took his own _____ while fighting with the Philistines.

Saul brought about his own failure because of his disobedience and lack of faith. As God had promised, David eventually was affirmed as king in Saul's place.

A story of true loyalty and friendship (1 Sam. 20). David and Jonathan were true friends. Jonathan showed his friendship to David though it meant that David might be the next king. Saul summed up the situation well. He told Jonathan that as long as David lived, Jonathan would never be king of Israel. Jonathan placed his ambitions behind him and remained loyal to his friend David. This story is a good example for believers. The characteristics of Jonathan should be adopted by all God's people. We are to remain loyal to the Lord and think of others above ourselves.

▶ To grasp the main points of this account of selfless love, read 20:1-7,24-34,41-42. Suggest a modern-day example of circumstances that might require a Christian to sacrifice personal ambition for the sake of loyalty to a friend or to God's plan. _____

_____

_____

RESPONDING TO GOD'S WORD

★ As you reflect on the ways Saul proved unfit to lead God's people, consider any tendencies you discern in your own life that could threaten to make you unfit for God's service. Ask God to cleanse you and to strengthen you in those areas of weakness.

★ Consider wrongs you have confessed to God. Have your attitudes and actions changed sufficiently to indicate true repentance? _____

_____

_____

★ Pray that God will convict you of any inconsistencies in your life and help you correct them.

---

[10]Answers: 1-c; 2-c; 3-b; 4-e; 5-f; 6-a.

DAY 5   The Kingdom of David (2 Samuel 1—24)

U N I T   7

You will see in this session that David proved to be a man after God's own heart. He earnestly sought to know and to follow God's will (2 Sam 2:1-4). You will see that David proved to be an able leader. Through much of his early life, he functioned as a master politician. As king over Israel, he made wise political decisions. He knew how to lead the people and how to influence them to do the right thing. He mourned the death of Saul and Jonathan. He refused to take advantage of Saul's inconsistency and personal difficulties. David showed proper respect for the things of the Lord.

You also will see that David had his failures. One is described in 2 Samuel 2:2-4. David took several wives, a weakness which encouraged his son, Solomon, to establish a large harem. Sometimes, David took advantage of events and people for his own personal purposes (Bathsheba and her husband).

David's Reign at Hebron

When David started to reign the tribes of Israel were divided and most of them followed another king. There were two kings. Both had their own military commanders and reigned over separate areas.

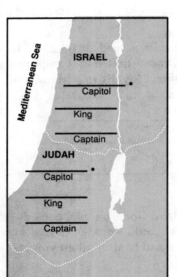

▶   **Use information in 2 Samuel 2:1-11 to discover the name of the other king, the two military commanders, and the two capital cities. Write these at the appropriate places on the map in the margin.**

Saul's kingdom lacked effective administration to lead the people of Israel. In his capitol at Hebron, David quickly began organizing and administering the workings of government. The conflict between Saul's household and David's continued. The effect was that David's forces became stronger and that Ish-Bosheth's became weaker. Ish-bosheth served as king of the northern tribes, but in reality Abner, the commander of the army, proved to be the power behind the throne. When Ish-bosheth displeased Abner, Abner volunteered to give the rest of the kingdom to David as well.

After Abner offered to throw his support to David, Joab killed him. With Abner gone, Ish-bosheth's power waned. He was soon killed by men seeking their own gain. After the death of Ish-bosheth, the other tribes of Israel came to David petitioning him to be their king.

▶   **A. Read 2 Samuel 5:1-3. Which of the following reasons did the northern tribes give for pledging their allegiance to David? Check your answer. Answers are at the bottom of the column on the next page.[11]**
   ☐ 1. We cannot win our war against you.
   ☐ 2. We are kinfolk.
   ☐ 3. You led us on military campaigns under Saul.
   ☐ 4. You were Saul's choice to succeed him as king.
   ☐ 5. You are the Lord's choice to be our ruler.

B. In view of their participation in the civil war against David, how do you view the statement of the northern tribes' leaders that the Lord said David would shepherd Israel? Check your answer:
☐ 1. They were sincere.
☐ 2. They were playing politics.
☐ 3. They had repented.

David's Reign at Jerusalem

After reigning seven years and six months in Hebron, David did two important things to unify the nation politically and religiously.

▶ **Study 2 Samuel 5—7 and answer the following questions. Use the paragraphs that follow to check your answers.**
1. What did David do to unify the nation politically? _____
_____

2. What did David do to unify the religious practice of the nation? _____
_____

3. What dream did David have that he was not permitted to fulfill? ____
_____

4. How do you interpret 2 Samuel 7:16? _____
_____
_____

Capturing Jerusalem and making it the capitol of his kingdom showed David's grasp of political realities. Consider:

(1) Much like Washington, D.C. is not located in any of the United States of America, Jerusalem belonged neither to the northern nor the southern tribes. Jerusalem served as a compromise location between the north and the south.

(2) Since David took the city, it rightly could be called the City of David. Associating his name with the capital city paid political dividends.

(3) Jerusalem was a well-fortified city. The city was easily defended and served well as a site of government.

David brought the ark of the covenant to Jerusalem. The ark symbolized God's presence among His people. Thus, His people came to Jerusalem to worship Him. He focused the attention of all the tribes on this city.

Throughout its history, Israel had only a tent to symbolize the place of God. David wanted to build a permanent house of God. God refused to let David build the temple but promised that David's son would do so.

When God refused to let David build the temple, He made a covenant with David to David's kingdom. One from the line of David would dwell on the throne of Israel forever. The passage rightly is interpreted to refer to Jesus. Only Jesus can fulfill such a magnificent promise. While born of the virgin Mary, Jesus' legal descent was traced through Joseph, a descendant of David. Jesus will completely fulfill God's promise when He comes again.

---

[11]Answers: A-2, 3, 5; B-I checked 2, but your opinion is as valid as mine.

▶ **Read 2 Samuel 8:15. In what sense was David an example for other kings to follow?**

_____

_____

Did you write that David consistently did what was just and right for the people? Good.

David's Later Years (2 Sam. 9—24)

Some biblical scholars call 2 Samuel 9—20 the succession narrative. In this section of 2 Samuel, the key question floating in the background is: Who will be king after David? Israel did not have a method for choosing a king. How would the people know who should be king after David? Solomon, of course, became king. But he gained the throne after a period in which several sons of David proved themselves unworthy and after a time of political maneuvering.

These chapters also contain accounts of personal sin and how sin affects other people. David's sin with Bathsheba led to sorrow and heartache within his own family. This sin occurred at a time of idleness (1 Sam. 11:1). David compounded his sin of adultery by trying to cover his tracks. He had Uriah, Bathsheba's husband, killed when Uriah failed to go along with David's plan to cover his sin. The Lord sent Nathan the prophet to confront David with his guilt. David's genuine repentance is evident in his response to God's prophet.

The Lord forgave David's sin, but the consequences of his act continued to affect his family life. Because of David's sin, he was unable to correct his son Amnon when he raped his half-sister. Since David had Uriah killed, he could hardly condemn the murder of Amnon by Absalom. Absalom later mounted a rebellion against his father and violated David's wives. Absalom was killed in the rebellion. God's words through Nathan were fulfilled.

▶ **Check the statements with which you agree.**[12]
   ☐ 1. Since God is willing to forgive sin, how I live does not matter.
   ☐ 2. My sins don't hurt anyone but me.
   ☐ 3. Eventually, sin always brings regrets.
   ☐ 4. God's forgiveness does not wipe out the influence of our sins on other people.
   ☐ 5. God can forgive sin, but the scars of sin remain.

Other rebellions occurred during this time, all of them failing to unseat David. Late in David's life, he designated Solomon to be king in his place. David left Solomon a kingdom at peace. The kingdom of Israel reached its largest size and greatest influence to date under David's reign. David served as the model by which Israel would judge all its kings.

---

[12]Answers: I hope you checked 3, 4, and 5.

▶ **SUMMARY REVIEW**

To review this week's study of the Old Testament, see if you can mentally answer the following questions. You may want to write the answers on a separate sheet of paper. Mark your level of performance on the left: circle "C" if you can answer correctly and circle "R" if you need to review.

C R 1. Write the Books of Law and of History through 2 Samuel.

C R 2. Who was Ruth's most famous descendant at the time the Book of Ruth was written?

C R 3. Name one purpose of the Books of Samuel.

C R 4. Name two roles that Samuel filled in serving Israel.

C R 5. How did Samuel view the people's call for a king?

C R 6. Give three ways Saul proved himself unfit to serve as king of Israel.

C R 7. What was David's motive in fighting Goliath?

C R 8. What is the meaning of David's being a man "after God's own heart"?

C R 9. Explain briefly the stages in David's becoming king after Saul's death.

RESPONDING TO GOD'S WORD

★ The Bible pulls no punches when it comes to describing its heroes. David was one of God's best, yet at times he failed God and his people. Answer the following by checking YES or NO.

1. Did God quit using David after his sins of adultery and murder?
   ☐ YES   ☐ NO

2. When Christian leaders sin and then repent, should they be disqualified from serving God?   ☐ YES   ☐ NO

3. When I discover faults in my church leaders or spiritual heroes, I should no longer put confidence in them.   ☐ YES   ☐ NO

★ Be prepared to discuss your responses in your group session. Pray for your church leaders right now.

God and the United and Divided Kingdoms *(1 Kings—2 Chronicles)*

The Books of Kings and Chronicles show how each decision in Israel's history affected the nation. These books show how God blessed the nation of Israel and how Israel's sins led to the nation's destruction. These books unfold how one decision affected another.

In this unit you will study the books of 1 and 2 Kings. You also will see how 1 and 2 Chronicles parallel the Books of 1 and 2 Samuel and 1 and 2 Kings.

1 and 2 Kings complete the story of the kingdom of Israel. These books pick up where 2 Samuel left off. Second Samuel left unanswered the question of who would serve as king after David. The Books of 1 and 2 Kings answer that question and tell the remainder of the history of the Northern Kingdom and the Southern Kingdom.

1 Chronicles generally parallels Samuel while *2 Chronicles* parallels Kings. Although Samuel-Kings are similar to Chronicles, there are apparent differences. Chronicles appear to have been written much later and as an interpretation of the history related in Samuel-Kings.

Kings:

   I. Solomon (1 Kings 1—11)
  II. The Divided Kingdom (1 Kings 12—2 Kings 17)
 III. Judah (2 Kings 18—25)

Chronicles:

    I. Genealogies (1 Chron. 1—9)
   II. David (1 Chron. 10—29)
  III. Solomon (2 Chron. 1—9)
  IV. Judah (2 Chron. 10—36)

WordWatch

Watch for these words as you study this unit.

Asherah—(or Astarte) was the goddess consort to Baal. The fertility of the land was believed to come from sexual relations between Baal and Asherah. To stimulate this, worshipers gathered at shrines, usually on the high places, and engaged in cult prostitution or sexual orgies as a part of their worship.

Asherah pole—pole or tree that marked a place of worship for Asherah.

DAY 1 Introducing the Books of Kings and Chronicles

U N I T 8   1 and 2 KINGS

The Books of 1 and 2 Kings pick up where 2 Samuel left off and complete the story of the kingdom of Israel. Second Samuel left unanswered the question of who would serve as king after David. The Books of 1 and 2 Kings answer that question and tell the remainder of the history of the Northern Kingdom and the Southern Kingdom. Take time now to look at the outline of these two books on page 122.

	SAMUEL	REIGN OF SAUL	REIGN OF DAVID	REIGN OF SOLOMON	DIVIDED KINGDOMS
1 SAMUEL					
2 SAMUEL					
1 KINGS					
2 KINGS					
1 CHRONICLES					
2 CHRONICLES					

Solomon served as king after David his father. He reigned over the same territory that David had brought into the kingdom of Israel. Solomon reigned in peace primarily because of what David had done.

After the death of Solomon, the kingdom of Israel divided into the Northern Kingdom and the Southern Kingdom. The Northern Kingdom, also called Israel, was made up of the 10 northern tribes. The tribes of Judah and Benjamin made up the Southern Kingdom, often called Judah.

This arrangement continued until the fall of the Northern Kingdom (Israel) in 722 B.C. The Southern Kingdom (Judah) continued until its fall to Babylon in 586 B.C.

➤ **Match the following words or phrases on the left with the correct words or phrases on the right. Write the correct letters in the blanks. Answers are at the bottom of the column.**[1]

_____ 1. Solomon	A. Northern Kingdom
_____ 2. Northern Kingdom	B. Southern Kingdom
_____ 3. Southern Kingdom	C. David's son
_____ 4. Ten tribes	D. Fall of Judah
_____ 5. Judah and Benjamin	E. Fall of Israel
_____ 6. 722 B.C.	F. Judah
_____ 7. 587 B.C.	G. Israel

Date and Authorship of 1 and 2 Kings

Jewish tradition credits Jeremiah with writing the Books of Kings. However, no one really knows who wrote them. First and Second Kings cover the time period from about 971 B.C. to 561 B.C. The last event in 2 Kings that we can date is when Evil-Merodach, the king of Babylon, allowed Judah's king Jehoiachin to receive favored treatment (2 Kings 25:27). We know that this happened in 561 B.C. So, the author or editor would have lived after that date. The author of Kings presents

---

[1]Answers: 1-C, 2-G, 3-F, 4-A, 5-B, 6-E, 7-D.

this event as a hopeful sign that Judah's exile would soon end. Since the book does not tell us about the end of the exile, we assume that the book must have been written before 539 B.C. when the Babylonian exile ended.

▶ **How would you explain to your Sunday School class the approximate time that 1 and 2 Kings were written?**

_____

_____

_____

Some of the material in 1 and 2 Kings came from contemporary sources in the courts of Israel and Judah.

▶ **Read the following verses and identify the sources of information mentioned. Answers are at the bottom of the column.²**

1. 1 Kings 11:41 _____

2. 1 Kings 14:19 _____

3. 2 Kings 8:23 _____

The Purpose of 1 and 2 Kings

At least three purposes for 1 and 2 Kings are evident.
● They continue the history of the Northern and Southern Kingdoms until their fall.
● They especially point out the wickedness of the northern kings in continuing the worship of the golden calves set up by Jeroboam and show why the Northern Kingdom fell so quickly.
● They clearly reveal the judgment of God on the sin of nations. Israel and Judah were not simply victims of international circumstances that worked against them. Their kings and people had rebelled against God. They turned from God to follow their own wicked way. Instead of worshiping the Lord alone, they worshiped other gods. God brought His judgment on them through hostile neighboring kingdoms. Both the Northern and Southern kingdoms fell because of God's judgment on the people's sins.

The Books of Chronicles

First Chronicles begins with a long genealogy (chaps. 1—9). These chapters set the stage for the chronicler's interpretive history of the people of Israel. The account begins with Saul and the Philistines (1 Chron. 10:1) and ends with Cyrus' decree that ended the Babylonian captivity. Cyrus gave this decree about 538 B.C. This means that 1 and 2 Chronicles cover a later period of history than do 1 and 2 Kings. Second Kings ends around 561 B.C., 23 years earlier than 2 Chronicles.

After a short section concerning Saul, the remainder of 1 Chronicles covers the reign of David, with emphasis on his planning and preparation for building the temple. Second Chronicles takes up the story of Solomon and his building the temple, then dwells on the history of the Southern Kingdom of Judah.

Chronicles probably was written after the Babylonian captivity. Its purpose is to emphasize religion and its practice. For example, the genealogy in 1 Chronicles 1—9 includes long lists of people who were to serve in the temple. In addition to

²Answers: Other translations may read differently, but the New International Version has:
1. the book of the annals of Solomon
2. the book of the annals of the kings of Israel
3. the book of the annals of the kings of Judah

Note: Some translations use the word *chronicles* instead of *annals* for the latter two sources. These books are not the same as 1 and 2 Chronicles.

temple personnel, the planning, construction, and dedication of the temple is given in great detail.

The major portion of material in the Chronicles is about David. Only favorable words are written of him. The author did not mention David's sin with Bathsheba.

▶ **To get an idea of how Chronicles roughly parallels Samuel and Kings, compare the outlines of Chronicles with those of Samuel and Kings (p. 122). Check the correct answer for each of the following questions:[3]**

BOOKS OF HISTORY

1. What section of the Chronicles outline is not found in Samuel or Kings?
☐ a. I.
☐ b. II.
☐ c. III.

2. What section of the Samuel outline is not found in Chronicles?
☐ a. I.
☐ b. II.
☐ c. III.

3. What section of the Kings outlines is not found in Chronicles?
☐ a. I.
☐ b. II.
☐ c. III.

4. Chronicles deals primarily with the history of the
☐ a. kings of Israel.
☐ b. kings of Judah.
☐ c. kings of Israel and Judah.

▶ **Let's end this session with another review of the books of the Bible. You should be able to supply the names of the missing books.**

DAY 2   The Reign of Solomon (1 Kings 1—11)

U N I T   8

Extent of Solomon's Empire

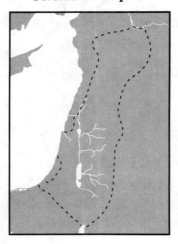

"Solomon reigned over all kingdoms from the river unto the land of the Philistines, and unto the border of Egypt: they brought presents, and served Solomon all the days of his life."
—1 Kings 4:21

Solomon reigned during the highest point of Israel's history. He inherited the kingdom from his father David. This inheritance included an era of peace and prosperity unparalleled in the history of Israel. The nation expanded its borders to the fartherest limits. It was a period of building and growth.

First Kings 1—2 explain how David designated Solomon as his successor. These two chapters of 1 Kings complete the account of 2 Samuel. Second Samuel shows that most of David's sons were unworthy to serve as king of Israel. First Kings 1—2 answers the question, "Who will serve as king after David?"

Power Politics (1 Kings 1—3)

Two of David's sons were shown as likely candidates for the kingship. Adonijah, the older of the two, demonstrated good characteristics and received solid backing from some members of David's court. Solomon, the son of Bathsheba, also received support from powerful members of David's inner circle.

▶ **Read 1 Kings 1:5-7 and answer the following questions:**

1. What was Adonijah's ambition? _____

_____

2. What did he do publicly to impress people that he should be king? ____

_____

3. What did he do privately to ensure his becoming king? _____

_____

Check your answers by information in the following paragraph.

Adonijah wanted to be king after David's death. He prepared both himself and the people to accept him as king by looking and acting as a king should in public. He had chariots and horsemen to run before him. In his attempt to become king, he privately enlisted the aid of Joab, David's army commander, and Abiathar the priest.

▶ **Read of Nathan and Bathsheba's plan in 1 Kings 1:11-14, and the result of that plan in 1:29-30. Do you think this is an example of applying the modern proverb, "All that is needed for evil to triumph is for good men to do nothing"? Circle your answer: YES   NO**

Does a worthy end justify lying to achieve it?

Nathan the prophet and Bathsheba, Solomon's mother, moved quickly to undercut the effort of Adonijah. Bathsheba told David that he earlier had said that Solomon would reign as king after him. As planned, Nathan came in as she was speaking and confirmed what she had said. In his old age, David accepted the words of his wife and his trusted advisor. He proclaimed Solomon to be the next king.

God blessed Solomon and the people of Israel. God also blessed Solomon with wisdom from above (1 Kings 4:29-34). First Kings 3:16-28 demonstrates his wisdom. He knew how to make delicate decisions. Solomon ruled the people of Israel with the wisdom of God.

Solomon's Government (1 Kings 4—5)

Solomon enlarged Israel's government. He appointed a large cabinet who functioned much the same way as modern secretaries of state and leaders in defense function (4:1-19).

Solomon burdened the people with taxes which were beyond the means of even a wealthy nation (10:14-15). Solomon gave each tribe the responsibility to provide for him and his household so that they could live extravagantly (4:7, 22-28; 10:14-29). He used much of the wealth of Israel for non-productive purposes.

Solomon's government also encouraged building projects. First Kings 7:1-8 describes different buildings Solomon built. The king erected a magnificent palace, taking 13 years to complete. In comparison he spent only seven years in building the house of the Lord.

▶ **Match the following Bible references on the left with the correct items on the right. Write the correct letters in the blanks. Answers are at the bottom of the column.[4]**

____ 1. 1 Kings 3:16-28	A. Solomon's wisdom
____ 2. 1 Kings 4:7	B. conscripted labor force
____ 3. 1 Kings 4:20-21	C. peace and prosperity
____ 4. 1 Kings 4:29	D. example of wisdom
____ 5. 1 Kings 5:13-14	E. heavy taxes
____ 6. 1 Kings 10:14-15	F. extravagant life-style
____ 7. 1 Kings 10:16-21	G. government officers

The Building of the Temple (1 Kings 6:1-38)

We remember Solomon best as the person who carried out the dream of his father, David, and built the temple. The temple symbolized the presence of God and gave permanence to Israel's religion. The temple also served as a rallying point for the nation. Coming to Jerusalem to worship and to celebrate the great feasts strengthened the people's loyalty to Jerusalem and to the idea of a united kingdom.

Solomon spared no expense on the house of the Lord. When the temple was rebuilt in the days of Haggai, those who had seen the old temple wept over the loss of Solomon's magnificent structure. The new building could not compare with the temple Solomon built.

Solomon and the people of Israel dedicated the temple of the Lord. Solomon's prayer of dedication is a wonderful statement of commitment to the Lord (1 Kings 8:22-53).

▶ **Read the following parts of Solomon's prayer of dedication: 1 Kings 8:27-30, 33-34,46-53. Mark the following statements as T (true) or F (false):[5]**

[4]Answers: 1-D, 2-G, 3-C, 4-A, 5-B, 6-E, 7-F.

_____ 1. Solomon prayed for God to dwell in the house he had built for Him.
_____ 2. Solomon prayed for God to hear prayers prayed toward the temple.
_____ 3. Solomon prayed that Israel would never be defeated in battle.
_____ 4. Solomon prayed that God would forgive His people of their sins if they would turn to Him in heart-felt confession and repentance.

God is a God of grace.   God is a God of mercy

The foundation stones of our relationship with God.

Solomon knew that no temple could contain the presence of God. Not even heaven could contain His glory. Solomon showed that he knew the Lord to be a God of grace and mercy and based his prayer on these great characteristics of God. Solomon also realized that all people are sinners and need God's forgiveness. After his prayer of dedication, he spoke to the people of Israel who were gathered for the temple dedication.

▶ **Read Solomon's address to the people in 1 Kings 8:56-61. Check the correct answer for each of the following questions:[6]**

1. Solomon said that not one word had failed of the promises God had given them through
☐ a. Abraham.
☐ b. Moses.
☐ c. David.

2. Solomon wanted all the peoples of the earth to know
☐ a. about the glorious temple.
☐ b. of God's blessings on His people.
☐ c. that the Lord is the only God.

3. Solomon hoped that the Lord would uphold His people according to each
☐ a. day's need.
☐ b. month's need.
☐ c. year's need.

4. To experience God's help, Solomon told the people that
☐ a. their hearts needed to be committed to obey God.
☐ b. they needed to make sacrifices.
☐ c. they needed to pray toward the temple.

The End of Solomon's Reign (1 Kings 9:10—11)

Solomon carried David's kingdom to its highest point. His reign was a time of great peace and prosperity, a time of building and of cultural achievement.

Solomon also started Israel down the road to destruction by making marriage alliances with foreign nations. Solomon sealed these alliances by marrying the daughters of the nations' kings (1 Kings 3:1; 11:1-8). This ensured peace but at a terrible price. These women turned his heart away from the Lord God and encour-

---
[5]Answers: 1-F, 2-T, 3-F, 4-T.
[6]Answers: 1-b, 2-c, 3-a, 4-a.

aged the worship of foreign gods in the city of Jerusalem. God told Solomon that after his death, God would take all but one tribe from his kingdom because of this sin. The divided kingdom was to be God's judgment on Solomon's sin.

RESPONDING TO GOD'S WORD

★ Read 1 Kings 11:1-6. Describe briefly how one act of disobedience led to other acts of disobedience. _____

_____

★ Read 1 Kings 11:11-13. Is this comment accurate: If I sin, I am hurting no one but myself? Underline your answer: YES   NO Explain your answer:

_____

_____

★ Praise God that His commandments have been given for our good. If you need to confess and repent of some wrong, do so now.

DAY 3   The Division of the Kingdom (1 Kings 12—20)

U N I T   8   Around 931 B.C., the nation of Israel divided into two kingdoms. Though Solomon had reigned 40 years in a time of prosperity and peace, he also had introduced practices that resulted in the division of the nation. Because of Solomon's worship of other gods, God told Solomon that after his death, the kingdom would be taken from his son, except for one tribe. What God had promised came to pass.

> **Factors that Contributed to the Division of the Kingdom**
> - Tribal jealousies
> - Solomon's heavy-handed approach in governing
> - Jeroboam's political ambition
> - Rehoboam's foolishness

▶ Read about the actual break between the northern tribes and Judah in 1 Kings 12:4-16. Match the items on the following page left with the corresponding item on the right. Write the correct letters in the blanks. Answers are at the bottom of the column.[7]

_____ 1. The people's request of Rehoboam
_____ 2. The elders' counsel to Rehoboam
_____ 3. The young men's counsel to Rehoboam
_____ 4. Rehoboam's answer to the people
_____ 5. The people's answer to Rehoboam

A. Lighten their load.
B. I will make your load heavier.
C. Lighten our load.
D. We will have no part in the house of David.
E. Make their load heavier.

Rehoboam was insensitive to the needs of the people. His father Solomon had levied heavy taxes and drafted large labor gangs. By Rehoboam's time, the people's resentment had hardened into resistance. Rehoboam failed to discern the mood of the people. He listened to his younger, inexperienced advisors and made even harder demands than his father had made. Rehoboam's policy drove the northern tribes to reject him and turn to Jeroboam as their king.

The division of the kingdom ended the greatest period of Israel's history. Under David, Israel had expanded its border to its farthermost limits. Solomon's reign brought a period of peace and prosperity never again approached in the Old Testament period.

From this time (931 B.C.) until the fall of Jerusalem in 587 B.C., Israel would exist as two kingdoms. The Northern Kingdom had its capital at Samaria and was known as the Kingdom of Israel. The Southern Kingdom had its capital in Jerusalem and was known as the Kingdom of Judah.

▶ **Fill in the blanks:**

1. The Northern Kingdom had its capital at _____
   and was known as the Kingdom of _____.

2. The Southern Kingdom had its capital at _____
   and was known at the Kingdom of _____.

Answers: See the above paragraph.

The Divided Kingdoms

The primary purpose of the Books of Kings is to teach religious truth, not to record historical facts.

The Books of Kings contain a great deal of history, but they were not written to be merely history books. They were written to be books of religion to instruct the people in right living before God. The writer of the Books of Kings wanted to show that people who put their trust in God and are obedient will endure as a nation and will receive God's blessings. People who reject God's leadership will face destruction.

▶ **Test the truth of the statements in the preceding paragraph.**

1. King Ahab did very little of political significance in the life of the Northern Kingdom. However, his actions had profound religious significance. How many verses in 1 Kings are devoted to telling about incidents involving Ahab, Jezebel, and Elijah? Begin counting at 1 Kings 16:29. _____

2. Omri was one of the most politically significant kings of the Northern Kingdom. Begin counting at 1 Kings 16:21. How many verses are devoted to Omri? _____

You should have seen by the exercise you just completed that the focus of the Books of Kings is not to convey historical fact, but to teach the religious significance of those facts.

---

⁷Answers: 1-C, 2-A, 3-E, 4-B, 5-D.

Read 2 Kings 10:28-29 and explain in one sentence what is meant by "the sins of Jeroboam son of Nebat, which he had caused Israel to commit":

_____

Worship Centers

Golden Calves

Mediterranean Sea

• Dan

ISRAEL

• Bethel

Jerusalem •

JUDAH

The Temple at Jerusalem

_____

Your answer should reflect that Jeroboam set up golden calves at Bethel and Dan for the people to worship.

As a sample of how 1 and 2 Kings describe the kings of the kingdom of Israel, read the references on the left and match them with the kings on the right. Put the correct letter by each reference:[8]

____ 1. 2 Kings 15:8-9   A. Pekah
____ 2. 2 Kings 15:17-18   B. Pekahiah
____ 3. 2 Kings 15:23-24   C. Menahem
____ 4. 2 Kings 15:27-28   D. Zechariah

When the kingdom divided, the temple was in Judah's territory at Jerusalem. Jeroboam feared that if his people returned there to worship, they would be influenced to shift their allegiance back to Solomon's son, Rehoboam. He placed golden calves at Dan and Bethel, the northern and southern extremes of his territory, and enticed the people of the Northern Kingdom to worship these false gods. Since all the northern kings followed Jeroboam's example, the biblical writers describe them as evil kings.

Are you aware of times when persons have used religion as a means of achieving personal or political ends? What can you do to guard against this failure in your own life?

_____

_____

The religious nature of the Books of Kings clearly is seen in the record of Omri's son, Ahab (1 Kings 16:29—22:40). Much space is devoted to Ahab because his rebellion against the Lord was opposed by the mighty prophet Elijah. Elijah spoke the words of God against the king and his wife Jezebel. Thus the writer of Kings used the story of Ahab to emphasize certain religious teachings.

Read 1 Kings 16:29-33; 17:1; 18:1,16-26,36-39, and mark the following T (true) or F (false):[9]

____ 1. Ahab built a special temple for the Lord in Samaria.
____ 2. Ahab's wife, Jezebel, worshiped Baal.
____ 3. Elijah announced to Ahab years of flooding as God's judgment on his sins and those of his people.
____ 4. Ahab sent for 950 prophets to meet on Mount Carmel.
____ 5. Elijah challenged the prophets to a debate.
____ 6. Elijah prayed from morning to evening for God to consume his sacrifice.
____ 7. When the Lord consumed Elijah's sacrifice, the people ran in terror.

In 1 and 2 Kings the story of the Northern and Southern Kingdoms intertwine. Sometimes this makes reading difficult. You may want to write "N" in the margin of your Bible by kings of the Northern Kingdom and "S" by kings of the Southern Kingdom. Some Bibles have subheads identifying the kings as ruling Israel or Judah.

---

[8]Answers: 1-D, 2-C, 3-B, 4-A.
[9]Answers: 1-F, 2-T, 3-F, 4-F, 5-F, 6-F, 7-F.

RESPONDING TO GOD'S WORD

★ Why do you think the writer of 1 Kings recorded the contest on Mount Carmel between Elijah and the prophets of Baal? _____

_____

Your answer could have indicated that this account was included for the religious truth it taught: Idolatry is empty; serve the true God.

★ Meditate for one minute on this question: Did your life this past week reflect the fact that you truly recognize the Lord as your God? Do not go farther until your minute is up.

Perhaps your meditation led you to conclude that sometimes your life reflected that the Lord is your God and sometimes it did not.

★ Meditate one minute on this question: What would need to be changed this week for your life to more completely show that the Lord is your God? Do not go farther until your minute is up. Record your response here.

_____

_____

_____

★ Ask God for His strength to make changes you need to make this week.

DAY 4 The Fall of the Northern Kingdom (2 Kings 12:20—17:41)

U N I T 8

The Northern Kingdom came into existence in 931 B.C. In spite of the courageous ministries of a number of prophets, especially Elijah and Elisha, the nation turned away from the Lord and worshiped false gods. Because of its rebellion against God, the Northern Kingdom fell to Assyria in 722 B.C.

Some of the Northern Kingdom's greatest years were those shortly before its fall to Assyria. Jeroboam II, the son of Jehoash, reigned over the Northern Kingdom for 41 years. During his reign, Jonah the prophet spoke of the return of the Northern Kingdom to some of its former glory. He had prophesied that Israel's boundaries would extend from Hamath in the north as far as the Arabah in the south.

▶ Read 2 Kings 14:23-25. Hamath is far north of anything you see on the map in the previous session. The Arabah is the valley that runs south from the lower end of the Dead Sea. If the Northern Kingdom controlled all that area, what relationship do you think existed during that period between the Northern and Southern Kingdoms? Write your answer here.

_____

In all probability, Israel dominated Judah during this period. This period of success simply preceded a time of great decline. Jeroboam II died in 747 B.C. That year the Northern Kingdom began a significant decline. In that one year, four different kings reigned. Jeroboam II was followed by his son, Zechariah, who reigned only six months before he was murdered by Shallum, who reigned in his place. Shallum was in turn murdered by Menahem who continued on the throne for 10 years. Someone has suggested that during the latter years of the Northern Kingdom, the question was not who is king but who has not been king.

▶ **Read 2 Kings 15:17-20 and answer the following questions. Answers are at the bottom of the column.**[10]

    1. How long did Menahem reign in Samaria? _____

    2. Who invaded the Northern Kingdom in his reign? _____

    3. How did Menahem gain the invader's support? _____

    4. What was Menahem's source of funds? _____
_____

    5. What did the invader finally do? _____

Second Kings 15—17 tells of the last years of the Northern Kingdom. During the reign of Menahem, the barbarous nation Assyria reached its peak under the reign of Tiglath-Pileser, who is often called Pul in the Bible.

The Assyrians ran roughshod over the Middle East. Pul threatened to destroy Samaria. Menahem appeased him by paying tribute of a thousand talents of silver. This act might have been the only thing that saved the Northern Kingdom at that time. After the death of Menahem, Pekahiah reigned in the place of his father. Pekahiah reigned only two years before being killed by Pekah, his captain.

▶ **Read 2 Kings 15:27-31. Check the correct answer for each of the following questions:**[11]

    1. Pekah reigned over Israel in Samaria
    ☐ a. 6 months.
    ☐ b. 10 years.
    ☐ c. 20 years.

    2. Tiglath-Pilesar came again to the Northern Kingdom and
    ☐ a. extorted more money.
    ☐ b. took Gilead and Galilee.
    ☐ c. took Dan and Beersheba.

    3. The Assyrians
    ☐ a. deported the population to Assyria.
    ☐ b. slaughtered the people.
    ☐ c. suddenly departed in fear.

    4. Pekah was succeeded by
    ☐ a. his son, Hoshea.
    ☐ b. his assassin, Hoshea.
    ☐ c. his brother, Hoshea.

Pekah reigned in place of Pekahiah for 20 years. At this time Tiglath-Pileser made another assault against the Northern Kingdom. Hoshea took advantage of the political unrest in Samaria to rise against Pekah and to kill him. Hoshea, who reigned nine years, served as the last king of the Northern Kingdom.

---

[10]Answers: 1-10 years; 2-Pul (also known as Tiglath-Pileser); 3-paid him a thousand talents of silver; 4-each wealthy man of the land was required to pay 50 talents of silver; 5-left the land.
[11]Answers: 1-c, 2-b, 3-a, 4-b.

At first, Hoshea remained a faithful vassal of Assyria. However, when Hoshea refused to pay tribute and started to make overtures toward the king of Egypt, he sealed Israel's fate.

► **Read 2 Kings 17:1-6 and mark the following statements as T (true) or F (false):[12]**
    ____ 1. Shalmaneser moved against Samaria because he was running low on funds.
    ____ 2. Shalmaneser put Hoshea in prison.
    ____ 3. Salmaneser beseiged Samaria for nine years.
    ____ 4. Salmaneser deported the Israelites to Assyria.

In about 725 B.C. Shalmaneser, Assyria's new king, besieged Samaria. After three years, the Israelites could stand the Assyrian siege no longer and Samaria fell in 722 B.C.

The Assyrian leaders carried out a cruel policy of exile. They removed many of the leading people of Samaria to foreign lands. In their place, they brought peoples from other conquered lands to Samaria. The descendants of these people were the Samaritans in the New Testament era.

Assyria's policy of exile carried out a political strategy. A nation without military leaders, political leaders, and people with the skills to develop weapons could not revolt against their conquerors. They imported foreigners to ensure that the land would remain productive enough to produce taxes.

Why did Samaria fall to Assyria? How could God allow His people to be conquered by an unrighteous nation? Was God defeated? Were the gods worshiped in the other nations greater than the Lord? The people of Israel probably asked these questions. The writer of the Books of Kings presented the reason for the fall of the Northern Kingdom.

► **Read 2 Kings 17:7-8,12-18 and check the following statements with which you agree:[13]**
    ☐ 1. Israel fell to Assyria because Assyria had a vastly superior military force.
    ☐ 2. Israel fell to Assyria because her people worshiped idols.
    ☐ 3. Israel may have been more faithful if God had warned them more than once against disobeying Him.
    ☐ 4. Israel was more influenced by neighboring nations than the commandments of God.
    ☐ 5. The Israelites even practiced human sacrifice.
    ☐ 6. The Lord was behind Israel's fall.

The Kingdom of Judah

From 722 B.C. onward, only the kingdom of Judah existed. The territory of the Northern Kingdom was under Assyria. In later times, Josiah, one of Judah's best kings, attempted to take some of the northern area into the kingdom of Judah. For the most part, all such attempts failed and Judah alone remained in the land of Palestine.

The Southern Kingdom suffered from the leadership of weak kings just as the Northern Kingdom had. Most of the kings failed to live up to God's high ideal. They allowed the worship of other gods in outlying regions on the high places. Some people worshiped the Lord at the high places. Others worshiped the gods of

---

[12]Answers: 1-F, King Hoshea had stopped paying tribute and was trying to make an alliance with Egypt; 2-T; 3-F, three years; 4-T.
[13]Answers: 1-disagree (v. 18 or v. 7); 2-agree (vv. 7, 15-16); 3-disagree (vv. 12-13, 15); 4-agree (v. 15); 5-agree (v. 17); 6-agree (v. 18).

Baal. Most of this worship was probably a combination of the worship of the Lord and the worship of foreign gods. In this kind of worship, the Lord was reduced in people's minds to the level of the nature gods worshiped by the Canaanites.

▶ **Read 1 Kings 14:22-24 to see what happened in the Southern Kingdom of Judah during the reign of Solomon's son, Rehoboam. Check the specific transgressions mentioned in those two verses:**

☐ 1. Set up sites for worship on the high places.
☐ 2. Practiced child sacrifice.
☐ 3. Stole from the poor.
☐ 4. Worshiped sacred stones and Asherah poles.
☐ 5. Kidnapped.
☐ 6. Used male prostitutes at the places of worship.

Did you check 1, 4, and 6?

RESPONDING TO GOD'S WORD

★ Underline your answer(s): Do you think the people of the Northern Kingdom in general
  1. did not believe God would ever judge their sins?
  2. did not believe in God?
  3. presumed on God's mercy in spite of their refusal to turn from their sins and obey Him?

★ Which of the above answers best describes the attitude of people you know who do not seek to obey God? Circle your answer: 1 2 3

★ Pray for God to help you and the other members of your study group take more seriously the promises and warnings in God's Word.

DAY 5 The Fall of the Southern Kingdom (2 Kings 18—25)

UNIT 8

While most of Judah's kings failed to serve the Lord with all their hearts, some kings, such as Hezekiah and Josiah, provided effective political and spiritual leadership. They tried to remove the worship at the high places. They called on the people by words and by example to obey the Lord and to do His will. Their leadership helped ensure the continuation of the Kingdom of Judah for a number of years.

HEZEKIAH (2 Kings 18—20)

Use the following exercise to guide you in a study of the reign of this good king.

◆ **Exercise A. Read 2 Kings 18:1-8.**

1. Circle the words below that characterize Hezekiah:[14]

weak   godly   zealous   superstitious   faithful

lucky   strong   successful   cautious   bold

2. What action did Hezekiah take that would anger the Assyrians? _____

_____

Exercise B. Read 2 Kings 18:17-25. Check the words listed below that describe elements in Sennacherib's message to Hezekiah in verses 19-25.

☐ 1. Bluff   ☐ 5. Misunderstanding
☐ 2. Threat   ☐ 6. Enticement
☐ 3. Ridicule   ☐ 7. Religious
☐ 4. Joke

Exercise C. Read 2 Kings 19:1-2, 5-7, 9-19. Write a one-word answer to each of the following statements or questions:

1. When Hezekiah heard Sennacherib's message, he was _____

2. Who was the prophet that reassured Hezekiah? _____

3. What did the prophet tell Hezekiah not to do? _____

4. Sennacherib's second message described hope in God as what? _____

5. Hezekiah responded to the second message by doing what? _____

6. Hezekiah declared that the Lord alone is _____

7. Hezekiah acknowledged that many of Sennacherib's claims were what? _____

8. Hezekiah's request was for what? _____

Exercise D. Read 2 Kings 19:35-37 to discover how God answered Hezekiah's prayer.

Manasseh (2 Kings 21:1-18)

Hezekiah had been one of Judah's best kings, but Manasseh his son proved to be one of the worst. Here is a list of some of his wicked deeds. He . . .

● Rebuilt the high places
● Erected altars to Baal
● Built an Asherah pole
● Built altars to other gods in the temple
● Sacrificed his son
● Practiced sorcery and divination
● Consulted mediums and spiritists
● Put Asherah pole in temple
● Led the people astray

---

[14]Answers to Exercise A: Godly, faithful, zealous, strong, successful, bold. 2-Hezekiah rebelled against the Assyrians.

Answers to Exercise B: I checked all but 1 and 4 (you may have described as a joke what I thought of as ridicule). The Assyrians were not (1) bluffing; already they had taken the Northern Kingdom (see 2 Kings 18:10). They (2) threatened to destroy the city; (3) ridiculed Judah's hope in Egypt and inability to provide even 2,000 fighting men; (5) misunderstood Hezekiah's removal of the high places; (6) enticed them to surrender by promising to take them to another fruitful land; (7) claimed to have come against Hezekiah at God's command.

Answers to Exercise C: 1-you may have put something like upset, depressed, or hopeless; 2-Isaiah; 3-fear; 4-deceit; 5-praying; 6-God; 7-true; 8-deliverance.

Josiah (2 Kings 22—23:30)

At Manasseh's death, his son Amon became king. He was assassinated after only two years. However, his assassins were killed and his son, Josiah followed him on the throne. Josiah was the last great and godly king in Judah. Josiah's desire to do what was right in the sight of the Lord set in motion a sequence of events that brought about Judah's last high hour.

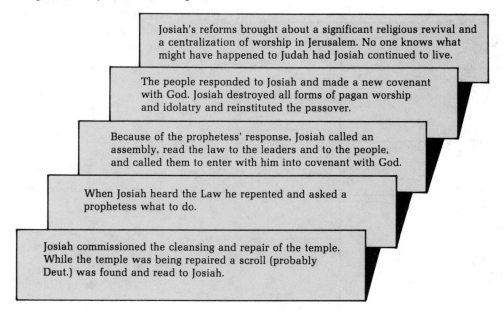

Josiah's reforms brought about a significant religious revival and a centralization of worship in Jerusalem. No one knows what might have happened to Judah had Josiah continued to live.

The people responded to Josiah and made a new covenant with God. Josiah destroyed all forms of pagan worship and idolatry and reinstituted the passover.

Because of the prophetess' response, Josiah called an assembly, read the law to the leaders and to the people, and called them to enter with him into covenant with God.

When Josiah heard the Law he repented and asked a prophetess what to do.

Josiah commissioned the cleansing and repair of the temple. While the temple was being repaired a scroll (probably Deut.) was found and read to Josiah.

International Turmoil, Decline, and Fall (2 Kings 23:31—25:30)

At this time a three-way struggle for power was taking place between Assyria, Babylon, and Egypt. Unfortunately, Judah was caught squarely in the middle geographically and politically. Josiah was killed and Judah started its final decline. Her kings were evil, weak, and ineffectual. Some of them were no more than puppet kings of Egypt or Babylon. Note this procession of kings on the time line on the next page. Those who tried to break away from the power that was controlling them were mercilessly slain and other puppets were installed in their places.

As the tides of war and world power swept back and forth Judah was aligned with Egypt. Jehoiachin hardly had taken the throne after his father's death when Nebuchadnezzar, king of Babylon, besieged Jerusalem. The young king surrendered to Nebuchadnezzar and was taken into exile in Babylon along with about 10,000 Judeans. This was the first phase of the Babylonian's taking Judeans into captivity (around 598 B.C.).

Nebuchadnezzar put Zedekiah, another son of Josiah, on the throne and he was king for 11 years (597-586 B.C.). Zedekiah failed not so much because of his wickedness but because of his weakness. He could not decide whether to cast his lot with the Egyptians or the Babylonians. When he finally decided to follow the Egyptians, Nebuchadnezzar moved speedily against Jerusalem. After a siege of about 18 months, Nebuchadnezzar broke through the walls of Jerusalem. He captured Zedekiah. The Babylonian king ordered Zedekiah's children killed before his eyes, and then had his eyes put out.

Nebuchadnezzar destroyed the walls of Jerusalem and burned the temple of the Lord. Another large group of citizens were taken into Babylon as exiles. It was Jerusalem's darkest day. Jerusalem fell to Babylon in 587 B.C. Jerusalem fell because of a series of wicked kings who defied the living Lord.

The Book of 2 Kings ends with a small glimmer of hope. The writer described how Evil-Merodach, the king of Babylon, graciously provided for Jehoiachin in exile.

Could the exile end? Would Israel be a nation again? Was God still with His people? The writer could not answer any of these questions. But he certainly hoped that God would work and would not forget His people Israel.

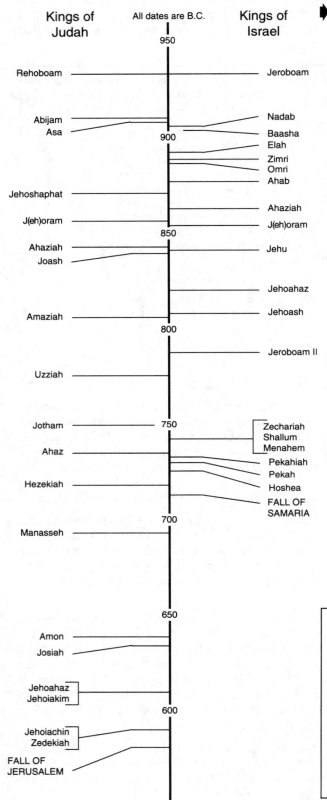

Kings of Judah	All dates are B.C.	Kings of Israel
	950	
Rehoboam		Jeroboam
Abijam		Nadab
Asa	900	Baasha
		Elah
		Zimri
		Omri
		Ahab
Jehoshaphat		
		Ahaziah
J(eh)oram	850	J(eh)oram
Ahaziah		Jehu
Joash		
		Jehoahaz
Amaziah		Jehoash
	800	
		Jeroboam II
Uzziah		
Jotham	750	Zechariah
		Shallum
		Menahem
Ahaz		Pekahiah
		Pekah
Hezekiah		Hoshea
		FALL OF SAMARIA
	700	
Manasseh		
	650	
Amon		
Josiah		
Jehoahaz		
Jehoiakim	600	
Jehoiachin		
Zedekiah		
FALL OF JERUSALEM		
	550	

▶ **SUMMARY REVIEW**

To review this week's study of the Old Testament, mentally answer the following questions. You may want to write the answers on a separate sheet of paper. Mark your level of performance on the left: circle "C" if you can answer correctly and circle "R" if you need to review.

C R 1. Fill in the blanks:

BOOKS OF HISTORY

J _____   1 & 2 C _____

J _____   Ezra

R _____   Nehemiah

1 & 2 S _____   Esther

1 & 2 K _____

C R 2. What are two differences in the Books of Chronicles and Kings?

C R 3. What were two strengths and two weaknesses of Solomon?

C R 4. What was Solomon's greatest contribution?

C R 5. What are three reasons the kingdom divided?

C R 6. What were the capitals of the two kingdoms?

C R 7. Why were more lines of Scripture given to Ahab than to Omri?

C R 8. Why is no northern king given a good report in the Books of Kings?

C R 9. What nation carried the people of the Northern Kingdom into captivity?

C R 10. How would you describe the state of Jerusalem and Judea at the end of the period described in 2 Kings?

RESPONDING TO GOD'S WORD

★ **Read 2 Kings 25:27-29. If you had been one of the Judean exiles in Babylon, would learning of those events make you feel hopeful? Circle one: YES NO**

The news probably gave the exiles a glimmer of hope for the future. Contrast that hint of hope with the confident hope in the present and for the future that we have through the Lord Jesus Christ. Lift your heart in a prayer of thanksgiving for God's grace that He has poured out on you.

God and the Exile and Restoration *(Ezra—Esther)*

How do you live in difficult times? The Books of Ezra, Nehemiah, and Esther describe people who lived in difficult times. They also show how God is present, even in the darkest hours in the lives of His children. As we study these books, we can learn how we too can handle life when times are tough.

In this unit you will study the Books of Ezra, Nehemiah, and Esther.

Ezra-Nehemiah should be considered together. Most biblical scholars believe that the books were written by the same author. In the Hebrew Bible they were one book, and several biblical scholars believe that Ezra himself was the author. The Books of Ezra and Nehemiah continue the story of the people of Judah who were carried into exile in Babylon. Little is known of the period between the destruction of Jerusalem and the return from exile. The Books of Ezra and Nehemiah pick up the story beginning with the return from exile shortly after 540 B.C. and continue through the resettling of Judah.

Esther continues the profound message of Ezra and Nehemiah. By blessing and caring for His people, God showed His concern for them. Though they lived outside Palestine, the Lord still reigned over them. His care for His people never wavered.

Ezra-Nehemiah:

    I. Return from Exile and Rebuilding the Temple (Ezra 1—6)
    II. Ezra's Work (Ezra 7—10)
    III. Nehemiah's Administration of Judea (Neh. 1—12)
    IV. Nehemiah's Second Visit to Judea (Neh. 13)

Esther:

    I. Esther Becomes Queen (Esth. 1—2)
    II. Haman's Plot and Esther's Intervention (Esth. 3—7)
    III. The Jews Prosper (Esth. 8:1-9:19)
    IV. The Feast of Purim (Esth. 9:20-32)
    V. Mordecai's Greatness (Esth. 10)

WordWatch

Watch for these words as you study this unit.

Jew—apparently came into use during the Babylonian exile. The Babylonians knew that the people had come from Judea. Instead of calling them Judeans, they shortened the name to Jew.

Purim—the Jews' celebration of the deliverance from Haman's plot. The word is the plural form of *pur*, the Persian word for lot or stone which Haman cast to decide the day on which he would carry out his plot (Esth. 3:7).

DAY 1   The Return and Reconstruction Begins (Ezra 1—6)

UNIT   9

You saw as you studied the unit page that Ezra and Nehemiah must be studied together because their narratives overlap as they tell the history of the Jewish people beginning with the return from exile and continuing through the resettling of Judah.

In this session you will study about the return from exile. If you have not studied the material on the unit page for this unit, please do so before proceeding.

▶ **There are 12 books of history. List the six which best relate the history of Israel from Samuel through the return from captivity. Answers are at the bottom of the column.[1]**

1. _____   4. _____

2. _____   5. _____

3. _____   6. _____

The first six chapters of Ezra relate the events that occurred between 540 B.C. and 514 B.C. Ezra apparently had not lived through those years, but was recording events that were already history to him. His known ministry began in 458 B.C. when he returned to Jerusalem. We do not know how long he had been active before that time.

Ezra related the events of world history to the work of the Lord. He knew that the Lord had worked in the past and was continuing to work in the present. The people in captivity had been praying for deliverance from Babylonian captivity and for an opportunity to return to their homeland. Ezra shows how God can work through events in the pagan world to bring His will to pass and answer the prayers of His people.

In his writing, Ezra showed that God worked through Cyrus to bring about the deliverance of His people from exile in Babylon. Babylon had been the dominant power in the Near East since 605 B.C. In 540 B.C. Cyrus, king of Persia, marched on Babylon, and the city fell the following year. Ezra 1:1 begins in the first year of Cyrus the Persian, 540-539 B.C.

▶ **Read Ezra 1:1-4 and answer the following questions.[2]**

1. What prophet foretold the return from captivity?_____

2. What king was God's instrument to end the captivity? _____

3. What was the king's stated purpose in allowing the return?_____

_____

4. Who was to return? _____

5. What role did the people who did not return play?_____

For his time Cyrus was known as an enlightened leader. He rejected the socially destructive policy of exile which both Assyria and Babylon practiced. He did not

---

[1]Answers: 1 Samuel, 2 Samuel, 1 Kings, 2 Kings, Ezra, Nehemiah.
[2]Answers: 1-Jeremiah; 2-Cyrus of Persia; 3-build a temple to God, 4-anyone, 5-give material support.

send captive people to exile. Instead, throughout the ancient world, Cyrus allowed captive peoples to return to their homes and to practice their religion. Ezra 1:2-4 gives the decree of Cyrus the Persian allowing the people of Jerusalem to return to their homeland and to rebuild the temple of the Lord.

Many leaders of the Jews, including priests and Levites, made plans to return to Jerusalem and to rebuild the house of the Lord. Cyrus boldly encouraged their going to Jerusalem (Ezra 1:5-11).

► **Read 1:5-11 and answer the following questions and check answers on the next page.**[3]

    1. What was the final factor that determined whether people chose to return or to stay?

    _____

    2. What did Cyrus send with them to Jerusalem?_____

    _____

BOOKS OF HISTORY

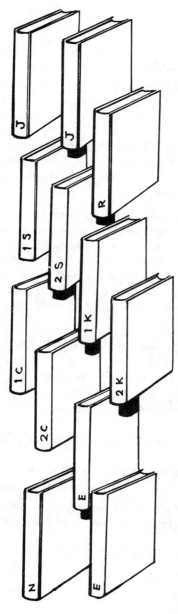

By 536 B.C. many Jews in Babylon began the return to Jerusalem. Cyrus allowed the returning Jews to take with them the articles which had been taken from the temple by the Babylonians (Ezra 1:7). Sheshbazzar led the returning group. The lists of those who went to Jerusalem is recorded in Ezra 2:1-70. The group totaled 42,360.

► **A. Read 3:1-5. Write the numbers 1, 2, or 3 beside the first, second, and third things the returning exiles did when they arrived in Judea. Answers on page 142.**[4]

    _____ a. Rebuilt the foundation of the temple.
    _____ b. Rebuilt the altar.
    _____ c. Wrote Cyrus a formal letter of appreciation.
    _____ d. Settled in their towns.
    _____ e. Began to make offerings and sacrifices.

    B. Check your response: The returning exiles felt welcomed and wanted by the present inhabitants of Judea.　☐ **Agree**　　☐ **Disagree**

Jerusalem lay in ruins. The wall, the temple, the houses, and even the altar of the Lord had been destroyed. Returning to Jerusalem was a major undertaking for the Jews. To compound the problem, many of the people who returned were the older and poorer exiles. Many Jews who had established successful businesses in Babylon probably remained in the land of Babylon.

► **Write one sentence describing how you might have felt had you been a returning exile and saw the conditions in Jerusalem and realized the hostility of the people then living in the area:**

    _____

    _____

The returning exiles lived in great fear for their own personal safety (Ezra 3:1-7). To the people who lived in Palestine, the returning Jews were invaders intent on taking their land. In spite of their fear, they immediately set up the altar in Jerusalem, dedicated it to the Lord, and began to offer sacrifices.

They had no idea of the difficulties they would face or how overwhelming their task of reconstruction would be. As you continue this study tomorrow you will see how God helped them deal with seemingly impossible situations.

► **Reenforce your memory of the books of the Bible that you are learning. You should now know all the books of history. Can you supply the titles to the books in the margin?**

RESPONDING TO GOD'S WORD

★ What significant victories has God helped you achieve? How can you commemorate those victories? Write a plan for remembering regularly one such victory:

_____

_____

★ Pray for God to grant you the courage to do what is right regardless of the personal risk. Commit yourself into His keeping as you faithfully pledge to serve Him in integrity.

DAY 2   Reconstruction and Revival (Ezra 4—10)

U N I T   9

Rebuilding the Temple (Ezra 4—6)

In yesterday's session you saw that the people laid the foundation of the temple during the second year of their return. They rejoiced and celebrated with praise and thanksgiving and hoped that the temple would soon be completed. Unfortunately, the temple was not completed for many years.

Ezra 4 explains why 14 years passed between laying the foundation and beginning work on the structure itself. The Jews faced opposition, especially from the people who lived in the area that would come to be known as Samaria in New Testament times. These people were the Jews who had been left in the land when others were carried off into captivity. These Jews considered themselves to be faithful followers of the law of Moses. However, the returning exiles did not recognize them as part of God's people because they had intermarried with other nations.

▶ Read 4:1-5 for the background of opposition that delayed the completion of the temple. Check statements with which you agree:
   ☐ 1. The offer by the people living in the land to help build the temple may have been a sincere offer of cooperation.
   ☐ 2. The claim by the present inhabitants to worship God probably was not accepted by the returned exiles.
   ☐ 3. The people of the land sought to encourage the Jews to rebuild the temple.
   ☐ 4. The people of the land were determined to frustrate all efforts of the returned exiles.

In the previous exercise, you probably agreed with all the statements except the third. Fourteen years passed without work continuing on the house of the Lord.

---

[3]Answers: 1-God's moving their hearts; 2-the temple vessels that Nebuchadnezzar had taken when he destroyed the temple and Jerusalem.
[4]Answers: A: 1-d, 2-b, 3-e. B:-disagree (v. 3).

We do not know all the reasons for the delay. We do know that the people suffered opposition and poverty. They probably struggled to eke out an existence for themselves. They faced hardships of many kinds which drained their emotional energy.

Four people who got things started

▶ **Read 5:1-2 to see how work again was begun on the temple. Fill in the blanks below. Answers are at the bottom of the column.[5]**

1. The two prophets that God used to lead the people to rebuild the temple were

_____ and _____ .

2. The two men that led the work were _____ and

_____ .

Who are the persons who have encouraged you and guided you in pressing on in the Lord's work?

▶ **Read 5:3-5 for another problem the builders had to face. Check the correct ending for each of the following statements:[6]**

1. The present governor of the area was
☐ a. Shealtiel
☐ b. Tattenai
☐ c. Shethar-Bozenai

2. The governor wanted to know (check two of the following)
☐ a. who issued the building permit.
☐ b. who was in charge.
☐ c. who was paying for the work.

Whom did you encourage and guide last?

3. Until authority from king Darius was received,
☐ a. the work was again halted.
☐ b. the work was delayed six months.
☐ c. the work continued.

4. The Jews felt confident that
☐ a. God was watching over them.
☐ b. the governor's local forces were weak.
☐ c. Darius was on their side.

When the present local governor questioned the building project, he was informed of Cyrus' decree. He wrote Darius, who had become king of Persia, asking that the information be checked. Darius had the archives searched.

▶ **Read 6:1-12 to see Darius' reply to the governor. Check the things that Darius instructed the governor and his men to do:[7]**
☐ 1. Stay away.
☐ 2. Do not interfere.
☐ 3. Pay for the construction out of their taxes.
☐ 4. Provide weapons for the Jews.
☐ 5. Provide what the priests needed for daily sacrifices.
☐ 6. Hold a feast for the Jewish leaders.
☐ 7. Do what I say or else!

Work continued on the temple for four years. Ezra 6:15 describes how the work was finished in the sixth year of the reign of Darius the king. In 516 B.C. the people of Israel celebrated the completion of the house of the Lord and dedicated the

[5]Answers: 1-Haggai and Zechariah, 2-Zerubbabel and Jeshua.
[6]Answers: 1-b, 2-a and b, 3-c, 4-a.
[7]Answers to exercise on chapter 6: You should have checked all except 4 and 6.

temple for use in worship of the Lord God of Israel. The people presented offerings and kept the Passover. It was a time of rejoicing and worship. The people had returned to their land and the house of the Lord had been rebuilt. The building program reflected genuine commitment to God and the desire to know Him and to do His will. The result of this commitment was cause for celebration and thanksgiving.

Revival Under Ezra (Ezra 7—10)

The story of events that involved Ezra begins at Ezra 7:1. The events recorded in Ezra began around 540 B.C. Ezra does not appear on the scene until 82 years later. Ezra loved the law of the Lord and sought to teach it to others. He wanted to teach the law in Jerusalem. Ezra journeyed to Jerusalem believing the good hand of God was on him.

▶ **Read Ezra 7:8-10. What was Ezra's three-fold commitment to the Law of the Lord?**

1. _____

2. _____

3. _____

You saw that Ezra's commitment was to study, obey (practice), and teach the law. How do you evaluate the strength of these three aspects of your commitment to God's word? _____

_____

_____

Ezra 7:11-26 is a letter containing Ezra's credentials given him by King Artaxerxes.

▶ **To focus on some significant information in the letter, match the following verses on the left with the correct statements on the right. Write the correct letters in the blanks.[8]**

____ 1. 7:13
____ 2. 7:15-16
____ 3. 7:17-18
____ 4. 7:21-23
____ 5. 7:24
____ 6. 7:25-26

A. Ezra carried considerable wealth with him.
B. Part of the wealth was for sacrifices.
C. Local government could not tax religious workers or institutions.
D. Other priests and Levites could return with Ezra.
E. Ezra was to appoint officers to administer God's law.
F. Local government was to support the temple worship.

The journey to Jerusalem proved difficult. You can imagine trying to take a journey of several weeks duration without benefit of restaurants, motels, law enforcement, or modern transportation. Ezra believed that God would lead them. At the same time, you can read his practical concern in Ezra 8:22. Ezra had proclaimed the power of God so much that he felt ashamed to ask for a band of soldiers for protection from possible enemies. Most of us can identify with Ezra at this point. He loved the Lord and put his faith in Him, but at the same time he was concerned about what could happen. Ezra and the other biblical characters faced real obstacles and felt the real emotions of fear and dread. He was wise to take his feelings to God in prayer and not to let them paralyze him.

---

[8]Answers: 1-D, 2-A, 3-B, 4-F, 5-C, 6-E.

▶ Shortly after Ezra arrived at Jerusalem, he was presented with a pressing problem. Read Ezra 9:1-2 to understand the problem. Check the correct answer or answers to the following questions:[9]

1. Who among the Israelites was involved in this problem?
☐ a. priests
☐ b. Levites
☐ c. the people, including priests and Levites

2. In what sense had the Israelites not separated themselves from neighboring peoples?
☐ a. They were in business with them.
☐ b. They had intermarried with them.
☐ c. They had entered into military and political alliances with them.

3. Who had led the way in these faithless practices?
☐ a. Leaders and officials
☐ b. Benjaminites
☐ c. Nehemiah

When God's leaders pray and call for repentance, God's people respond.

Many of the men had married foreign wives. Ezra was appalled at this violation of the law. From the time the law was given, God forbade His people to intermarry with other tribes (Deut 7:1-4). This prohibition was to guard against pagan wives influencing their husbands to practice idolatry. Ezra's response was intense public grief and prayer. This public display on his part produced a response on the part of the people.

▶ A. Read 10:1-4 for the response of many people to Ezra's grief and prayer. Check the statements that correctly reflect that response:[10]

☐ 1. They wept with Ezra.
☐ 2. They confessed their sins.
☐ 3. They said they would not make any more foreign marriages.
☐ 4. They felt that Israel no more had hope.
☐ 5. They agreed they should send away foreign wives with their children.
☐ 6. They agreed to support Ezra as he led in this matter.

B. Study the repentance recorded in 10:7-17. Mark the following statements as T (true) or F (false):

_____ 1. All the male Jews were called to assemble in Jerusalem.
_____ 2. They gathered on a bright, sunny day.
_____ 3. Ezra denounced marriages to foreign women.
_____ 4. The people disagreed with Ezra.
_____ 5. The people agreed to put away their foreign wives immediately.
_____ 6. Ezra dealt with each case personally.

No leader can call God's people to a level of living higher than the one on which he stands!

The leaders called a national assembly, and Ezra called on the men to confess their sins and to separate themselves from their foreign wives. (Ezra's is not the last word on marriages of God's people with unbelievers; see 1 Cor. 7:12-16.)

While this action may seem harsh, it served to keep the religion of Israel alive and to make the people of Israel a stronger people with a stronger commitment to obey the Lord. Many Bible students believe that Ezra should be credited with the survival of Judaism.

---

[9]Answers: 1-c, 2-b, 3-a.
[10]Answers: A- You should have checked all except 4. B- 1-T, 2-F (they were uncomfortable in the rain), 3-T, 4-F (they agreed they should put away foreign wives), 5-F (they asked for time to deal properly with each case), 6-F (he appointed leaders to handle the cases).

Ezra's ministry extended for several more years. In the Book of Nehemiah we find Ezra reading the word of the Lord and the people responding to it in genuine concern. Ezra helped preserve the law of the Lord and God used him to preserve His own people.

▶ **Think of the things you have learned about Ezra. What do you think was his greatest contribution to God's work? Write your answer here:**

_____

_____

Be prepared to share your answer at the next group session.

RESPONDING TO GOD'S WORD

★ **Reflect on how you feel when you do something that you know God wants you to do.**

★ **Have you been delaying some action that God has put on your heart?**

★ **Prayerfully plan right now to obey the Lord.**

DAY 3 The Ministry of Nehemiah

U N I T   9

Nehemiah's ministry began around 13 years after Ezra had journeyed to Jerusalem. Nehemiah 1:1 dates Nehemiah in the twentieth year of Artaxerxes, king of Persia, almost 100 years after the first exiles returned to Judea. I assume that this was Artaxerxes I who reigned beginning in 465 B.C. Therefore, the twentieth year would place Nehemiah at 445 B.C. This is the traditional date for Nehemiah.

Nehemiah, a Jew living outside Palestine, exhibited the kind of faith God desires for His people. Apparently he never had been to Israel. He served as cupbearer in the court of King Artaxerxes I (Neh. 1:11b). This title may mean that he tasted the king's food to ensure it was not poisoned, but it probably meant more than that. He served at the right hand of the king as an advisor. Nehemiah was a trusted associate who gave faithful service to his king.

▶ **Read Nehemiah 1:1-4 and answer the following questions. Answers are at the bottom of the next page.**[11]

1. Who wrote the Book of Nehemiah?   _____

2. How did Nehemiah learn of the situation in Judah?   _____

_____

3. Using no more than three words, describe the situation in Judah:

_____

4. How did Nehemiah respond to the news from Judah?   _____

_____

Nehemiah's Prayer

Nehemiah 1 records Nehemiah's concern for Jerusalem and describes how he felt when he heard how Jerusalem lay in ruins. Word came to him that the walls of Jerusalem had not been rebuilt. The survivors in Jerusalem lived in peril. When Nehemiah heard this news, he wept, mourned, fasted, and prayed.

Elements of Nehemiah's Prayer

- Praise to God (1:5)
- Confession of sin (1:6-7)
- Petition based on God's promises (1:8-11)

Complete each statement in 10 words or less:

Lord, I praise you because . . .

_____

_____

_____,_____

Lord, I confess that . . .

_____

_____

_____

Lord, I beseech you that . . .

_____

_____

_____

▶ **Meditate on each element of Nehemiah's prayer. Try to internalize that element and feel the full weight of the significance of that particular element. Write your responses in the margin at the left.**

Such prayer inspires believers today to call on God in times of need. God is faithful. He hears our prayers and cares for our deepest needs and our heaviest burdens. As we pray, the elements of Nehemiah's prayer can remind us to praise and to adore God who has blessed us so wonderfully. Nehemiah's prayer can encourage us to confess our own sin so that God may forgive our sins and cleanse our hearts (see 1 John 1:9). His prayer can remind us to base our prayers on God's promises in His Word. Confidently we may ask God to help us in His service.

▶ **Rank the following elements according to how much you use them in your own personal prayer life. Place a 1 by the element in which you are strongest, 2 by the element next strongest, and 3 by the element in which you are weakest.**

_____ PRAISE   _____ CONFESSION   _____ PETITION

Pray a brief prayer right now giving more emphasis to the area in which you are weakest.

Nehemiah's Return (Neh. 2:1-20)

At a time which seemed appropriate to Nehemiah, he asked King Artaxerxes for permission to go to Jerusalem. He wanted to build the walls of Jerusalem to provide security for the city. The king granted Nehemiah's request and encouraged his servant in his work (Neh. 2:6).

▶ **Read 2:1-6 to see how God answered Nehemiah's prayer (1:5-11). Mark the following statements as T (true) or F (false):**[12]
_____ 1. Nehemiah let his concern show in his face.
_____ 2. Artaxerxes thought Nehemiah was sick.
_____ 3. Nehemiah stated the object of his concern with great confidence.
_____ 4. Nehemiah told the king exactly what he wanted to do.
_____ 5. The king agreed for Nehemiah to do as he desired.

Having received the king's permission to return to Jerusalem, Nehemiah asked for letters from the king. These letters would ensure safe passage in his travels. He

---

[11]Answers: 1-1:1 cites Nehemiah as the writer; 2-he talked with men who had been there; 3-your response probably reflects bad news, sad state, trouble and disgrace; 4-he mourned, fasted, and prayed.
[12]Answers: 1-T, 2-F, 3-F, 4-T, 5-T.

knew that traveling beyond the river (the Euphrates) would involve a long and dangerous journey. They also would enable him to get materials needed for the building projects. The king also graciously sent officers of the army and horsemen to accompany Nehemiah.

Identify two who did not want to help the Jews (2:10).

▶ **In view of the king's response to Nehemiah's requests, how do you think the king felt about Nehemiah?**

_____

_____

Be prepared to share your answer at the next group session.

Some people in Palestine did not share Nehemiah's enthusiasm for rebuilding Jerusalem's walls. A weak Jerusalem served their interests. They did not wish to see the city become secure and strong.

▶ **What did Nehemiah do first when he arrived in Jerusalem? Write a brief description here and explain why you think he did it.**

_____

_____

_____

_____

_____

_____

_____

Nehemiah sought to win the people's support. He identified with the people, describing their troubles as his trouble. He asked the people to work with him. He said: "Come, let us rebuild the wall of Jerusalem, and we will no longer be in disgrace" (Neh. 2:17). Nehemiah also described how the hand of God had been upon him and how God would help them rebuild the walls of Jerusalem.

Rebuilding the Walls (Neh. 3—6)

Though Nehemiah and the people of Jerusalem made swift progress, they encountered significant opposition from their enemies.

▶ **A. Match the following references on the left with the correct form of opposition on the right. Write the correct letters in the blanks.[13]**

____ 1. 4:1	A.	plot of an open attack
____ 2. 4:8	B.	ridicule
____ 3. 4:11	C.	rumors of planned attacks
____ 4. 4:12	D.	plot of a sneak attack
____ 5. 6:2	E.	threats of accusations to the king
____ 6. 6:5-7	F.	attempt to discredit Nehemiah
____ 7. 6:10-13	G.	attempted ambush

B. To see how Nehemiah dealt with this opposition from his enemies, read the following references. Beside each reference write no more than three words to describe what was done:

1. 4:6 _____

2. 4:9 _____

3. 4:14 _____

4. 4:16 _____

5. 4:17 _____

6. 4:19-20 _____

7. 6:3 _____

8. 6:8 _____

9. 6:11 _____

Nehemiah and his faithful workers continued to build in the face of opposition. Nehemiah 4:6 demonstrates why the work progressed—the people worked hard and gave their best effort. Soon the wall was half-finished.

Nehemiah knew that he had to provide for the safety of the workers. Half the servants worked on the construction while half stood guard as protection for the workers. Though having half the men working must have slowed down the progress, the tactic probably boosted the morale of the people.

In addition to coping with opposition from enemies, the people also faced significant internal dissension.

➤ **Read 5:1-12 to get a picture of the problems among the Jews. Check the correct answer for each of the following questions:**[14]

1. What was the main problem?
   □ a. A famine and taxes
   □ b. Poor management of resources
   □ c. Work on the wall kept people from farming

2. What were some people having to do in order to get enough food to survive?
   □ a. Stealing
   □ b. Raiding neighboring tribes
   □ c. Mortgaging property and homes

3. What had some done in order to get money for taxes?
   □ a. Sold children into slavery
   □ b. Killed
   □ c. Cheated

4. Who did Nehemiah blame for the difficulty?
   □ a. The king
   □ b. God
   □ c. The nobles and officials

5. What charge did Nehemiah bring against the wealthier Jews?
   □ a. Slave trading
   □ b. Extortion
   □ c. Usury

6. What tactic did Nehemiah use to put pressure on the guilty parties?
   □ a. He threatened to take away their wealth.
   □ b. He dealt with them publicly.
   □ c. He said he would sell them into slavery.

---

[13]Answers to A: 1-B, 2-A, 3-D, 4-C, 5-G, 6-E, 7-F. Answers to B: 1-worked hard, 2-prayed, posted guard, 3-challenged to faith, 4-half guarded, 5-armed the workers, 6-established alarm system, 7-avoided an ambush, 8-called a bluff, 9-stood firm.

7. What was the basis of Nehemiah's appeal to the guilty ones?
☐ a. Moral and spiritual
☐ b. Financial
☐ c. Physical

8. What response did the guilty people make?
☐ a. They were angry.
☐ b. They were silent.
☐ c. They were repentant.

Nehemiah served as a benevolent and wise governor (Neh. 5:14-19). This was a period of building and hope for the people living in Jerusalem.

Nehemiah's Good Leadership (5:14-19)

- Did not follow the example of previous governors
- Did not permit his assistants to lord it over the people
- Acted in all things out of his reverence for God
- Devoted himself and his assistants to the work
- Paid personally the expense of feeding 150 Jews plus guests
- Did not accept the governor's food allotment

Nehemiah refused to put heavy burdens on the people. His good policy as governor came from his relationship with God. He refused to overburden the people he served because of his fear of God. A person's relationship with God will determine how the person treats other people. God intends for our commitment to Him to affect our jobs, our schools, and our families.

▶ **What ultimately determines how a person relates to others?[15]**

_____

Nehemiah sought to carry out his work with singleness of purpose. When Sanballat and Geshem wanted to meet with Nehemiah in the plain of Ono, Nehemiah knew that they intended to harm him. He responded with the classic statement; "I am carrying on a great project and cannot go down. Why should the work stop while I leave it and go down to you?" (Neh. 6:3).

Nehemiah's words should be a reminder to God's people that we have a great work to do. God's work should not be interrupted by pettiness and littleness. God has given to us the responsibility of proclaiming Jesus Christ to all the world. When we live selfishly, thinking only of ourselves, we harm the work of God. When the church sees its purpose as proclaiming Christ, then we have the opportunity to work together and to make Him known.

I am convinced that the church that sees its common goal as proclaiming Christ, being the people of God, and accomplishing His purpose will live harmoniously together. Without this purpose, we have little to hold us together and to make us live peacefully. Nehemiah had a singleness of purpose which helped him to accomplish his great work.

▶ **1. Why is the work God has assigned to the church the most important work in the world?**

_____

---

[14]Answers: 1-a, 2-c, 3-a, 4-c, 5-c, 6-b, 7-a, 8-c.
[15]Answer: That person's relationship with God.

2. **Which of the following hindrances to God's work do you think causes more harm? Check your answer:**
☐ Opposition from without
☐ Dissension from within

3. **What can help church members rise above pettiness and selfishness?**

_____

Be prepared to share your answer during the next group session.

In an amazing feat, Nehemiah and his workmen finished the walls in 52 days because God helped them. Jerusalem could dwell securely because of the efforts of Nehemiah.

Nehemiah's Second Visit to Jerusalem (Neh. 13:1-31)

Nehemiah returned to serve king Artaxerxes, but he was still concerned for the people of Jerusalem. In 433 B.C. he learned that the people of Jerusalem had broken their covenant with God. Nehemiah loved the Lord and His people too much to remain uninvolved. He went back to Jerusalem.

▶ **Read Nehemiah 13:4-7,10,15,23 and circle the correct objects of his reforms.**[16]

Sabbath observance   idolatry   tithing   marrying pagans

adultery   polluting the temple   mistreating the poor

During Nehemiah's second visit to Jerusalem, he dealt with the problems. After this trip to Jerusalem, Nehemiah's work was completed. He had reached out to the people of Jerusalem helping them to live securely in the land which God had given to the people of Israel. He helped preserve Judaism and he promoted true worship of the Lord God. He lived in difficult times and faced many obstacles. But his faithfulness helped to preserve the people of God in the land of Israel.

We will face much opposition during our lives. If we faithfully follow God, obeying His words and serving Him with all of our hearts, minds, and beings, we too can be effective witnesses for God in our time.

RESPONDING TO GOD'S WORD

★ **What does the example of Nehemiah say to you when you feel like giving up? When you feel like compromising your convictions? When you are opposed by people who hate you? When you are hindered by people who should be helping?**

★ **Pray for God to give you a spirit of faithfulness that will enable you to keep on keeping on in obedience to God.**

---

[16]Answers: You should have circled Sabbath observance, idolatry, tithing, marrying pagans, polluting the temple.

DAY 4   The Book of Esther

UNIT   9   The Book of Esther continues the profound message of Ezra and Nehemiah. By blessing and caring for His people, God showed His concern for them. Though

Have faith in God when
   your pathway is lonely,
He sees and knows all
   the way you have trod;
Never alone are the least
   of His children;
Have faith in God, have
   faith in God.

Have faith in God when
   your pray'rs are
   unanswered,
Your earnest plea he will
   never forget;
Wait on the Lord, trust
   his Word and be
   patient,
Have faith in God, he'll
   answer yet.

B. B. McKinney, "Have Faith in God." © 1934. Renewal 1962. Broadman Press. Used by permission.

Doing God's will begins with being at the place where He wants us to be at the exact time He wants us to be there.

When the wicked seem to prevail, remember that God is moving beneath the surface and behind the scenes to preserve and bless His children.

they lived outside Palestine, the Lord still reigned over them. His care for His people never wavered.

This book resolves any question concerning God's power. He is the sovereign Lord over the universe. All lands are His lands. He intends to care for His people wherever they might be.

Though we cannot date Esther precisely, the book fits generally into the time period of Ezra and Nehemiah. The author is unknown. Esther is set in Susa, the Persian capital, during the reign of Xerxes (486-465 B.C.). The Book of Esther is unique in that the name of God does not appear in any form. This is the only Bible book which does not use God's name.

The following activities will guide you through the heart of the Book of Esther. Be sure to work each activity.

▶ **A. Read Esther 2:5-7 and answer the following questions:**[17]

   1. What was Mordecai's relationship to Kish who had been carried into exile by Nebuchadnezzar?

   _____

   2. Why had Mordecai raised his cousin Esther? _____

B. Esther 1:1-22 tells of King Xerxes banishing his queen. Read 2:1-4 to learn how a new queen was to be chosen.

C. Read 2:19-23 and select the correct response:
1. Esther kept secret that
   ☐ a. she was raised by Mordecai.
   ☐ b. she was a Jew.
   ☐ c. she was broken-hearted.

   2. After Esther became queen, Mordecai's relationship with her was
   ☐ a. maintained.   ☐ b. non-existent.   ☐ c. closer than ever.

   3. Mordecai foiled a plot to
   ☐ a. raid Xerxes' harem.
   ☐ b. steal the royal treasure.
   ☐ c. assassinate the king.

   4. Mordecai's means of warning the king was
   ☐ a. the eunuch.   ☐ b. Esther.   ☐ c. Teresh.

   5. Mordecai's action was
   ☐ a. recorded in a book.   ☐ b. secretly rewarded.   ☐ c. Esther's secret.

D. To grasp the relationship between Haman and Mordecai, read 3:1-6.

E. Read 3:8-14 to understand Haman's plot. Mark the following statements as T (true) or F (false):

_____ 1. Haman's description of the Jews was false.
_____ 2. Haman's description of the Jews was true.
_____ 3. Haman's description of the Jews was true and false.
_____ 4. The King let Haman decide how to destroy the Jews.
_____ 5. Haman's plan was to destroy all Jews over a week's time.
_____ 6. The right to plunder the Jews' goods was an incentive to encourage the people to carry out the decree.
_____ 7. Haman and the king knew Esther was a Jew.

F. Read 4:1, 6-8 for Mordecai's reaction upon learning of Haman's plot. Check the actions below that Mordecai carried out:

☐ 1. Privately mourned.
☐ 2. Publicly mourned.
☐ 3. Visited Esther.
☐ 4. Told Esther's servant of Haman's plot.
☐ 5. Sent a letter urging Esther to intercede with the king.
☐ 6. Asked the servant to urge her to intercede with the king.

G. Read 4:9-10 for Esther's immediate reply to Mordecai's appeal. Write here what risk she would have to take in order to intercede with the king on behalf of her people:

_____

H. Read 4:12-14. In your opinion, which of Mordecai's arguments carried most weight with Esther? Check your response:

☐ 1. Living in the king's house will not protect you from Haman's decree.
☐ 2. If you do not help, help will come from elsewhere (probably he meant God) but not for you.
☐ 3. You probably have come to royal position to help in this time of crisis.

Be prepared to share your reasoning at the small-group session this week.

I. Read 4:15-17. Why do you think Esther wanted the Jews and her maids to fast with her for three days before she approached the king?

_____

"If I ascend up into heaven, thou art there: if I make my bed in hell, behold, thou art there. If I take the wings of the morning, and dwell in the uttermost parts of the sea; Even there shall thy hand lead me, and thy right hand shall hold me."
—Psalm 139:8-10

J. Read 5:1-7 for the king's response to Esther. Why do you think she wanted Haman present when she planned to tell the king her request on the next day?

_____

K. Read 5:9-14. How do you think Haman felt after he ordered the gallows built?

_____

L. Read 6:1-10,12-13.
1. What do you think Haman might have said to himself when the king gave him the order?

_____

2. Why did Haman's wife say that since Mordecai was a Jew, Haman would surely come to ruin?

_____

We ought to ask God regularly:

Is this where I am supposed to be right now?

Am I here right now because someone else here needs me?

M. Read 7:1-10 for the climax. Check the correct answer for each of the following questions:

1. Why did Esther say she would not have bothered the king if she and her people merely were being sold into slavery?
☐ a. She was willing to be a slave.
☐ b. That's the way you talk to kings.
☐ c. She really would not have risked her life over that.

2. What was Esther implying by saying she and her people had been sold for destruction, slaughter, and annihilation?
☐ a. Haman had hidden motives for suggesting the Jews be destroyed.
☐ b. Haman had offered money to pay for his plot.
☐ c. Haman would add to his wealth by looting the Jews' possessions.

3. What was ironic about Haman's death?
☐ a. He had been the king's favorite.
☐ b. He did not intend to assault the queen.
☐ c. He was hanged on the gallows he intended for Mordecai.

You may want to read chapters 8 and 10 for the rest of the story. With the support of the king, Mordecai warned the Jews of the pending attack on them. When people knew that the king was supporting Mordecai, the massive uprising against the Jews never happened. The Jews attacked their enemies and won a great victory. The victory was commemorated by establishing an annual feast called Purim (9:18-28).

RESPONDING TO GOD'S WORD

★ **1.** Recall a time when you knew God was caring for you and directing you in a dark hour in your life. How did you come to be aware that God was watching over you? _____

_____

_____

★ **2.** Identify a time when God put you at a certain place at a certain time because He wanted to work through you to meet another person's need.

_____

_____

★ **3.** Pray now thanking God for the way He has always been there for you and for the way He has brought you to others who need your ministry.

---

[17]Answers: A: 1-great-grandfather; 2-her parents died. C: 1-b, 2-a, 3-c, 4-b, 5-a. E: 1-F, 2-F, 3-T, 4-T, 5-F, 6-T, 7-F. F: 2, 4, 6. G: Her life could be required. I: The fast was a time of spiritual preparation for Esther and a time of prayer for God's help. J: She wanted Haman present when she revealed that the plot against the Jews included her. She hoped that the king would vent his wrath on Haman. L: 1-Oh no! (Your response is probably better.) 2-Haman's plot was against Jews, and Mordecai the Jew had just been given an exceptional honor by the king. M: Maybe these were a bit tricky. 1-b, but a case could be made for any of the three; 2-a, but b or c could be right; Esther certainly was implying that Haman had advanced the plot to gain some advantage for himself; 3-c.

DAY 5   The Messages of Ezra, Nehemiah, and Esther

U N I T   9

God speaks to us in all the experiences of life. Each book of the Bible contains profound messages that teach us about God and help us live for Him each day. The messages of the Bible continue to be relevant because the messages are from God and the word of God came to people in real, historical situations. Neither human nature nor human needs have changed. We need to hear the messages of the Books of Ezra, Nehemiah, and Esther.

To Jews living in 539 B.C. or 450 B.C., God may have appeared to have little control over the world. The truth of Ezra is that God remains in charge. The Lord remembered His people in exile, raising up Cyrus the Persian to conquer Babylon and to allow the captive Jews to return to their homeland and rebuild Jerusalem and the temple.

God put the needs of Jerusalem on Nehemiah's heart. God then led Nehemiah to Jerusalem, having gained for him authority to obtain materials and rebuild the walls of Jerusalem. Thus God showed His concern for His people. Through Nehemiah He provided leadership and protection for the city.

The Book of Esther shows us that we do not have to hear the direct mention of God's name to clearly see His hand in history. God saved the Jews through Mordecai and Esther.

God Is Always with His People

You can take hope in knowing that God never forsakes His own. At times you may feel forsaken, but human feelings often are misleading. You may feel that your prayers are never answered and never heard. You may feel that God is far from you. The Books of Ezra, Nehemiah, and Esther show that God never forsakes His people. They reveal that God always cares for His people. He watches over them in all the circumstances of life. Whether in Palestine or Babylon or where you are right now, God is present.

▶ **Meditate a moment on your own past experiences. Can you recall a time you felt forsaken? Looking back, can you see how God was working for your good in that time? Pause to pray a prayer of thanksgiving for His always being with you.**

The Word of God Leads People to Greater Faith and Spiritual Blessings

Ezra's reading from the book of the law shows the power of God's Word to help and bless us throughout life. When the people heard and obeyed God's Word, they experienced great joy. When we allow Bible study to become a significant part of our lives, and when we earnestly seek to obey God's Word, we will find greater faith and daily blessings. As you have worked faithfully through the units of this study in the Scriptures, you probably have gained insights and experienced blessings from God.

▶ **List two insights that have blessed you since beginning this study through the Old Testament:**

1. _____

2. _____

Be prepared to share these in the small-group session.

God's Laws Affect All of Life

Many people think of God only on Sunday. The Bible plays a significant part in their lives but only on specific days and under certain circumstances. They do not allow God's Word to affect all of life. Even for some Christians, their commitment to God seems reduced simply to one more good thing to do. They live at a hectic pace. Each afternoon the children participate in some worthy activity. They play soccer, take piano, participate in library activities. Mom and Dad have their work, clubs, and hobbies. On Sundays they attend church.

I am afraid that church is viewed as only one more good activity that helps make a well-rounded life. The Books of Ezra and Nehemiah remind us that God is the Lord of all of life. God's Word touches every aspect of our lives. Only when we allow Him to be Lord over all areas of life can we find life's richest meaning and the greatest fulfillment.

▶ **List one teaching in the Bible that in some way affects the following areas of life:**

1. Home: _____

2. Work: _____

3. Civic life: _____

4. Church: _____

5. Neighbors: _____

God Helps His People Accomplish Their God-given Goals

Nehemiah finished the work on the walls of the city of Jerusalem because God's hand was on him. If we will pray and seek God's leading, He will help us in all we do.

Ask God to guide you in developing your long-range plans. As He guides you, pray for Him to help you accomplish your goals.

Should you pray for God to help you be successful in your job? Why should we pray for help with a Sunday School lesson and not pray for help with a business deal? God cares for all of life. As we turn each part of our life over to Him, we find strength for living and a guide for treating people correctly. God will help us live for Him wherever we are and in whatever we do.

▶ **Check the following things you will do:**
   ☐ 1. Pray daily for God to reveal His purposes for you each day.
   ☐ 2. Pray daily for God to reveal His long-range purposes for your life.
   ☐ 3. Pray for guidance and help in your daily work.
   ☐ 4. Pray for guidance and help in your family relationships.
   ☐ 5. Pray for guidance and help concerning your church relationships and your role in the life and ministry of your church.

SUMMARY REVIEW

To review this week's study of the Old Testament, see if you can mentally answer the following questions. You may want to write the answers on a separate sheet of paper. Mark your level of performance on the left: circle "C" if you can answer correctly and circle "R" if you need to review.

C R   1. List the Old Testament books of law and history.

C R   2. List three primary events in Ezra and Nehemiah.

C R   3. What is unique about the Book of Esther?

C R   4. Define the origin and meaning of the term "Jew."

C R   5. Identify Ezra and a major problem with which he had to deal.

C R   6. What was Nehemiah's primary contribution to God's work?

C R   7. Name three ways in which Nehemiah showed he was a good and able governor of his people.

C R   8. What was the key to Nehemiah's behavior?

C R   9. Name three messages given through Ezra, Nehemiah, and Esther.

RESPONDING TO GOD'S WORD

★ **Reflect on the messages from Ezra, Nehemiah, and Esther. Commit yourself anew to letting the Lord be the Lord of your everyday life.**

UNIT 10

God and Wisdom (Job—Song of Songs)

When you ask: "How can I live the best life possible?" you are asking about wisdom. Wisdom relates to every aspect of life and every relationship of life. Everyone in every age needs wisdom. The wisdom literature shows us the way of wisdom and points us to God who gives life and instructions to those who follow Him. (These books are also identified as the books of poetry.)

In this unit you will study the Books of Job, Psalms, Proverbs, Ecclesiastes, and the Song of Songs (or Song of Solomon).

Job deals with the problem of suffering. Because everyone suffers, studying the Book of Job can be helpful to everyone. The book approaches suffering from a personal rather than from a philosophical viewpoint. Job's suffering is a starting point from which we can approach our own hardship and suffering.

The Psalms speak to people in need because they were written by people with needs. The psalms express the deep, innermost feelings of people's hearts and speak to their hearts about matters of life and faith. Those who read them find strength and encouragement for daily living.

Proverbs provide wisdom for daily living. They guide people to follow the ways of the Lord, allowing Him to lead their lives. They are brief conclusions about life drawn out of the experiences of life.

Ecclesiastes raises the questions that grow out of the search for the joy and meaning of life.

Song of Songs (Songs of Solomon) is a series of love poems which rejoice in the love of a man and a woman.

With the exception of the Book of Job, none of the Books of Wisdom lend themselves to outlining. These outlines of Psalms and Proverbs are workable but not entirely satisfactory. No attempt is made to outline Ecclesiastes and Song of Songs.

Job:

    I. Prologue (Job1—2)
   II. Dialogue (Job3—31)
     A.First Cycle of Speeches (Job 3—14)
     B.Second Cycle of Speeches (Job 15—21)
     C.Third Cycle of Speeches (Job 22—31)
  III. Speeches of Elihu (Job 32—37)
  IV. Speeches of the Lord (Job 38:1—42:6)
   V. Epilogue (Job 42:7-17)

Psalms:

    I. Psalms mostly associated with David (Ps. 1—72)
   II. Psalms mostly associated with Korah (Ps. 73—89)
  III. Psalms mostly untitled (Ps. 90—106)
  IV. Psalms used in worship (Ps. 107—150)

Proverbs:

> I. Proverbial Discourse (Pro. 1—9)
> II. Proverbs of Solomon (Pro. 10:1—22:16)
> III. The Words of the Wise (Pro. 22:17—24:22)
> IV. A Proverb on Laziness (Pro. 24:23—34)
> V. The Proverbs of Solomon that the Men of Hezekiah Copied (Pro. 25—29)
> VI. The Proverbs of Agur (Pro. 30)
> VII. The Proverbs of King Lemuel (Pro. 31:1-9)
> VIII. A Proverb Concerning the Virtuous Woman (Pro. 31:10-31)

WordWatch

Watch for these words as you study this unit.

Selah—occurs 71 times in the Book of Psalms. The most popular interpretation is that it indicates either a pause during which instruments are played or a change from speaking or singing softly to full volume.

Maskil—a poem that is intended to teach or to instruct.

Zion—originally one of the hills on which Jerusalem was built. The term was later enlarged to include all of Jerusalem. The use of the term is intended to communicate the special place of God's presence.

DAY 1   The Book of Job

U N I T   10

THE CYCLE OF THE DIALOGUES

Authorship and Date of the Book of Job

Neither the date nor the author is given anywhere in the Scripture. Some assume that Job himself wrote the book since he was the one who suffered so greatly. However, Job could not possibly have written chapters 1, 2, and 42. We cannot be sure who the author of Job was, but most authorities agree that he was a brilliant poet who understood the deep sufferings of human beings and the problems associated with their sufferings.

Determining when the Book of Job was written is as difficult as determining who wrote it. It could have been written as early as 1200 B.C. or as late as 200 B.C. The setting of the book certainly is early in Israelite history, though Job was not an Israelite (Uz, his homeland, was probably in an area northeast of Palestine).

In my view, the setting of the Book of Job is during the time of the patriarchs. The Book of Job was not written until much later. No one can be certain of the date of the book. I think of the book as having been written after the Jewish exile in 587 B.C. At this time the people of Israel faced personal suffering and corporate suffering. They focused on the problem of suffering and why seemingly righteous people suffer. This time period certainly fits the circumstances of the Book of Job.

The Purpose of the Book of Job

Bible students suggest several purposes for the Book of Job. Here are three of the most popular.

Purposes for the Book of Job

- To answer questions concerning why good people suffer. The only answer given in the book is that suffering tests one's faith.
- To refute the idea that all suffering is a punishment for sin.
- To show God is present with His people in the midst of their suffering.

▶ **Which of the three possible purposes of the Book of Job seems to you the real purpose for which it was written? Check your response:**

☐ 1. To answer the question, Why do good people suffer?

☐ 2. To refute the idea that all suffering is the result of sin.

☐ 3. To show that God is with His people even when they are suffering.

The Prologue: Job's Suffering (chaps. 1—2)

Both the prologue and the epilogue of Job are written in prose. The dialogue is in poetry. The prologue sets forth Job's suffering. Job, a righteous and wealthy man, suffered greatly when God permitted him to be tested by Satan. Satan is presented as one who is in heaven accusing the righteous before God. Satan accused Job of living righteously only for what he could get from God. God allowed Satan to afflict Job to prove that Job's faith was genuine.

▶ **Use these activities to guide you through a study of the prologue. Answers to the questions are at the bottom of the column.[1]**

A. Read Job 1:1-5. For which of the following purposes were these verses primarily written? Check your answer.
☐ 1. To show that Job was wealthy.
☐ 2. To show that Job was blessed by God.
☐ 3. To show that Job was righteous and religious.

B. Read 1:6-12 and answer the following questions:

1. What was God's evaluation of Job? _____

2. How did Satan explain Job's behavior? _____

3. What did God permit Satan to do? _____

C. Read 1:13-22. List the things Job lost:

_____

_____

D. Read 2:1-6. Write here what Satan was given permission to do:

_____

E. Read 2:7-10 and mark the following statements as T (true) or F (false).

_____ 1. Job was shaking with fever.
_____ 2. Job was covered with sores.
_____ 3. Job's wife had more faith than Job had.
_____ 4. In spite of his losses and pain, Job did not cry out against God.

---

[1]Answers: A-Probably 3 is the best answer. B-Your answers probably reflect the following ideas: 1-most godly man on earth; 2-he is faithful only because you bless him; 3-take away Job's blessings except for his health. C-oxen, donkeys, servants, sheep camels, sons, daughters, house. D-To do anything to Job physically short of killing him. E-1-F, 2-T, 3-F, 4-T.

The Dialogue (Chaps. 3—31)

The dialogue sections are written in poetry. They consist of a series of speeches delivered by Job and his friends. Each of Job's friends spoke in turn and Job responded to each speech. For example, Eliphaz spoke in Job 4—5; Job responded in Job 6—7. This dialogue is followed by the speech of Bildad in Job 8 to which Job replied in chapters 9 and 10. Zophar finally spoke in Job 11, followed by the long reply of Job in chapters 12—14.

The dialogue consists of three cycles of speeches. The first two follow this pattern.

▶ **In order to see the basic argument used by each of Job's friends, work through the following activities on the dialogue:[2]**

A. 1. ELIPHAZ: Read Job 4:7-9,17. In one sentence, summarize what Eliphaz was saying to Job:

_____

_____

2. Read Job's reply to Eliphaz in 6:24-30. In one sentence, summarize his reply:

_____

_____

B. 1. BILDAD: Read Job 8:3-4,11-13,20. Did Bildad have the same basic argument that Eliphaz had? Circle one: YES   NO

2. Read Job's reply to Bildad in 10:1-7. Check the following statements with which you agree:

☐ 1. Job was becoming bitter.
☐ 2. Job wondered whether God punished the righteous and blessed the wicked.
☐ 3. Job felt that God knew he was innocent.
☐ 4. Job was questioning God's justice.
☐ 5. Job was turning away from God.
☐ 6. Job maintained that he was innocent and did not deserve the terrible things that were happening to him.
☐ 7. Job was feeling frustration and impatience.

C. 1. ZOPHAR: Read Job 11:1-6,13-20. Is Zophar's basic position different from that of his friends? Write those differences here:

_____

2. Read Job's reply to Zophar in 12:1-5; 13:2-5,19. Mark the following statements as T (true) or F (false):

_____ 1. Job was impressed with his friend's wisdom.
_____ 2. Job acknowledged that his friends had a superior education.
_____ 3. Job knew that people who had not suffered great misfortune had compassionate insight and understanding of those in situations like his.
_____ 4. Job said that his friends' words were a healing balm to him.

---

[2]Answers: A-1—Your answer probably suggests that if Job were innocent, he would not be suffering. A-2—Your answer should have the idea that Job asked his friend to name Job's sin. B-1—Yes. B-2—You could have checked all but 5. C-1—No basic differences. C-2—all are false.

The pattern of the dialogue is broken in the third cycle of speeches. Zophar does not speak and Bildad's speech is brief. Why? I believe that the arguments of the friends had been exhausted. They had no other insights to offer. Job continued to maintain his innocence, and their position was that innocent people do not experience what Job was experiencing. Therefore, Zophar had nothing more to say and Bildad spoke only sparingly.

Have you noted that God has been silent through these endless exchanges of dialogue? Have you found yourself wondering why there is no word from God? When you resume your study tomorrow, one more speaker will enter the dialogue. Then God will speak.

RESPONDING TO GOD'S WORD

★ Think of a person who is experiencing severe suffering at the present time (it could be you). Pray for God to use your study of Job today and tomorrow to give you insights that will help you face suffering (your own and that of others) with faith.

DAY 2 Job and Psalms

U N I T 10

Recall from yesterday's session that Job's three "friends" had completed three cycles of dialogue with him. Today you will see a new speaker enter the dialogue. Then God will speak to Job's suffering.

Elihu Speaks (Chaps. 32—37)

Elihu appears in the Book of Job suddenly and without warning. In Job 32, he speaks only after expressing his respect for Job and his friends because they are older. Elihu is an angry young man whose lengthy and wordy speech adds nothing new to the argument.

▶ **Read Job 32:1-12. Check the correct ending for each of the following statements.[3]**

1. Elihu was angry with Job because
   □ a. he had embarrassed Elihu's friends.
   □ b. he had justified himself rather than God.
   □ c. he had blasphemed against God.

2. Elihu was angry with his friends because
   □ a. they had sided with Job.
   □ b. their speeches had been too long.
   □ c. their words had failed to answer Job's arguments.

3. Elihu had come to the conclusion that
   □ a. he knew more than his older friends.
   □ b. wisdom belonged to older people.
   □ c. wisdom was not the issue.

---

[3]Answers: 1-b, 2-c, 3-a.

God Speaks to Job (38:1—42:16)

Finally God spoke to Job. Chapters 38—41 contain a long series of questions God addressed to Job.

▶ **Read Job 38:1-6,17,31-33,35; 39:19,26-27, and answer the following questions:**

1. Which of God's questions was Job able to answer?

_____

2. What effect do you think all those questions had on Job?

_____

Of course, you saw that Job had no answers. And, did you notice also that God did not tell him what the answers were. The result of God's confronting Job was Job's recognition that only God is the Lord. Job acknowledged his dependence on the Lord.

▶ **Read 40:1-5; 42:16. Check the following statements that reflect what you think Job learned from his encounter with God:[4]**

☐ 1. Humans cannot predict what God might do, for He acts according to His whims.
☐ 2. God's ways were beyond Job's understanding.
☐ 3. God had nothing to do with Job's problems.
☐ 4. To hear about God and to experience His presence are two things that cannot be compared.
☐ 5. In God's presence Job understood his own unworthiness.
☐ 6. God will carry out His purposes.
☐ 7. Job learned why he had suffered.

By means of his sufferings and by God's answer to Job, Job came to a deeper faith in God. Job's response to God's speech seems to reveal the main teaching of the book. God never gave Job a reason for his suffering. The book does not answer the question of why people suffer, but it does demonstrate that suffering can be a test of one's faith and that God will help us in the midst of our suffering. God is always available to His people.

▶ **What does Job's response to God's speech imply to be the main teaching of the Book of Job?**

_____

Your answer to the preceding question probably expressed the idea that God is available to help in times of suffering. When you and I suffer, we should look for ways in which God can be glorified. We should look for ways in which He can make us stronger people because of our difficult circumstances. We probably will never know fully why we suffer. We only can know that God is with us to help us, strengthen us, and guide us when we face the difficulties of life.

The Epilogue (42:7-17)

The epilogue tells how God restored Job's fortune and gave him a new family. The epilogue shows that Job is proven to be a righteous man, and Job's friends recognize that God indeed has blessed Job.

▶ **Suffering is a fact of life. You must face it and deal with it in your own life and in the lives of others. List three lessons you have learned about dealing with suffering from this study of Job.**

---

[4]Answers: 2, 4, 5, 6.

1. _____

2. _____

3. _____

NATURE PSALMS

CHARACTER PSALMS

PRAISE PSALMS

ASSURANCE PSALMS

MESSIANIC PSALMS

LAMENT

ENTHRONEMENT PSALMS

PSALMS OF VENGEANCE

Introduction to the Psalms

Date and authorship. The date and authorship of the Psalms must be approached in two ways. First, we must consider each psalm individually and ask when it was written. A few psalms such as Psalms 51 and 137 can be dated easily because they are associated with known historical events. However, most psalms cannot be assigned specific dates. Some psalms mention David, Moses, Solomon, the Sons of Korah, and Asaph. However, these titles do not necessarily indicate authorship. They do make a connection between the person or persons mentioned in the title and the individual psalm. We cannot be sure what the connection is. For example, the Hebrew preposition used with the name David in the title could mean that the psalm was written *to* David, *for* David, *by* David, or *about* David. It also could mean that the psalm belongs to the group of psalms associated in some way with David.

Here is another question. When were all the different psalms brought together into a collection and who collected them? The Book of Psalms could not have been compiled before the Babylonian exile. Psalm 137 has its setting in the Babylonian exile (the time period between the fall of Jerusalem in 587 B.C. and the decree of Cyrus that allowed the Jews to return to Jerusalem in 539 B.C.). The Book of Psalms certainly was brought together before the first century A.D. Jesus knew the Psalms and spoke of them on several occasions (for example, Luke 24:44). Probably the collection was complete before 300 B.C.

► **Based on the preceding paragraph, what is the range of dates within which the Book of Psalms was probably compiled? Answers are at the bottom of the column.[5]**

Earliest possible date: _____.

Latest probable date: _____.

No one knows who collected the Psalms. The collecting probably occurred over a long period of time with the help of many people. As in the case of all of the Old Testament canon, scholars, priests, and religious leaders did not determine which psalms would be included in the collection. People of faith determined the contents of the Book of Psalms. God used certain psalms to speak to people's hearts about the matters of life and faith. The people's use of the psalms led religious leaders to include them in the collection.

Types of Psalms

The psalms have been grouped and classified in a variety of ways by different scholars. No one way is correct. For our study purposes we will group the psalms into eight categories.

Nature psalms. Nature psalms describe the beauty of nature and the even greater beauty of the Creator of nature. Both Psalm 8 and Psalm 19 have been called nature psalms. Strictly speaking, they should be seen as psalms of the Creator. While they look at the beauty of nature, they ascribe praise and honor to the One who has created the beauty of the universe.

---

[5]Answers: 587 B.C. and 300 B.C.

Psalm 19

"The heavens declare the glory
     of God;
   the skies proclaim the work of
     his hands.
Day after day they pour forth
     speech;
   night after night they display
     knowledge."

▶ **Read Psalm 8 and write each verse reference that contains some mention of nature. The first mention of nature is in verse 1.**

Verses: _____

Psalm 8 describes the beauty of the heavens and compares human beings to the greatness of God. How little and insignificant we are! God is the wonderful Creator who has blessed His people so greatly. You probably identified verses 1, 3, 7, and 8.

▶ **Read Psalm 19:1-6. Write here what aspect of nature is highlighted in this Psalm:**[6]

_____

_____

RESPONDING TO GOD'S WORD

★ **What in the natural world has made you aware of the greatness of God?**

_____

★ **Meditate on the words of "Great Is Thy Faithfulness."**

> Summer and winter, and springtime and harvest,
>   Sun, moon, and stars in their courses above
> Join with all nature in manifold witness
>   To thy great faithfulness, mercy, and love.
>   —Thomas O. Chisholm

★ **Praise God for His wonder revealed in His world.**

---

[6]Answer: The heavens.

DAY 3   The Book of Psalms (continued)

U N I T   10

Yesterday you began studying the Book of Psalms. Without looking back, use the following exercise to review the important background information you learned.

▶ **A. What do we know about who wrote the Book of Psalms?**

_____

_____

B. What do we know about when the book was written?

_____

_____

Your answer should have dealt with the matter of both the authorship of individual books and the compiler of the individual psalms into one book. You also should recall that our approach to studying the psalms is to examine the different types of psalms. Yesterday we studied the first of eight types, the nature psalms.

Psalm 1

"Blessed is the man who
does not walk in the
counsel of the wicked
or stand in the way of
sinners
or sit in the seat of
mockers."

Character psalms. Psalm 1 and Psalm 15 are good examples of the character psalm. Character psalms describe the kind of character people who love God and seek to serve Him ought to strive to develop.

Psalm 1 may have been placed deliberately at the beginning of the Book of Psalms. It indicates the kind of character faithful people in all ages ought to have and draws a brief contrast between the godly and the wicked. The psalm is divided into two parts. Verses 1-3 describe righteous people; verses 4-6 describe the wicked.

▶ **Read Psalm 1. Match the following verses on the left with the correct phrase on the right. Write the correct letters in the blanks. Answers are at the bottom of the column.[7]**

_____ 1. 1:1-3	A.	What the righteous do not do
_____ 2. 1:4-6	B.	The righteous person
_____ 3. 1:1	C.	The wicked described
_____ 4. 1:2	D.	The wicked person
_____ 5. 1:3	E.	What the righteous do
_____ 6. 1:4	F.	The result of being wicked
_____ 7. 1:5	G.	The result of being righteous

The righteous people are blessed. They react negatively to evil and positively to good. They shun the counsel and the way of the wicked. The righteous meditate on the law of the Lord day and night. They seek to know and do God's will. Therefore, all they do will prosper. The psalmist concluded Psalm 1 with the beautiful word of assurance: "For the Lord watches over the way of the righteous, but the way of the wicked will perish" (Ps. 1:6).

Psalm 15 begins with the question: "Lord, who may dwell in your sanctuary? Who may live on your holy hill?" (Ps. 15:1). The psalmist answers his question in a series of specific, concrete statements.

▶ **Read Psalm 15 and list below some of the characteristics of the one who may dwell in God's sanctuary.**

_____

_____

_____

The character psalms encourage correct living that ensures wholeness of life. Notice that Psalm 1 and Psalm 15 end with similar promises. The person who lives for God is known by God and will never be moved.

Praise psalms. Psalms 50, 66, 103, and 107 are good examples of praise psalms. Psalm 103 is a favorite of many people. The psalm begins by praising God. The psalmist called for everything within him to praise the Lord. The reason for the praise is twofold. The psalmist praises God for the wonderful way He worked in history through Moses and blessed him. Psalm 103:8 is similar to Exodus 34:6-7. The psalmist told how God is compassionate and gracious, slow to anger, and abounding in love. The psalmist praised God for the way He relates to His people.

Psalm 104

"Praise the LORD, O my soul.
O LORD my God, you are
very great."

▶ **Read Psalm 103:3-19. List below the three benefits mentioned in the psalm that seem most precious to you right now:**

1. _____

2. _____

3. _____

Be prepared to share your responses in the next small-group session.

---

[7]Answers: 1-B; 2-D; 3-A; 4-E; 5-G; 6-C, 7-F.

Psalm 27

"The LORD is my light and my
salvation—
whom shall I fear?
The LORD is the stronghold of
my life—
of whom shall I be afraid?"

Other Types of Psalms

_____

_____

_____

Psalms of Assurance. God's people experience many difficulties in life. Through the ages, the Lord has spoken through the psalms to people in need of comfort and assurance. Psalms 23; 27; 46; 90; 121; 125; and 126 are good examples of assurance psalms. Many of these psalms describe the Lord as a shepherd, a rock, or a redeemer.

▶ Select one of the psalms cited in the preceding paragraph and search that psalm for a promise you will claim to help you through a difficult situation you are facing. Record that promise here.

_____

Without looking back, see if you can recall and list the four types of psalms you have studied.

N _____   P _____

C _____   A _____

Now look back to check your answers.

Other types of psalms. So far you have studied four types of psalms and I have classified them for you. I would like for you to classify the last four.

▶ Read Psalm 2:2,6-7,12. Now read Psalm 110:1,4,6. How would you classify the psalms from which these verses come? Write your classification here.

_____

You have just looked at two psalms from a group that can be interpreted as referring to Christ. My classification for this group is *Messianic*. It is all right if you used a different word if you got the idea correct. Your answer need not be exactly as mine as long as you referred to the coming of Christ.

▶ Now enter a classification on the first line under Other Types of Psalms in the margin.

Read Psalms 3:4,7; 5:1-3,8,11; 16:1. How would you classify the psalms from which these verses come? Write your classification here.

_____

The psalms you just examined are pleas for help. Sometimes the danger is physical; other times it is spiritual. The unifying factor in these psalms is a cry to God to come to the aid of the psalmist. Does the term you chose express this idea? I classify this group *Laments*.

▶ Write the classification you chose on the second line under Other Types of Psalms in the margin.

Read Psalm 93:1; 96:10; 97:1. How would you classify the psalms from which these verses come? Write your classification here.

_____

Each of the psalms in this group contain the phrase "the Lord reigns" and pictures God as the enthroned deity. Did your classification express this idea? I call this group the *Enthronement Psalms*.

▶ Write your choice for a classification on the third line under Other Types of Psalms in the margin.

You have one more type of Psalm to study tomorrow and that will conclude your study of the Book of Psalms.

RESPONDING TO GOD'S WORD

★ Now it is your turn to be the psalmist. Compose a psalm of at least four lines. It may be any one of the seven types you have studied, but it should express the feelings of your heart. Take a moment to pray. Ask God to help you give expression to what your heart is feeling at this moment. Be prepared to share your psalm with your group.

_____

_____

_____

_____

_____

_____

DAY 4   The Books of Psalms and Proverbs

U N I T   10

At the end of yesterday's study, you still had one more type of psalm to examine.

▶ **Read Psalm 137. How would you classify this psalm? Write your classification here.**

_____

The few passages in the Psalms that reflect genuine bitterness and anger give interpreters the greatest difficulty. Keeping the following facts in mind will help you as you study this type.

- These are expressions of real feelings being experienced by people—*not by God*. Because these feelings are recorded in the Bible does not mean that they are right or acceptable to God. The Bible records the wrong actions and attitudes of God's people as well as the right ones.
- These were temporary feelings that would moderate in time. From your own experience, you know that feelings of anger and bitterness heal with time.
- These feelings were expressed before Christ's more complete revelation of God's nature. Such feelings are based on the law of retribution, "an eye for an eye," and not on the law of love taught by Christ.
- Bitterness and hatred have no place among Christians.

▶ **List eight types of psalms and use work done in previous sessions to check your answers.**

N _____   M _____

C _____   L _____

P _____   E _____

A _____   V _____

The Book of Proverbs

Strictly speaking, the word "proverb" comes from a Hebrew word meaning "to compare" or "to be like." The exact concept in the use of this word for the title is unclear. However, there is no doubt about the nature and purpose of the book. The Book of Proverbs is a collection of conclusions that have been reached out of the experiences of life. They are brief, attention-getting, rhythmic ways of expressing conclusions about who God is and what He is like, about the world, and about human nature. Their purpose is to help us know how to relate to people and to God. The Proverbs provide wisdom for daily living. They guide people to follow the ways of the Lord, allowing Him to lead their lives. More than anything else, the wisdom writers want us to know that awe and reverence for God is the beginning of wisdom.

Since the Book of Proverbs contains 31 chapters, some have recommended that believers read a chapter of Proverbs each day of the month. While you may or may not want to do that over an extended period of time, you might try it for one month.

Date and Author

Date. Like the Book of Psalms, the proverbs are difficult to date for they contain several collections of proverbs.

▶ **Read the following verses and explain why these verses have led Bible students to see several collections of proverbs in the Book of Proverbs:**

Proverbs 1:1; 10:1; 25:1; 30:1; 31:1

_____

_____

_____

Your answer probably expresses the idea that each verse you examined identifies a group of proverbs and states the name of the person who wrote or collected them. Proverbs 1:1 begins: "The proverbs of Solomon son of David, king of Israel." Proverbs 10:1 has "The proverbs of Solomon" for a heading. Proverbs 25:1 identifies its collection as "proverbs of Solomon, copied by the men of Hezekiah king of Judah."

Hezekiah reigned about 200 years after Solomon. While some of the material in the book is quite ancient and certainly goes back to the time of Solomon, other materials evidently come from a later time period. Some scholars feel that the Book of Proverbs in its present form was completed between 700 B.C. and 400 B.C.

Author. While Solomon made a significant contribution to the Book of Proverbs, he probably was not the author of Proverbs in its present form. For centuries, the Book of Proverbs has been associated with Solomon for two reasons:
1. He had a reputation for writing and collecting proverbs and is noted for his great wisdom (see 1 Kings 3:16-28).
2. The title verse attributes the book to him. The verse probably refers to the early sections of Proverbs rather than to the entire book. Certainly Solomon inspired generations of wise men and women to consider the wisdom which comes from God and to speak words which contain timeless validity.

A. Check the two reasons the Book of Proverbs has been associated with Solomon.[8]

☐ 1. Solomon's many wives.
☐ 2. The Book of Proverbs says clearly that Solomon wrote it.
☐ 3. Solomon's reputation for wisdom.
☐ 4. The New Testament says that Solomon wrote Proverbs.
☐ 5. The first verse of Proverbs.

B. Give one reason that supports the idea that Solomon was not the author of Proverbs in its final form:

_____

Two Styles of Proverbs

The Book of Proverbs contains two distinct styles of proverbs. Chapters 1—9 and 30—31 are a series of narratives. Each narrative is built around a different theme and may be only a few verses or an entire chapter.

Study the following narratives and match each with the correct theme listed in the column on the right.[9]

____1. 1:8-19   a. The pitfalls of immorality
____2. chap. 4   b. The enticements of sinners
____3. chap. 5   c. Heeding parental advice
____4. 31:10-31   d. Description of a worthy woman

Chapters 10—29 are pointed, concise one-, two-, or four-liners that usually state an important truth by placing one thing in contrast with another.

A. Study these one-liners: 16:3; 24:10; 26:7.

B. Study these two-liners: 13:18; 15:21; 20:4; 28:1-2.

C. Study these four-liners: 22:24-25; 24:13-14; 24:21-22.

D. Now, let's write our own proverbs. I will start each one and you complete it. Remember, simply state a truth that you know to be a fact from personal experience.

A well-heeded Scripture is a guide to the soul,
    but a dust-covered Bible is

_____

A prayer from the heart is like a sweet sacrifice to the Lord,
    but ears that itch for praise

_____

You have studied three of the five books of Wisdom. See if you can recall them and complete the blanks below.

THE BOOKS OF WISDOM

J __ __

P __ __ __ __ __

P __ __ __ __ __ __

E __ __ __ __ __ __ __ __

S __ __ __   __ __   S __ __ __ __

---

[8]Answers: A-3 and 5; B-You may have indicated that Hezekiah lived around 200 years after Solomon, and one section of Proverbs was recorded by his men.
[9]Answers: 1-b, 2-c, 3-a, 4-d.

DAY 5   The Book of Ecclesiastes and Song of Songs

UNIT   10

Proverbs and Ecclesiastes differ in one important aspect. The Proverbs are basically optimistic; Ecclesiastes is basically pessimistic. The Book of Ecclesiastes examines life and asks the popular question: "Is this all there is?"

The writer of Ecclesiastes wanted to know the significance of life. He wanted to find joy and meaning in the midst of his life. Modern men and women seek the same answers and the same meaning in life.

▶ Ecclesiastes 1:1-11 seems to set the mood for the entire book. Read that passage and write here one or two words to describe the feeling or mood those verses create:

Authorship, Date, and Title of Ecclesiastes

Authorship. Though the Book of Ecclesiastes is anonymous, many passages in the book hint that Solomon is the author. For example, Solomon, son of David, served as king in Jerusalem (Eccl. 1:1). Solomon faced problems of wealth and leisure time that are mentioned in Ecclesiastes. He could have written or at least inspired many of the questions raised in the book. Solomon was either the author or the inspiration of the author who wrote Ecclesiastes.

Date. The date of the book necessarily will follow the idea of authorship. If Solomon wrote the book, the date would be about 1000 B.C. If someone else wrote the book to answer the kinds of questions Solomon's life inspired, the date could be as late as 200 B.C.

Title. The Hebrew name for the Book of Ecclesiastes is "Koheleth," which comes from a word that means "to bring together." Some people have interpreted the meaning as that of calling together a congregation. Thus the English title stated in 1:1 is "The Preacher" (NIV uses "Teacher"). The title we use is the Greek title from the Septuagent and means "a member or speaker of an assembly."

The Structure and Meaning of Ecclesiastes

The Book of Ecclesiastes contains reflections on a number of questions. The author wanted to know, "Is life worth living?" He also wanted to know, "What makes life worth living?"

These questions make the Book of Ecclesiastes relevant for today. Many people today, young, old, and in between, want to know how to make life worth living. As we explore the Book of Ecclesiastes, we ask the same questions the author asked.

▶ **Find in the following references some of the things the writer of Ecclesiastes discovered NOT to be the key to a meaningful life. Match the reference on the left with the correct response on the right. Write the correct letters in the blanks.**[10]

——— 1. 1:16-17	A. wine
——— 2. 2:1-2	B. wisdom and knowledge
——— 3. 2:3	C. great projects
——— 4. 2:4-5,11	D. pleasure

The preacher's questions led him to a number of temporary conclusions.

▶ **A. Read 3:12-13. Summarize this conclusion about the meaning of life:**

_____

_____

B. Decide why you agree or disagree with this conclusion.

In 3:13 and 5:18 the meaning of life is expressed as enjoying food, drinking, and toiling. The author came to his final and best solution in 12:13.

THE BOTTOM LINE

The conclusion, when all has been heard, is: fear God and keep His commandments, because this applies to every person.

Ecclesiastes 12:13, NASB

The Song of Songs

The Song of Songs is a series of love poems which rejoice in the love of a man and a woman. The most serious question of the book concerns how the Song of Songs is to be interpreted.

Interpreters normally follow one of three approaches:

1. Allegorical. Many Jewish rabbis viewed Solomon as symbolizing God and the maid as a symbol of the people of God. Some Christian interpreters adopted a similar approach, seeing Solomon as a symbol of Christ and the maid as a symbol of the church.

To me, the allegorical method seems to be a dangerous way to interpret Scripture. In an allegory, the meaning is imposed by the interpreter. The interpreter is free to make each character stand for what he or she thinks best. The interpretation can be based on personal bias or even a whim.

2. Typical. A type is a likeness, a sort of object-lesson, by which God reveals His grace and saving power. In the middle ages, some Christian interpreters began to teach that the Song of Songs was a literal love poem, but that it was meant to help us understand the relationship between Christ and His church. The lover was viewed as a type (likeness) of Christ. However, nowhere in Scripture is found any indication that this figure should be viewed as a type of Christ.

---

[10]Answers: 1-B, 2-D, 3-A, 4-C.

3. Literal. The literal approach views the song as a celebration of the kind of love that God has established between husband and wife. This interpretation exalts the biblical ideal of sexual relationships being limited to one man and one woman who commit themselves to each other for life.

The literal approach seems best because it respects the integrity of the book. The song is taken at face value. The book proclaims the profound message of the joy of two people whom God has brought together in commitment.

▶ **List the five Old Testament books of wisdom. Look back at this week's work to check your answers.**

_____   _____

_____   _____

_____

SUMMARY REVIEW

To review this week's study of the Old Testament, see if you can mentally answer the following questions. You may want to write the answers on a separate sheet of paper. Mark your level of performance on the left: circle "C" if you can answer correctly and circle "R" if you need to review.

C R   1. List the Old Testament books of law, history, and wisdom.

C R   2. What question reflects the meaning of wisdom?

C R   3. What are two possible reasons for Job's being written?

C R   4. What was the basic argument of Job's friends?

C R   5. List four types of psalms.

C R   6. What type are Psalms 1 and 15?

C R   7. What significance do titles of psalms have?

C R   8. Define "proverb."

C R   9. What is the primary message of Ecclesiastes?

C R   10. What is the primary message of Song of Songs?

RESPONDING TO GOD'S WORD

★ **In your opinion, how should a Christian view sex? Check your answer:**
☐ 1. As a gift from God that is to be expressed fully only in marriage
☐ 2. As something that is wrong
☐ 3. As something to be avoided
☐ 4. As a gift from God that is to be enjoyed for its own sake
☐ 5. As the main thing in life

☐ 6. Other _____

★ **Pray for God to help you maintain a biblical view and practice of sex.**

God and the Major Prophets I *(Isaiah)*

Many people think of prophets and prophecy in terms of predicting what God will do in the future. Today, prophecy often is interpreted to mean predictions about the second coming of Christ and the events at the end of time. These ideas are not wrong, just inadequate.

In these final three units we will look at the Old Testament prophets. We will consider the nature of prophecy and what God has to say to us through the prophets of the Old Testament.

In this unit you will study the Book of Isaiah.

Isaiah had an impact on his world and a significance that endures beyond his times. Isaiah's message from the Lord saved Judah from certain doom in perilous times. When events looked bleak, Isaiah counseled the people to have faith. Judah endured because the people heard the word of the Lord from Isaiah.

Isaiah:

    I. The Book of Judgment (Isa. 1—39)
       A. Judgment against Judah and Jerusalem (Isa. 1—12)
       B. Judgment against the nations (Isa. 13—23)
       C. Judgment against the world (Isa. 24—35)
       D. Events surrounding Hezekiah (Isa. 36—39)
    II. The Book of Comfort (Isa. 40—66)

WordWatch

Watch for these words as you study this unit.

Prophecy—a message from God, not necessarily restricted to end-time events.

Prophet—is the person who delivers that message with God's authority.

Major prophets—designates the first five books of prophecy. These books are called major because of their length as compared to the other 12 prophetic books. Lamentations often is grouped with the major prophets because it is associated with Jeremiah.

Minor prophets—designates all the books of prophecy except the first five. The minor prophets are minor only in size, not in importance. These prophets proclaimed God's message to people of their day with powerful words from God. The minor prophets and the Hebrew Book of the Twelve are the same. We will study these prophets in Unit 13.

Sovereignty—in reference to God, this term expresses the absolute, supreme, and ultimate authority of God. The concept of God's sovereignty appears throughout the Scripture although the word does not.

Remnant—in Scripture, this term has a two-fold meaning. The most immediate meaning in the Old Testament refers to the nucleus of Israelites that would survive the captivity and dispersion in Babylon to return to Palestine. The hope for the righteous remnant was one of the promises of the prophets, particularly Isaiah. The Messianic aspect of this prophecy is affirmed by the New Testament. Paul, particularly, pointed to the church as the righteous remnant.

Holy/holiness—completely separated and apart, different. As applied to God, the word takes on implications of moral purity and perfection. By association, God then declares to be holy all those persons, places, things, and events that He has called and set apart for His purposes.

DAY 1 The Prophets of the Old Testament

U N I T   11

What comes to your mind when you hear the terms *prophet* or *prophecy*?

▶ **Use a pencil to complete this activity because you may want to adjust it later.**

A. Write your description of a prophet: _____

_____

B. Write your definition of prophecy: _____

_____

You may recall from our first unit of study that the Jews organized the Hebrew canon into three divisions. The third division, the writings, includes most of the wisdom literature, the poetic books, and books like Chronicles, Ruth, and Daniel.

As you worked through this study, you discovered that in our English Bibles, the Old Testament canon is normally divided into five sections.

● Law
● History
● Wisdom (or Poetry)
● Major Prophets
● Minor Prophets

▶ **What books of prophets in the Hebrew canon do we usually consider books of history? Write those six books below:[1]**

_____   _____

_____   _____

_____   _____

The Hebrew included Joshua, Judges, 1 & 2 Samuel, and 1 & 2 Kings among the prophetic books because prophets wrote the books or because the books (especially Samuel and Kings) contain stories about prophets.

_____
[1]Answers: Joshua, Judges, 1 & 2 Samuel, 1 & 2 Kings.

THE LAW
GENESIS
EXODUS
LEVITICUS
NUMBERS
DEUTERONOMY

THE PROPHETS
FORMER: LATTER:
JOSHUA   ISAIAH
JUDGES   JEREMIAH
1 SAMUEL   EZEKIEL
2 SAMUEL   BOOK OF
1 KINGS   THE TWELVE
2 KINGS

THE WRITINGS
WISDOM LITERATURE
POETIC BOOKS
OTHER BOOKS LIKE
   1 CHRONICLES
   2 CHRONICLES
   RUTH
   DANIEL

See how well you remember the the books of law, history, and wisdom. Fill in the book titles in the chart below. Then use the table of contents in your Bible to check your work and to fill in the titles of the books classified as major prophets and minor prophets.

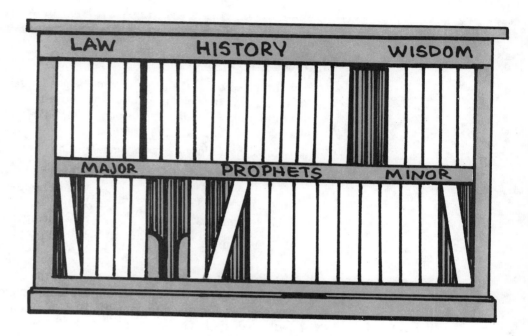

The Nature of Prophecy

The nature of prophecy may be the most misunderstood concept in the Old Testament. Many people think of the prophets of the Old Testament as mere fortune tellers. Other people think of the prophets as weird and unusual individuals who used strange methods to convey strange messages. Some people even think that the prophets gave encoded or cryptic messages which were to be understood by people living in later times. All of these views miss the real significance of the prophets of the Old Testament.

Prophecy is basically a message from God. The prophet is the person who delivers that message with God's authority. Some of the prophetic passages in the Old Testament clearly speak of future events. However, the prophets usually were proclaiming strong, relevant messages to the people of their day. They called for righteous living and just actions. They condemned abuse of the weak and poor in society.

These prophets demanded that the people give more than lip service to God. They expected people who worshiped God to obey God in everyday life. The prophets exhorted the people to worship the Lord, but they wanted this worship to be a genuine experience of faith which issued in new and right behavior. They called for justice and righteousness to be at the center of the people's religion. Worship that does not change our actions toward God and toward other people is not genuine worship.

The message of the Bible is truly timeless. The prophetic messages were spoken thousands of years ago, and most of the messages were spoken to people of that day about conditions of that day. Yet the message of the prophets still speaks to us today for at least four reasons:

> ### Prophecy Still Speaks
>
> - The message came from God.
> - The message is rooted in real life.
> - The message speaks to human nature.
> - The message addresses the problem of sin.

Predictive Prophecy

From time to time, the prophets' messages contained clear predictions of future events. Some of those predictions foretold the work of Jesus, but many of them foretold events in the lives of people just like you and me. Occasionally, a sign was given to validate the prediction.

▶ **Read the following prophecies and answer the questions on the right.[2]**

A. 2 Kings 13:14-19

B. Isaiah 7:10-14

C. Jeremiah 31:31-34

D. Micah 5:2

_____ 1. Which passage prophesied events that would happen in the life of an individual?

_____ 2. Which two prophecies speak of the Messiah's birthplace and covenant?

_____ 3. Which prophecy mentioned the virgin birth?

The important thing to remember is that the prophets' predictions grew out of God's message for that day. Jeremiah predicted the new covenant because of the people's loss and discouragement after the fall of the Southern Kingdom. To the people in despair, God promised a new day when He would deal with His people according to a new covenant.

The prophets did not predict for the sake of satisfying curiosity. Any predictions they made grew out of God's message for the people of their day.

Do the prophets speak of the coming of Christ? Yes. The coming of Christ into the world is the greatest event in human history. I believe that when the prophets spoke of the days when God would deliver His people and give them a new covenant, they were talking about Christ's coming, His death on the cross, and His resurrection.

▶ **Look back at the definitions you wrote at the beginning of the session. Make any changes you think you should make so that they reflect what you have learned in this session.**

RESPONDING TO GOD'S WORD

★ **Pray for God to speak to you from His prophets as you study His Word this week.**

---

[2]Answers: 1-a; 2-c, d; 3-b.

DAY 2   The Book of Isaiah

UNIT   11

Background Information

Date. Two events bracket the ministry of Isaiah. We know that he began his ministry around the time Uzziah died (6:1-8). We also know that his last recorded activity was during the Sennacherib crisis (36:1—37:8). Although the dates are not precise, we know that Isaiah prophesied between 742 B.C. and 700 B.C. We can assume that Isaiah had a long and significant ministry that may have extended beyond the Sennacherib crisis.

Authorship. The traditional view of the authorship of Isaiah is that the entire book comes from Isaiah. The messages in 1—39 were addressed to the contemporary situations of his day, and his messages in 40—66 were both a messianic prediction and a prediction about the future of Israel. Remember this important fact about Isaiah and all the other prophets: Isaiah was a messenger, not an author. His message was spoken first and recorded later. Some scholars suggest that some of the messages Isaiah delivered may have been collected and recorded later by his disciples.

Scholars have debated the relationship between chapters 1—39 and 40—66. The setting for Isaiah 1—39 fits the time period of Isaiah in Jerusalem. However, the setting for chapters 40—66 is the Babylonian captivity 100 years after Isaiah probably died.

Some scholars believe that chapters 40—46 are not prophetic passages written by Isaiah. They argue that these chapters were written by an anonymous prophet who lived in Babylon during the exile and who later returned to Jerusalem.

Understanding the setting of the messages in Isaiah is essential. To understand the book, you must understand that the setting of chapters 1—39 is Jerusalem and the setting of chapters 40—66 is Babylon.

Isaiah the man. Most prophets functioned outside the religious and political institutions of their day. Isaiah functioned within them. While we cannot be certain, Isaiah may have grown up within the royal circle in Jerusalem. According to tradition, Isaiah's father was a brother to Amaziah, an earlier king of Judah. This relationship reflects Isaiah's royal background. If this were true, Isaiah would have felt at ease among kings and leaders of Judah, and we can see why he sought to work within the system.

▶ **Isaiah worked from within the system, Elijah from without. This exercise will help you see the contrast. Read Isaiah 7:3-4 and 1 Kings 18:16,18; 19:1-2. Write an E by the following statements that apply to Elijah and an I beside those that apply to Isaiah:[3]**

_____ 1. The prophet had a good relationship with the king.
_____ 2. The prophet was viewed as an enemy by the royal family.
_____ 3. The prophet had an encouraging word for the king.
_____ 4. The prophet rebuked the king.
_____ 5. The prophet could be described as a prophetic statesman.
_____ 6. The prophet was a political outsider.

---

[3]Answers: 1-I, 2-E, 3-I, 4-E, 5-I, 6-E.

We know more about Isaiah than we do about most of the prophets. He married a woman later called the prophetess. She may have prophesied herself, or the name could indicate simply that she was the prophet's wife. Isaiah had at least two sons to which he gave significant names. You will learn more about that in a future session.

Historical Background

Understanding the events that took place in Isaiah's lifetime helps us understand the man and his message. Isaiah proclaimed the word of God during the reigns of four kings of Judah.

▶ **Place Isaiah in historical context. Turn to the timeline on page 138. Read Isaiah 1:1 and circle the four kings to whom he prophesied. Write "Isaiah" by those kings.**

All of Isaiah's ministry and most of his messages revolved around three significant political and military crises. Understanding these crises helps us understand Isaiah's message.

The first crisis: **the threat from Syria and the pact with Assyria.** The first crisis occurred early in Isaiah's ministry. Ahaz served as king of Judah in the place of his grandfather Uzziah. The Northern Kingdom entered an alliance with Syria and the two nations mounted a campaign against Judah. The Bible records Ahaz's reaction to this threat: "The hearts of Ahaz and his people were shaken, as the trees of the forest are shaken by the wind" (7:2).

▶ **A. Read Isaiah 7:1-16. What was the message Isaiah brought to Ahaz from God?[4]**

_____

_____

B. Read 2 Kings 16:7-9. What did Ahaz do instead of following Isaiah's advice?

_____

_____

Ahaz asked for the help of the ambitious and cruel king of Assyria, Tiglath-Pileser, who proved only too happy to assist. Ahaz was soon to see that Isaiah had been right. Part of his dramatic prediction came to pass only three years later when Tiglath-Pileser ravaged Damascus, the capital of Syria. Ten years after that, he completely destroyed Samaria and sent the people of the Northern Kingdom into exile. The word of the Lord had been fulfilled. (Of course the ultimate fulfillment of the prophecy of a child named Emmanuel, meaning God with us, was the birth of Jesus Christ.)

The second crisis: **the Ashdod rebellion.** In 713 B.C. the city of Ashdod was the center of a rebellion against Assyria by several small states. Apparently Egypt had promised to support this rebellion.

▶ **Read Isaiah 20. What dramatic thing did Isaiah do to demonstrate to Judah that they should put their trust in God instead of Egypt?**

_____

_____

Because of Isaiah's intervention, Judah did not take part in the revolt. That wise decision avoided what could have been a disastrous alliance.

---

[4]Answers: A-Don't be afraid; don't be discouraged. God will defeat your enemies. B-Entered an alliance with Assyria.

The third crisis: the Sennacherib crisis. King Sennacherib of Assyria besieged Jerusalem during the reign of Hezekiah. (You may want to review the material on the Sennacherib crisis in Day 5 of Unit 8). Events in Jerusalem looked hopeless. How could Jerusalem survive? Isaiah 28—33 and 36—37 record the preaching of Isaiah during the Sennacherib crisis.

▶ **A. Read Isaiah 30:15-18. Answer the following questions in as few words as possible:[5]**

1. How did some of the people want to handle the crisis? _____

2. How did Isaiah say to handle the crisis? _____

_____

3. How did God want to deal with the people of Judah? _____

_____

B. Read Isaiah 37:33-38 and fill in the blanks:

1. Isaiah prophesied that the king of Assyria would not _____ Jerusalem.

2. The city was defended by _____   _____.

3. The angel of the Lord put to death 185,000 _____

_____.

4. Sennacherib returned to _____.

5. Sennacherib was cut down in his pagan _____.

For the third time, Isaiah called for faith. He knew that trusting God provided the only defense for the people of Jerusalem. During this time, Isaiah proclaimed that Jerusalem would not be violated. He knew that faith was the key to the city's defense. The Lord miraculously intervened to spare Jerusalem.

RESPONDING TO GOD'S WORD

★ **Read Isaiah 6:1-8. Spend a few minutes meditating on God's call to Isaiah and his willing response. Consider the relationship between being cleansed (forgiven of sins) and being willing to serve the Lord.**

★ **If you are aware of sins in your life that you have not confessed or repented, take those sins to the Lord right now. If you are aware of some task God has for you that you are not doing, commit yourself to obeying Him now.**

★ **What is your first response when you face a crisis? Check one:**
  ☐ 1. Panic   ☐ 4. Call a friend
  ☐ 2. Retreat   ☐ 5. Talk to a family member
  ☐ 3. Pray   ☐ 6. Attack

★ **What did you learn from Isaiah's advice to Judah that will help you face crises in your life?**

_____

_____

★ **Ask God to help you practice Isaiah's advice.**

---

[5]Answers to A: 1-to flee; 2-to repent and trust God to help them; 3-God wanted to save them, to show compassion on them and to bless them. Answer to B: 1-enter; 2-the Lord; 3-Assyrian soldiers or men; 4-Nineveh; 5-temple.

DAY 3   The Teachings of Isaiah

UNIT   11

Isaiah's teachings provide rich insights into the nature and character of God. We will look at his teachings under the following headings:

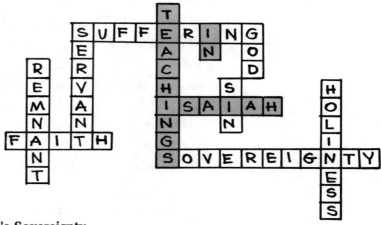

The Lord's Sovereignty

What have we to fear from what the future holds when we know that God holds the future?

▶ **Read Isaiah 37:21-26. Who determines the course of history?** _____

Isaiah knew that God is the Lord of history. History is not thwarted by tyrants like Tiglath-Pileser or rebellious kings like Ahaz of Judah.

▶ **Read Isaiah 37:18-19. What was Isaiah's teaching about idols, the gods of other nations?**

_____

Isaiah's teachings permitted no other god but the Lord. He said that the idols of the nations were "not gods."

▶ **Read Isaiah 10:5-6,12. For what purpose did God use Assyria?** _____

_____

Isaiah taught that the Lord would use Assyria as the rod of His anger to punish Judah. He also stated that Assyria would be punished because of its arrogance (Isa. 10). Clearly, the God is Lord of history.

The Holiness of God

Isaiah knew that God is holy. Isaiah 6:3 records the words of the seraphim who announced God as the holy one. They cried out, "Holy, holy, holy is the Lord Almighty; the whole earth is full of His glory" (Isa. 6:3).

The concept of holiness was not unique to Israel. Other nations had their gods whom they described as holy, but Isaiah gave a new meaning to the idea of holiness. In calling their gods holy, other nations meant that their gods were not human; they were gods and not men. To Isaiah, the holiness of God indicated His perfect moral purity and His being far above and beyond all that humankind can fully understand. The other nations had gods who were not men, but they did not have gods who had perfect moral purity.

▶ A. The Bible states that God's purpose for us is that we should be a holy people. The New Testament expresses the same idea with the terms *saint* and *sanctify*. Write your own explanation of what the Bible is saying when it refers to us as saints or holy or sanctified persons.

_____

_____

The Doctrine of Sin

▶ Read Isaiah 1:1-4. Based on those verses, write a definition of sin:[6]

Sin is _____

_____

To Isaiah, sin was rebellion against the Lord. Isaiah knew that all of society was tainted with sin. He also knew that sacrifices were no remedy for sin (Isa. 1:10-16). Only God could forgive sin.

▶ Read Isaiah 1:11-20. Mark the following statements as T (true) or F (false):[7]

_____ 1. God never has enough sacrifices.
_____ 2. Some offerings to God are meaningless.
_____ 3. God hates some religious assemblies.
_____ 4. God always hears prayers.
_____ 5. An unrepentant evil person's worship is not acceptable to God.
_____ 6. God offers His forgiveness to people who are willing and obedient.
_____ 7. God will extend His mercy to people who resist and rebel.

The Place of Faith

Throughout his ministry, Isaiah called the people of Israel to put their faith in God. In every crisis, Isaiah's message remained the same. People must trust God. Isaiah spoke these famous words which further illustrate his call to faith: "See, I lay a stone in Zion, a tested stone, a precious cornerstone for a sure foundation; the one who trusts will never be dismayed" (Isa. 28:16).

▶ Read Isaiah 12:2-3; 26:3-4; and 50:10. Because of the crises the people faced, they needed Isaiah's encouragement to exercise faith. Sometimes the faith of the people held, at other times it did not.

1. When you are facing a crisis, what factors challenge your faith and make it difficult for you to trust and follow God's leadership?

_____

_____

2. What persons have been an encouragement to your faith in times of crisis and what did they do or say to encourage and strengthen your faith?

_____

_____

The Doctrine of the Remnant

Isaiah named his first son Shear-Jashub, meaning "a remnant will return." Early in his ministry, Isaiah used this son as an object lesson. He foretold the coming

---

[6]Compare your answer to mine: Sin is rebelling against God. You may have written that sin is forsaking the Lord, spurning the Lord, turning one's back on the Lord.
[7]Answers: 1-F, 2-T, 3-T, 4-F, 5-T, 6-T, 7-F.

Teachings of Isaiah

judgment against Judah's sins. The judgment would be so severe that only a remnant would return. Later in his ministry Isaiah used the name to indicate the hope which God gave to people of faith. In the midst of tragedy and fear, Isaiah said that surely a remnant would return.

▶ **Read Isaiah 11:11 and 37:31-32.**

A. **Underline the words that best describe the purpose of these verses:**[8]

Judgment   Warning   Hope   Reassurance   Lament[8]

B. **How was survival of a remnant of God's people guaranteed?** _____

_____

▶ **In the box in the margin, draw five visual symbols which you think represent the five major teachings you have studied in this session. Leave room to add one more as you study tomorrow's session.**

RESPONDING TO GOD'S WORD

★ 1. **Recall and list some of the actions, thoughts, values, and so on that were separated from your life when God made you holy.**

_____

Does your life contain actions, thoughts, values, and so on that need to be separated from your life because God has made you a saint? Pray now asking God to help you achieve the holiness to which He has called you.

★ 2. **Who do you know who may need encouragement? What will you do to help strengthen that person's faith?**

_____

_____

_____

---

[8]Answer: A. You could have underlined hope and reassurance. B. Your answer probably carries the idea that the Lord would accomplish it.

DAY 4   The Teachings of Isaiah (conclusion)

U N I T   11

Yesterday you studied five of the major teachings in Isaiah. Today you will study one more major teaching and then begin a study of some of the major passages in the book.

The Messiah/Suffering Servant

Isaiah looked for a king who would come and reign over Judah in truth and righteousness. This teaching is found particularly in Isaiah 9:1-7; 11:1-9; and 32:1-8. These chapters describe a coming king.

▶ **Read the promise of a king in 11:1-9 and 32:1-8.**

Some people think these chapters originally referred to either the birth of Hezekiah or to the ascension of Hezekiah to the throne. Many Christians, including myself, believe that these verses are fulfilled in Jesus Christ. These chapters certainly point to a king which Judah never had, a king reigning in justice and righteousness. Only Jesus can fulfill perfectly such promises.

Isaiah's messianic hope resulted from faith in God. Because they believed God, the people could believe that God would work in wonderful ways in the future. Jesus is not mentioned by name in Isaiah. Nor do these passages give us any specific information about the time of Jesus Christ. The passages tell us about God and His magnificent work He would do in the future. The prophet was sure that God was at work and He would deliver His people in some future time.

You and I are privileged to live in that new era. We live rejoicing in the Lord's presence with us. We worship and serve the king whose coming Isaiah anticipated.

In Isaiah 40—66, the message about the Messiah takes on different characteristics. In these chapters, the prophet described the Messiah as a servant who would suffer voluntarily for the people of Israel. Isaiah 42:1-9; 49:1-6; 50:4-9; and 52:13—53:12 are known as the suffering servant poems in Isaiah. These passages speak of one who has served the Lord in humility and faith.

▶ **A. Match the following prophetic references on the left with the correct fulfillment references on the right. Write the correct letters in the blanks.**[9]

_____ 1. Isaiah 53:3	a. Matthew 27:38
_____ 2. Isaiah 53:7	b. Matthew 27:57-60
_____ 3. Isaiah 50:6	c. Matthew 26:62-63
_____ 4. Isaiah 53:12	d. Mark 14:65
_____ 5. Isaiah 53:9	e. Luke 2:32
_____ 6. Isaiah 42:6	f. John 1:10-11

B. Read Isaiah 42:1-4 and check the characteristics that you think those verses describe:

- ☐ 1. Power
- ☐ 2. Humility
- ☐ 3. Wrath
- ☐ 4. Just
- ☐ 5. Kind
- ☐ 6. Authority
- ☐ 7. Compassion

Isaiah described the servant as humble: "He will not shout or cry out, or raise his voice in the streets. A bruised reed he will not break, and a smoldering wick he will not snuff out. In faithfulness he will bring forth justice" (Isa. 42:2-3).

▶ **Read Isaiah 49:5-6 and mark the following statements as T (true) or F (false):**[10]

- _____ 1. The Servant's purpose was only to restore Israel to God's fellowship.
- _____ 2. The Servant's purpose was only to bring Gentiles into God's fellowship.
- _____ 3. The Servant's purpose included bringing Israel and Gentiles into God's fellowship.

---

[9]Answers: A; 1-f, 2-c, 3-d, 4-a, 5-b, 6-e. B; You could have checked all but 3; certainly you checked 2 and 4.
[10]Surely you checked 3 as True and the others False.

The prophet also believed that the servant would make God known to the nations: "I will also make you a light for the Gentiles, that you may bring my salvation to the ends of the earth" (Isa. 49:6).

The prophet indicated the individual nature of the servant in Isaiah 50:4-9. The servant declared his faithfulness to God. Christians often have thought of Jesus as they read these words: "I offered my back to those who beat me, my cheeks to those who pulled out my beard; I did not hide my face from mocking and spitting" (Isa. 50:6).

Isaiah 53 is one of the high points of the Old Testament. In this passage the servant voluntarily gave himself for his people.

▶ **Read Isaiah 53:4-6. Explain in your own words how these words relate to Jesus and to you:**

_____

_____

Isaiah 53 closes with the affirmation that the servant's death solved men's sin problem: "He bore the sin of many, and made intercession for the transgressors" (Isa. 53:12). In the Hebrew text, "he bore" occurs in a verb form indicating that something is certain to be completed or finished. The servant bore the sin of many. The next verb "made intercession" is a verb form which indicates something is incomplete or continuing.

When I read this verse in the Hebrew text, I find it hard not to think of Jesus who on the cross bore our sin and who continues to make intercession for us. All who trust in Christ may experience this forgiveness of sin and newness of life.

▶ **Select a symbol to represent the Suffering Servant and add it to the ones you selected yesterday.**

Read again Isaiah 53:12 and answer these questions:[11]
1. What aspect of the Suffering Servant's work would be completed:

_____

2. What aspect of the Suffering Servant's work would continue:

_____

Many of the favorite passages in the Old Testament come from the Book of Isaiah. We turn now to a study of some of those passages. The book contains various types of literature and often surprises us with its profound messages for our lives. Today, we will review several major passages in the Book of Isaiah.

Isaiah 9:1-7

The ninth chapter of Isaiah interests believers because of its Messianic implications. The passage finds its fulfillment in Jesus Christ.

▶ **Read Isaiah 9:1-7.**
1. Write in the blanks the number of the verse that describes the benefit promised under the reign of the coming King in verses 1-5:[12]

____ A. Enlightenment   ____ D. Deliverance
____ B. Joy   ____ E. Peace
____ C. Freedom

---

[11]Answers: 1-He bore the sin of many; 2-making intercession for transgressors.

2. Write here the names of all the kings of Israel and Judah who match the description in verses 6-7:

_____

The historical background of this messianic passage is the time when Syria and the Northern Kingdom teamed up against Judah. In response to a plea from Ahaz, king of Judah, the king of Assyria ravaged the Northern Kingdom (9:9; compare 2 Kings 16:5ff.) This passage speaks graphically about the condition of the Northern Kingdom after Assyria's assault. Isaiah described that condition as walking in darkness. Could there be any hope for the northern region? Did God still work? The prophet responded that God was at work and that they would see the light of a great hope. That hope and deliverance was a promise that would not be fulfilled until the coming of Christ.

➤ **Do you think the word *hopeless* belongs in the vocabulary of one who belongs to the Lord? Explain your answer here:**

_____

Be prepared to discuss your answer in this week's small-group session.

Isaiah described the peace and joy that comes from God by telling of the birth of a child who would usher in a period of peace, justice, and righteousness. Only in Christ do we find a "Wonderful Counselor, Mighty God, Everlasting Father, Prince of Peace" (v.6).

RESPONDING TO GOD'S WORD

★ **Read Hebrews 7:25. What ministry is Jesus carrying on today in behalf of believers?**

_____

Thank God for the faithful intercession of the Lord Jesus in your behalf.

---

[12]Answers to 1: A-2, B-3, C-4, D-4, E-5. Answer to 2: None; only the Lord Jesus Christ in His second coming will fulfill this promise.

DAY 5   Major Passages in the Book of Isaiah (continued)

U N I T   11   Isaiah 56:1-8

➤ **A. To gain a perspective on Isaiah's message in 56:1-8, read Deuteronomy 23:1-8. Check the groups of people named in the Deuteronomy passage who were excluded from the assembly of the Lord:**[13]

☐ 1. Philistines
☐ 2. Those who had been emasculated (eunuchs)
☐ 3. Ammonites
☐ 4. Those born of forbidden marriages
☐ 5. Moabites
☐ 6. Those who lived East of the Jordan
☐ 7. Egyptians
☐ 9. Edomites

B. Now read Isaiah 56:1-8 and answer the following questions:

1. What two groups will not be excluded from God's people?

A. _____   B. _____

2. What will be given to eunuchs who are committed to God that will be worth more to them than the sons and daughters they cannot have?

_____

3. What is promised to foreigners who are committed to God?

_____

4. What does God want His house to be called?

_____

The setting for Isaiah 56 probably reflects life in Jerusalem after the return from the Babylonian exile. The message concerned foreigners (non-Jews) and those with mutilated bodies (eunuchs). Isaiah emphasized the acceptance of foreigners and eunuchs. His only stipulation involved worshiping the Lord and keeping the Sabbath.

During Isaiah's time eunuchs could not worship God in the temple, but he saw a time when both foreigners and eunuchs who kept the Sabbath of the Lord would become a part of the covenant community. They would worship God on His holy mountain. Their burnt offerings and their sacrifices would be accepted on the altar of God. The house of the Lord truly would become a house of prayer for all nations (Mark 11:17).

Isaiah looked for the day when all people would become the people of God. The barriers of race, gender, and nationality would be erased. People would become the people of God based only on their acceptance of His love.

God is the Lord of all the nations. All people are His people. He wants everyone to know Him, to love Him, and to serve Him.

Isaiah 6:1-13

The last passage you will study is probably one of the most familiar passages in all the Old Testament and probably has as much to say to your life as any other passage. For that reason, it has been reserved for your final study.

Worship is important. Through worship we express our feelings toward God and toward other human beings. In times of worship, we are able to deal with the deepest emotions of life. Worship reminds us of what really makes a difference in the world and what really matters in life. Worship plays its most important role when it brings us into an encounter with the living God.

Isaiah worshiped God in the midst of his grief over the death of king Uzziah. In his worship experience, he probably dealt with his own emotions. How could the

---

[13]Answers: A. 2, 3, 4, 5. B. 1-Eunuchs and foreigners (Gentiles); 2-an everlasting name that will not be cut off; 3-joy in the temple worship; 4-a house of prayer for all nations.

nation continue without its great leader who had been king for 52 years? Who would take his place? These questions must have been going through Isaiah's mind as he worshiped in the temple.

This experience in Isaiah's life often has been outlined in three parts:
(1) Isaiah saw God (6:1-4)
(2) Isaiah saw himself (6:5-7)
(3) Isaiah saw a world in need (6:8-13).

Isaiah saw God (6:1-4).

Vision +
Self—awareness +
Cleansing +
Call =
 Worship

▶ Read Isaiah 6:1-4 and check the statements with which you agree. Use the material that follows the exercise to check your answers.

☐ 1. While Isaiah agonized about an empty earthly throne, God showed him that God still was on His throne.
☐ 2. Isaiah described God's appearance.
☐ 3. During the vision, an earthquake occurred.
☐ 4. Isaiah's experience was not a vision but an actual experience.
☐ 5. Isaiah actually experienced the presence of God.

As Isaiah mourned the loss of an earthly king, he began to focus on the heavenly king. As he worshiped, he probably began to think about the Holy Place and the Holy of Holies. Surely he thought about God whose presence was symbolized in the Holy of Holies.

The earthly king died; the heavenly King reigns. Isaiah had a profound experience with God that led him to look at the world in a different way.

Though Isaiah seemed to have been describing God, he actually described those things around God. For example, he described the throne but not the one sitting on the throne. He described the seraphim—burning, fiery creatures who bore witness to the holiness of God. Isaiah described how he felt and what he heard but he never described God.

God is Spirit; people who worship Him must worship Him in spirit and in truth (John 4:24). No person has seen God at any time (John 1:18; 1 John 4:12). Isaiah's experience fits these New Testament teachings perfectly.

Isaiah described an experience with God without describing God. Human beings cannot know God in His fullness. No matter how often someone may tell you that he knows all about God, the Bible tells us that we never can quite know God in His fullness. He is infinite; we are finite. God is perfect moral purity; we are sinful human beings. We can know God's leadership and God's forgiveness. Isaiah experienced both.

Isaiah saw himself (6:5-7).

▶ Read Isaiah 6:5-7 and answer the following questions. Use the material that follows the exercise to check your answers.

1. In God's presence, how did Isaiah see himself? _____

_____

2. What did Isaiah think was his fate? _____

_____

3. What solved Isaiah's problem? _____

_____

In response to his vision of God, Isaiah saw himself in his true condition: a sinner. He expressed his sin in terms of being a man of unclean lips who dwelled among a people of unclean lips. This curious expression probably indicated the darkness of his sin which expressed itself in his words.

Isaiah recognized his need for forgiveness. God responded to that need in a symbolic way. A seraph flew to the altar, removing a burning coal. The seraph touched the prophet's lips, declaring that "your guilt is taken away and your sin atoned for" (Isa. 6:7).

Isaiah saw a world in need (6:8-13).

Note the progression in Isaiah 6. First the prophet saw God, then he recognized his own sin and received forgiveness. Once his sin was forgiven, Isaiah could look to the world in need of God's forgiveness. The last section of the chapter deals with Isaiah's response to God's call.

▶ **Read Isaiah 6:8-13 and check the correct answer for each of the following questions:**[14]

1. Before Isaiah answered God's call,
   ☐ a. God had clearly spelled out exactly what He wanted Isaiah to do.
   ☐ b. he had experienced God's cleansing.
   ☐ c. he asked several key questions.

2. When Isaiah knew God was seeking someone to speak for Him,
   ☐ a. he wondered if God could use someone else.
   ☐ b. he immediately volunteered.
   ☐ c. he said he would go later on.

3. God's assignment indicated that Isaiah
   ☐ a. would have little outward success.
   ☐ b. would become one of the best-known of God's prophets.
   ☐ c. would be a failure.

4. Isaiah was to continue his ministry until
   ☐ a. the people repented of their sins.
   ☐ b. God healed the hurt of His people.
   ☐ c. until no people were left to hear.

5. The message about a stump being left was a message of
   ☐ a. judgment.
   ☐ b. hope.
   ☐ c. mystery.

To the question of "Whom shall I send?" (6:8), Isaiah responded eagerly. Having experienced God's forgiveness, he could anticipate joyfully sharing the message of God with the people of Judah. The prophet faced opposition and difficulties, but God promised to be with him and help him in his ministry. God promised that though judgment may come, He would restore Israel, preserving a holy remnant.

When the eyes of our hearts have seen God, the ears of our hearts hear the voice of God in every human need saying "Whom shall I send? And who will go for us?"

---

[14]Answers: 1-b, 2-b, 3-a, 4-c, 5-b.

▶ **SUMMARY REVIEW**

To review this week's study of the Old Testament, see if you can mentally answer the following questions. You may want to write the answers on a separate sheet of paper. Mark your level of performance on the left: circle "C" if you can answer correctly and circle "R" if you need to review.

C R   1. List the books of the Bible through the major prophets.

C R   2. List two reasons why the messages of the prophets still speak to us today.

C R   3. What are the two main divisions of Isaiah and the setting and theme of each?

C R   4. What was Isaiah's relationship to the leaders of Judah?

C R   5. Describe one crisis during which Isaiah ministered.

C R   6. Name three basic teachings of Isaiah.

C R   7. Name one reference in Isaiah that speaks of the Suffering Servant.

C R   8. What are two of the three points in Isaiah's experience and call in the temple (Isa. 6:1-13)?

RESPONDING TO GOD'S WORD

★ Consider your church. Can you describe your church as a house of prayer for all nations? Pray for God to help your church reach out to all people with an inclusive love and concern.

God and the Major Prophets II

(Jeremiah—Daniel)

In this unit you will see how God spoke through His prophets to people facing exile, discouragement, and disillusionment. He spoke to people whose lives had been changed forever by the events of the day. The message of these prophets is an ageless message to people who fear life and despair for the future.

Theme

Jeremiah was the prophet who wept over the sins of the people and their refusal to repent while he held out a strong message of hope. The book itself may be more difficult to understand because it is not written in chronological order.

Lamentations is made up of five dirges or funeral songs. These songs cry from the depths of despair and discouragement and address the question: Is it possible to believe in God anymore?

Ezekiel faithfully proclaims the message of God to the exiles. God used Ezekiel's distinctive personality to proclaim His message in the midst of difficult times.

Daniel emphasizes the sovereignty of God and the importance of being faithful to Him. Earthly kings and human tyrants cannot destroy the people of God. Faith is the key. Faith in God is the emphasis of the entire book, but particularly chapters 1—6.

Outline

Jeremiah:
    I. Prophecy against Jerusalem and Judah (Jer. 1—25)
    II. Biographical narrative about Jeremiah (Jer. 26—45)
    III. Prophecy against the foreign nations (Jer. 46—51)
    IV. Historical background of the Book of Jeremiah (Jer. 52)

Lamentations:
    I. The desolated and forsaken Jerusalem (Lam. 1)
    II. Reasons for the Lord's grief (Lam. 2)
    III. A personification of the nation (Lam. 3)
    IV. Contrast between the former glory and the present condition of Zion (Lam. 4)
    V. The nation appeals to the Lord to take notice of its trouble (Lam. 5)

Ezekiel:
    I. Prophecy of judgment against Jerusalem (Ezek. 1—24)
    II. Prophecy against foreign nations (Ezek. 25—32)
    III. Restoration passages (Ezek. 33—39)
    IV. Ezekiel's picture of the restored community (Ezek. 40—48)

Daniel:
    I. Change brings temptation (Dan. 1:1-7)
    II. Experience teaches faithfulness and perseverance (Dan. 1:8—6:28)
    III. Faithfulness and perseverance ultimately win (Dan. 7:1—12:13)

DAY 1   The Books of Jeremiah and Lamentations

U N I T   12

Who was Jeremiah? To many people Jeremiah remains a puzzle. He mystified many people of his day, and some who today study the man and his message also are mystified. Jeremiah has been called the weeping prophet because he wept for the people of Jerusalem. Some have interpreted his weeping as an indication that he was a weak, wavering, complaining prophet.

Neither perception is correct. Jeremiah was neither a puzzle nor a complainer. He wept over his people, but so did Jesus. He denounced the people's sin and proclaimed God's message of judgment. His message centered around Israel's refusal to repent. Jeremiah also had a strong message of hope for the people of his day.

▶ **Read Matthew 16:13-14. In light of those verses, circle the following words that could be used to describe Jeremiah:**[1]

loving	angry	honest	impatient	dedicated	righteous
caring	cowardly	weak	courageous	indifferent	
weak	unselfish	shallow	spiritual	longsuffering	

Author and Date

Jeremiah. While the material in Jeremiah is his, Jeremiah personally may not have written or collected the messages contained in the Book of Jeremiah. Jeremiah 36 mentions prominently the work of Baruch. When the Lord told Jeremiah to write all the words He had given Jeremiah, he dictated the words to Baruch who copied them on a scroll. When Jehoiakim destroyed the scroll, Jeremiah dictated a second scroll to Baruch (36:32). Later Baruch could have helped collect Jeremiah's messages into the book we now have.

Jeremiah's prophecy and ministry stretched over a long period of time. He began his ministry in the thirteenth year of King Josiah's reign, around 626 B.C. He remained active as a prophet until after the fall of Jerusalem in 587 B.C. While some people would date the beginning of Jeremiah's ministry differently, 626-586 B.C. is generally accepted. His messages probably were written and collected during that time.

Lamentations. Tradition associated the Book of Lamentations with Jeremiah for two reasons. First, Lamentations probably refers to the destruction of Jerusalem, the same period in which Jeremiah lived. Second, Lamentations consists of words of woe and lament, an association which people have made with the prophet Jeremiah.

The Books of Jeremiah and Lamentations have many similarities, and Jeremiah easily could have been the author of both books. The Book of Lamentations probably was written shortly after the destruction of Jerusalem in 587 B.C.

Historical Background

To understand the Book of Jeremiah, we must understand the historical background of his time. Basically, that background is the fall of the Southern Kingdom (you may want to review that material in Unit 8, Day 5).

---

[1]Answer: In his day, Jeremiah possessed what we would describe as a Christlike spirit. Any words that describe Jesus could have been used to describe Jeremiah.

Jeremiah received his call from God in the thirteenth year of Josiah's reign. Josiah became king of Judah in 639 B.C., so Jeremiah's call was in 626 B.C. Josiah instituted a reform movement in Jerusalem. This movement was intensified when the book of the law was found around 621 B.C. Apparently Josiah already had begun the reform and used the law book to encourage the people to reject idols and the worship of other gods.

In his early preaching, Jeremiah called for repentance and looked forward to the people's returning to the Lord. Apparently he supported Josiah's reform with enthusiasm. Jeremiah's idealism was abruptly dashed when Pharaoh Neco of Egypt killed Josiah at the battle of Megiddo.

➤ **Read an example of Jeremiah's early preaching in 2:14-19. (Note: "Israel" is used in these verses to describe God's people, not the Northern Kingdom which had been destroyed.) Check the correct answers to the following questions:[2]**

   1. What nation dominated Israel when Jeremiah preached these words?
      ☐ a. Persia
      ☐ b. Babylon
      ☐ c. Egypt

   2. For what reason did Jeremiah say Israel had become a servant to another nation?
      ☐ a. Forsaking the Lord
      ☐ b. Uninformed political decisions
      ☐ c. Poorly armed troops

   3. What two possible allies did Israel have against Babylon?
      ☐ a. The Philistines and Amorites
      ☐ b. Egypt and Persia
      ☐ c. Egypt and Assyria

   4. What does "to drink water" (v. 18) imply?
      ☐ a. to live there
      ☐ b. to make an alliance
      ☐ c. to enjoy recreation there

A few months after Josiah's death, Jehoiakim became king in Jerusalem. He ruled from 609-598 B.C. When he sided with Egypt against Babylon, the Babylonians quickly besieged Jerusalem and threatened to destroy it. While the city was under siege, Jehoiakim died. Jehoiachin followed his father on the throne and immediately surrendered the city. Many of the inhabitants of Jerusalem were taken away to Babylon. Jehoiachin's action saved the city, but he was taken captive to Babylon.

Zedekiah, another son of Josiah, took the throne. He reigned for eleven years. He decided to side with Egypt, and the Babylonians quickly rose against Judah. This time, Nebuchadnezzar crushed Jerusalem (587 B.C.). He destroyed the temple and tore down the city walls.

Through all these years, Jeremiah continued to preach the word of the Lord. He called for the people to trust God and not Egypt. His consistent counsel, in line with God's word to him, was to yield to the domination of the Babylonians. Jeremiah was branded a traitor because this counsel was regarded as treason. At one point in Zedekiah's reign Jeremiah was imprisoned. Many people wanted to take his life.

After the destruction of Jerusalem, Jeremiah proved his concern for the people. When the Babylonians offered to take him to Babylon and to treat him well, Jeremiah chose to stay with the poorest people of the land in Jerusalem. Gedaliah, the

---

[2]Answers: 1-c, 2-a, 3-c, 4-b.

governor appointed by the Babylonians, was murdered by a pretender to the throne of Judah. Then the people around Jerusalem asked Jeremiah what they should do. They were afraid the Babylonians would wipe them out to avenge Gedaliah's death, and they were considering settling in Egypt.

➤ **A. To learn what happened, read Jeremiah 42:1-18; 43:1-7. Check the statements with which you agree:**[3]

☐ 1. The people pledged to do whatever God told Jeremiah they should do.
☐ 2. God's message came to Jeremiah two weeks later.
☐ 3. God promised to deliver the people from the Babylonians.
☐ 4. God promised to bless the people in Egypt.
☐ 5. God promised to establish the people in Judah.
☐ 6. God promised death to the people if they settled in Egypt.
☐ 7. The people concluded that Jeremiah was lying and wanted them to fall into Babylonian hands.
☐ 8. The people went to Babylon and surrendered.

When the word came from the Lord, Jeremiah told the people to stay in Judah and they would prosper and be secure. The people refused to listen to Jeremiah and took him against his will into Egypt. There the prophet continued to preach God's truth. He died in Egypt, a faithful servant of the Lord.

Does serving God always bring comfort? It didn't in the life of Jeremiah. Jeremiah suffered many indignities. Not many people accepted him or believed his preaching. He gained few converts. For Jeremiah success meant following God even when others refused to do so.

Yet Jeremiah experienced the joy of knowing God in a personal way. He received God's affirmation. I think God would have said to the prophet: "Well done, good and faithful servant! . . . Come and share your master's happiness" (Matt. 25:21).

➤ **Now, use the timeline on page 138 to locate Jeremiah in historical context. Using information that you have just studied, circle the kings and the time period that were a part of Jeremiah's ministry. Write "Jeremiah" on the timeline.**

RESPONDING TO GOD'S WORD

★ **On a scale of 1 to 10, with 1 being least and 10 being most, how open and honest with God are you in your praying? Write your response here:**

_____.

Check your answer to the following questions:[4]
1. Do you think God was angry with Jeremiah for his prayer in 20:7-18?
☐ YES ☐ NO

2. Do you think God did not know how Jeremiah was feeling until he prayed?
☐ YES ☐ NO

3. Do you think God knows what you are feeling right now?
☐ YES ☐ NO

In the next few minutes, open your heart to God. Tell Him exactly what is troubling you, your doubts, your recurring questions, your frustration. As you open areas of yourself to God, you give Him the opportunity to begin to work in your life in those areas. Watch for the ways in which He begins to answer your deepest needs.

---

[3]Answers: 1, 3, 5, 6, 7.
[4]Answers: Your response. My response was 1-no, 2-no, 3-yes.

DAY 2   The Teachings of Jeremiah

U N I T   12

Can we really expect to find God in the calamities of life when we are unable to see Him in the events that surround our lives every day?

Your studies for today and tomorrow will be a sampling of the teachings in the Book of Jeremiah. This sampling highlights some of the book's major emphases. You should begin your study of each sample by carefully reading the Scripture reference at the beginning of the sample.

Inspiration and Revelation (1:11-16; 18:1-12)

Jeremiah learned that God can speak to individuals through ordinary experiences of life. On one occasion he saw a lesson from God in an almond rod and a boiling pot. Through this very ordinary experience, God gave him a message about the judgment that was to come upon the people for their apostasy and about the protection He would provide for Jeremiah. On another occasion, Jeremiah went to the potter's house and saw the potter rework a marred pot on his wheel into another pot. He realized that God had a message for Judah and for the people of Jerusalem about how He would break and remold them.

▶ **Record a time when God spoke to you through a common, everyday event in your life.**

_____

What did you do in response to what God was saying to you? _____

_____

Be prepared to share your answers with your group.

Personal Religion (3:16; 7:9-15; 20:7-18)

Jeremiah showed that the externals of religion are not necessary in order to hear the word of God. At one point the religious leaders barred Jeremiah from worshiping in the temple. Yet, Jeremiah experienced a deep and abiding relationship with God. Jeremiah condemned the sacrificial system of his day and spoke of the day when the ark of the covenant would no longer exist (3:16). He knew that God would destroy the temple because of the gross wickedness of the people. Even with the loss of the institutions of religion, Jeremiah remained close to his God and grew in his relationship with God.

Jeremiah affirmed that in every experience of life God is present to care for His people. Whether at work on Monday morning or at recreation on Saturday night, the message of God is available. God is the same Lord on Saturday night as He is on Sunday morning. God expects the same values on Monday morning as on Sunday morning.

Jeremiah learned that he could bare his heart to God. He could tell God exactly how he felt. He could even question God. God deals honestly with honest questions. Out of Jeremiah's personal experience of being open and honest with God and seeking God's guidance, he came to a greater faith in the Lord.

The Inner Nature of Sin (17:1-9)

Jeremiah shows us that sin is not just external, but it also is internal. Sin proceeds from a heart that is turned away from God. Because of inner rebellion, human beings rebel outwardly, choosing to commit acts of disobedience to God. Some of the most insightful texts in the Scripture about the nature of sin come from the Book of Jeremiah. Jeremiah 17:9 is an example.

Prayer

Jeremiah used prayer as a means of settling his doubts. In a series of laments or complaints called the confessions of Jeremiah, he prayed to God about the difficulties that he faced. These confessions are found in 11:18—12:6; 15:10-21; 17:12-18; 18:18-23; and 20:7-18.

"Oh, what peace we often
forfeit,
Oh, what needless pain we
bear,
All because we do not carry
Everything to God in
prayer."

—Joseph Scriven

We can go to God with any of our needs. Reading Jeremiah's confessions has helped me in my personal prayer life. When we are honest with God in prayer, He helps us grow and become stronger in our relationship with Him. Jeremiah prayed and God answered his prayers. God did not always do what Jeremiah wanted Him to do, but Jeremiah grew because he was willing to call on God in prayer.

A. Study one of Jeremiah's prayers and see how he opened himself to God and how God helped him process his feelings. Read Jeremiah 32:6-15. Mark the following statements as T (true) or F (false).[5]

—— 1. God told Jeremiah to buy a field in Judah even though the Babylonians were about to overthrow the nation of Judah.
—— 2. Jeremiah secretly bought the field.
—— 3. Jeremiah did not bother with a deed.
—— 4. Jeremiah told Baruch to preserve the documentation of the sale.
—— 5. Jeremiah prophesied that a time would come when property would again be bought and sold in Judah.

B. Read Jeremiah 32:16,24-25 to see the thrust of Jeremiah's prayer. Check the following questions Jeremiah could have had in mind as he prayed:

☐ 1. Did God really want me to buy that field?
☐ 2. Have I made a fool of myself?
☐ 3. Is God for me or against me?
☐ 4. How will I be vindicated before the people?

C. Read God's answer to Jeremiah in 32:36-44 and check the following statements with which you agree:

☐ 1. God affirmed that the city would fall to Babylon.
☐ 2. God said that every person would die.
☐ 3. God promised to gather His people back to Jerusalem.
☐ 4. God declared that no more would He have a covenant with His people.
☐ 5. God said He would make an everlasting covenant with His people.
☐ 6. God promised that once again His people would be prosperous and would buy and sell property in the land.

After Jeremiah had bought the field, he doubted that God wanted him to buy it. Out of these doubts, God replied and revealed to Jeremiah the restoration and the new covenant. Jeremiah's doubt provided him an opportunity to commune with God and for God to reveal Himself to Jeremiah.

Repentance (chaps. 3—4)

For Jeremiah, repentance went beyond sorrow for sin and included returning to God. Chapters 3—4 contain Jeremiah's greatest preaching about repentance. He compared repentance with breaking up unplowed ground. He called the people to return to the Lord. Sin is against God; repentance must be toward God (Jer. 4:1). This verse uses the word "return," the word for repentance in the Old Testament. The word means turning from one direction to another. Jeremiah wanted people to turn to the Lord by rejecting their sins and yielding their lives to Him.

Externals of Religion

True religion is not dependent on external religious facilities, objects, or rituals. True religion is primarily a matter of the heart. Jeremiah knew that. The ark of the

---

[5]Answers to A: 1-T, 2-F, 3-F, 4-T, 5-T. Answers to B: I checked all four responses. Answers to C: 1, 3, 5, and 6.

covenant represented God's presence to His people. Jeremiah foretold a time in which the ark of the covenant would be no more, but he explained that its absence would be of no consequence.

In previous times, the ark had been seen as the Lord's throne. Jeremiah prophesied of a time when Jerusalem would be called the throne of the Lord and all nations would gather to the presence of the Lord in Jerusalem. They would no more stubbornly follow their own evil hearts.

One of the most important religious "externals" was the temple. Jeremiah 7 and 26 record Jeremiah's temple sermon in which he proclaimed that the temple would be destroyed. Yesterday you read part of this sermon. Now look at 7:1-15.

▶ Read Jeremiah 7:1-15 and mark the following statements as T (true) or F (false).[6]

_____ 1. The people were trusting in the presence of the temple in Jerusalem for their security.

_____ 2. God's message was that faith in Him, shown by righteous living and obedience to Him, was the people's only hope of security.

_____ 3. God values a person's presence in a place of worship.

_____ 4. God preserved Shiloh because it was an ancient place of worship.

_____ 5. To ignore the warnings of God's Word is to invite disaster.

The people had made the temple little more than a robbers' hideout. They returned to the temple after committing their evil and acted as if they had done nothing wrong. Jeremiah warned that unless the people repented, God would destroy the temple and it would be no more. However, the people would not accept Jeremiah's warnings about God's judgement because they were convinced that Jerusalem was forever safe.

With the temple gone, the people were left with only their personal relationship with God to rely on. We are better off having God without the building than having the building without God. Programs and buildings are wonderful, but when we put them in the place of God, they are worthless and even hindrances to our religion.

▶ Study Luke 10:30-37 and John 4:19-20. How was worship of God hindered by preoccupation with religion and the place to practice it? Be prepared to share your answer with your group.

RESPONDING TO GOD'S WORD

★ 1. What struggles are you experiencing that you have not been open and honest about with God? Will you list at least one here? Use code words so that no one else will understand what you have written. _____

_____

God knows your code just as He has known your heart all along. Will you trust His love enough to talk with Him now about those struggles?

★ 2. Is it possible that you are having difficulty overcoming some habit in your life because you are failing to deal with the inner condition that produces that habit? Ask God to help you understand how to deal with the real source of the things that may be depriving you of a close relationship with Him.

---

[6]Answers: 1-T, 2-T, 3-F (not presence only; the person's heart must be right with God), 4-F, 5-T.

DAY 3   The Teachings of Jeremiah (continued)

UNIT   12

The Individual

For the most part, in Israel corporate religion was emphasized over individual religion. Examples of corporate religion are abundant in the Old Testament. Achan sinned against God, and as a result the whole nation stoned him and his whole household (Josh. 7:22-26).

Religion has a definite corporate sense. For example, our worship is enhanced when we join with other believers in worship. Real religion can never be solo religion. It should include other people and relate to their needs. Without rejecting the true emphasis on corporate responsibility, Jeremiah emphasized the importance of the individual's relationship with God.

▶ **Read Jeremiah 31:29-30 and note what these verses say about corporate and individual responsibility. Check in each of the following pairs of statements the one that you think is accurate:**[7]
    ☐ 1a. The people blamed their present difficulties on their parents.
    ☐ 1b. The people felt that their present difficulties were a judgment of God on the sins of their ancestors.

    ☐ 2a. Jeremiah stressed that individuals were not to be held responsible for the sins of others.
    ☐ 2b. Jeremiah stressed that parents were responsible for their children's sins.

    ☐ 3a. Each person is accountable to God for his or her sins.
    ☐ 3b. Some people are accountable to God for their own sins and also for the sins of other people they influenced.

In Jeremiah's day, people often quoted a popular proverb: "The fathers have eaten sour grapes, and the children's teeth are set on edge" (31:29). By this saying the people meant that they were receiving judgment from God because of what their ancestors had done. This statement denied any wrongdoing on their part. Jeremiah said that the day was coming in which that proverb would no longer be quoted, but everyone would die for his or her own sin: "Whoever eats sour grapes—his own teeth will be set on edge" (Jer. 31:30). Each individual is important to God. God cares for each one, and each one must respond to God as an individual.

The Messiah

Jeremiah used the term "righteous branch" as his favorite designation for the Messiah (Jer. 23:5-6; 33:4-16).

▶ **Read Jeremiah 23:5-6 and answer the following questions:**[8]
    1. Of whose lineage will the righteous Branch be? _____
    2. What will be His title? _____
    3. What three words describe His reign? _____
    4. By what name will He be called? _____

Jeremiah described the King whom God would give, who would deal wisely and execute justice and righteousness in the land. Jeremiah declared that in those

---
[7]Answers: 1-b, 2-a, 3-a (while we are accountable to God for our influence on others, each individual is accountable to God for his or her own sins).
[8]Answers: 1-David's; 2-king; 3-wise, just, right; 4-The Lord Our Righteousness.

future days God would save Judah and Israel would dwell securely. The name for this king would be: "The Lord Our Righteousness."

Jesus Christ fulfilled this prophecy. He is God's required righteousness for each of us who has received Him as Lord of our lives.

The New Covenant

In Jeremiah 31:31-34, Jeremiah described a day when God would make a new covenant with the house of Israel and the house of Judah. Israel's rebellion broke the old covenant. The people rejected the Lord and His leading for their lives. Their rebellion resulted in the destruction of the nation. In despair the people assumed that hope was gone. Jeremiah renewed their hope when he talked about the new covenant.

Jeremiah 31:31-34 does not speak of a messianic figure at all. No person is named. The hope of the future is based on God who has not given up on His people. Christians believe that Jesus, the Messiah, fulfilled the promise of the new covenant.

▶ **Read Jeremiah 31:31-34 and Hebrews 8:8-12.**

A. Match the following characteristics of the old covenant on the left with the corresponding new covenant characteristics on the right.[9]

_____ 1. Law written on tablets of stone

_____ 2. Broken covenant

_____ 3. Mediation of priests and prophets

A. All people, from least to great, will know Me

B. Law written on hearts

C. I will be their God

B. What do you think is the meaning of "I will put my law in their minds and write it on their hearts"? Read Acts 2:38-39 and Philippians 2:13 before you write your answer here:

_____

_____

Jeremiah foretold the new covenant. Read Luke 22:20 for the fulfillment of that prophecy.

Jeremiah saw a day when God would work in a new and different way with His people. He would give them a new covenant. He also would give them the ability to keep the covenant. Jeremiah 31:31-34 brings to Christians' minds their experience in Christ. The New Testament writers thought the same way. In a verse which probably refers to Jeremiah 31, Jesus told His disciples at the time of the last supper: "This cup is the new covenant in my blood" (Luke 22:20). Hebrews 8:8-12, the longest Old Testament quotation found in the New Testament, quotes Jeremiah 31:31-34 almost word for word. A shorter version of that Jeremiah passage is found in Hebrews 10:16-17.

What Was *New* About the New Covenant?

- It is written on the heart, not on stone tablets.
- It fulfills the ideal of the old covenant by establishing a new relationship between God and His people.
- Barriers between all people finally are broken down.
- It is based solely on the forgiveness of sin.

---

[9]Answers for A are: 1-B; 2-C; 3-A; For B, you perhaps wrote something like this: When we enter into the new covenant through faith in Christ, we receive the Holy Spirit to live in our hearts. He gives us the motivation and the ability to do what pleases Him.

The Structure of the Book of Lamentations

The word *lamentation* means a dirge. As you saw on the unit page for this unit, the Book of Lamentations is made up of five dirges or funeral songs. The Hebrew title for the book is "How." This name is taken from the first word of each of the first four chapters. The first four chapters of the Lamentations are written in acrostic style. Each verse in the chapter begins with a letter of the Hebrew alphabet, beginning with the first letter and going to the end.

➤ **Choose one chapter of Lamentations to read. After reading the chapter, write three to five words that describe the mood of that chapter. Be prepared to share your list of words at the small-group session this week.**

_____

_____

RESPONDING TO GOD'S WORD

★ In light of Jeremiah's life and work, how would you define success? Write your definition here:

_____

_____

I hope you wrote something to the effect that success is being faithful to do whatever God leads us to do.

★ On a scale of 1 to 10, with 10 being the most and 1 being the least, rank yourself in the following areas:

- I am doing what God wants me to do: _____
- I am seeing results of obeying God: _____
- I am encouraged in my service to God: _____
- I am fruitful _____

★ In prayer, rededicate yourself to doing faithfully what God has shown you He wants you to be doing.

DAY 4   The Book of Ezekiel

U N I T   12

God works through many different kinds of people. Studying Isaiah, Jeremiah, and Ezekiel strongly affirms that fact. All three prophets functioned differently. God worked through each prophet's individual personality.

Ezekiel's personality differed from that of both Isaiah and Jeremiah. Isaiah lived in Jerusalem and functioned as a statesman for the people of Israel. He called the kings, the leaders, and the people to faith in God. Jeremiah grew up in the small town of Anathoth and called the nation to repentance as an outsider rather than as an insider. Ezekiel came from a line of priests. Had Judah and Jerusalem survived, he probably would have served as a priest in the temple at Jerusalem.

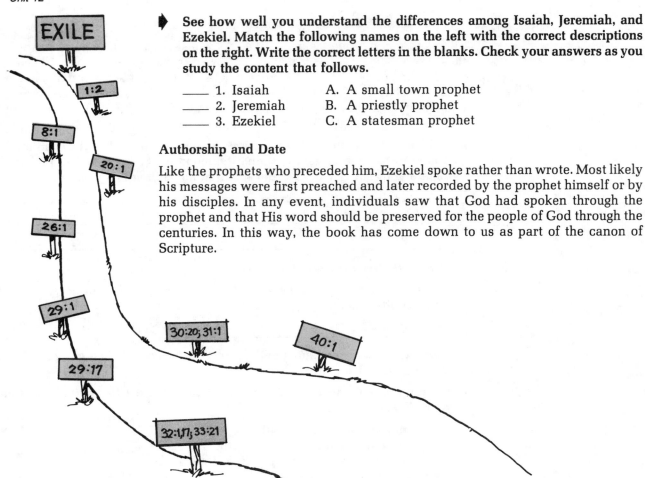

See how well you understand the differences among Isaiah, Jeremiah, and Ezekiel. Match the following names on the left with the correct descriptions on the right. Write the correct letters in the blanks. Check your answers as you study the content that follows.

_____ 1. Isaiah   A. A small town prophet
_____ 2. Jeremiah   B. A priestly prophet
_____ 3. Ezekiel   C. A statesman prophet

Authorship and Date

Like the prophets who preceded him, Ezekiel spoke rather than wrote. Most likely his messages were first preached and later recorded by the prophet himself or by his disciples. In any event, individuals saw that God had spoken through the prophet and that His word should be preserved for the people of God through the centuries. In this way, the book has come down to us as part of the canon of Scripture.

The Book of Ezekiel is organized around a series of dates. Ezekiel follows this precise plan of dating throughout the book, and the entire book is organized around those dates. Note the drawing in the margin to see how Ezekiel flagged certain dates. These flags are almost like signposts along a highway through history beginning at the year that Jehoiachin, king of Judah, was deported. Take time now to examine the reference designated by each marker.

The years relate to the exile of Jehoiachin, the deported king of Judah ("the fifth year," 1:2; "the sixth year," 8:1; "the seventh year," 20:1; and so on). God spoke to Ezekiel in 592 B.C., the fifth year of the exile of king Jehoiachin (1:2).

The statement that this was in the thirtieth year (1:1) probably means the thirtieth year of Ezekiel's life. According to the Old Testament, a priest began his ministry in the thirtieth year of his life. Therefore, Ezekiel was 30 years old when God called him to proclaim the word of the Lord to the people in exile in Babylon.

Ezekiel stated that this call came in the fifth year of Jehoiachin's exile (1:2) which began about 597 B.C. This means that he began his ministry around 592 B.C. and continued until about 570 B.C. (29:17).

Ezekiel, whose name means "God strengthens," ministered to the people of Judah in Babylon. They were in different and difficult circumstances. He preached the judgment and fall of Jerusalem until it actually happened and the temple was destroyed by the Babylonians. After the destruction of the city, Ezekiel preached comfort and reform.

Ezekiel's Unusual and Dramatic Messages

Ezekiel exhibited the most unusual behavior of the biblical prophets. Ezekiel's behavior has caused some commentators to suggest that Ezekiel suffered from some mental disorder. They refer to his lying on one side for 390 days and then lying on the other side for 40 days as symptoms of his disorder.

I strongly reject the idea that Ezekiel exhibited or suffered symptoms of psychological disorder. Ezekiel certainly displayed a different personality from the other prophets, but he did not demonstrate irrational behavior. Ezekiel acted out messages as He was instructed by God.

▶ **Read Ezekiel 4:1-8. Check the correct answer for each of the following questions.**[10]

  1. What did God command Ezekiel to create?
     ☐ a. a model of Jerusalem under siege
     ☐ b. a model of Babylon under siege
     ☐ c. a model of Damascus under siege

  2. How long was Ezekiel to lie on his left side?
     ☐ a. 100 days
     ☐ b. 365 days
     ☐ c. 390 days

  3. What was the significance of the days spent on his left side?
     ☐ a. Each day symbolized a year of sin for Judah.
     ☐ b. Each day symbolized a year of sin for Babylon.
     ☐ c. Each day symbolized a year of sin for Israel.

  4. What was the significance of the days spent on his right side?
     ☐ a. Each day symbolized a year of sin for Judah.
     ☐ b. Each day symbolized a year of sin for Babylon.
     ☐ c. Each day symbolized a year of sin for Israel.

  5. What method did Ezekiel use primarily to communicate God's message?
     ☐ a. preaching
     ☐ b. drama
     ☐ c. writing

To demonstrate that Jerusalem would face certain destruction, Ezekiel created a model of the city. He erected siege works against his model city. He showed the coming destruction of Jerusalem. His acting out prophecy may have been much more effective than simply telling the events which would soon come to pass. Ezekiel's unusual behavior was carried out in obedience to God. For example, in Ezekiel 24:15-27 we find one of the most unusual, yet most tender, acts to be found in Scripture.

▶ **Read Ezekiel 24:15-27 and answer the following questions:**[11]

  1. What heartbreaking event happened to Ezekiel? _____

  2. How did Ezekiel react to this event? _____

  3. What was the message to Israel in this behavior? _____

_____

The command for this behavior came from God, not from Ezekiel. God told Ezekiel that He would take away the delight of His eyes. Ezekiel's wife died. Ezekiel's response signaled the response the people in Babylonian exile should have toward the fall of Jerusalem. God instructed Ezekiel not to weep or lament over the loss of his wife. This restraint would indicate to those in exile that they should not mourn over the destruction of Jerusalem. The temple served as the delight of

---

[10]Answers are 1-a, 2-c, 3-c, 4-a, 5-b.
[11]Answers: 1-his wife's death; 2-he did not formally mourn but groaned quietly; 3-not to mourn formally the destruction of the temple or the deaths of kin left in Jerusalem.

the people's eyes, but God would destroy His own temple. They were not to mourn, for this was an act of God's judgment on their sins. God did not mourn; they were not to mourn.

RESPONDING TO GOD'S WORD

★ **Thank God that He uses varied personalities and multiple means of speaking to the hearts of people.**

DAY 5   The Book of Ezekiel (continued) and The Book of Daniel

---

U N I T   12   **A Summary of Ezekiel's Preaching**

Ezekiel's Themes

A. Hope for the Future
B. Responsibility for Others
C. Individual Responsibility
D. God's Sovereignty

▶ **Below, you will look at four passages that represent different themes of Ezekiel's preaching. After you read each passage, decide which of the themes listed in the box above best describes the theme of that passage. Write that theme on the line beside the reference. Then read the comments that follow the reference and the title you have written in. Be sure you choose a title for a passage before you read the comments about it.**

1. (3:16-19; 33:1-9): _____

Ezekiel was concerned for the life of the individual and for the nation. God called Ezekiel to view himself as a watchman. God wanted Ezekiel to be faithful to his calling. When God spoke to the house of Israel, Ezekiel faithfully should proclaim the word of the Lord.

▶ 2. (11:8-9): _____

Ezekiel knew that God is the Lord of history. He holds the future in His hands. The temple and Jerusalem fell to Babylon because the people rebelled against God. The Babylonians did not take the city because of their might, but because of the people's wickedness and the will of the Lord.

▶ 3. (18:1-20): _____

You will recall from the third day in this unit how the people sought to escape personal guilt by blaming their problems on God's judgment of their forefathers' sins (18:2). Ezekiel quoted the words of the Lord: "You will no longer quote this proverb in Israel" (Ezek. 18:3). All people belong to God (18:4), meaning that each individual is accountable to Him. The individual that sins will die. No longer would the destiny of the children be viewed as bound up in the destiny of the parents.

Ezekiel presented the message of individual responsibility: "The soul who sins is the one who will die. The son will not share the guilt of the father, nor will the father share the guilt of the son. The righteousness of the righteous man will be credited to him, and the wickedness of the wicked will be charged against him" (Ezek. 18:20).

▶ 4. (11:17-21; 36:22-32): _____

In words similar to Jeremiah's, Ezekiel spoke of the way God would restore the people of Israel after the time of testing and purifying in exile was completed. He knew that the day was coming when God would give the people a heart to know Him. He promised that God would give His people responsive hearts (a heart of flesh) that they might walk in His statutes and obey His words (Ezek. 11:19-20).

Ezekiel 36:22-32 approaches the high spiritual plateau of Jeremiah in the new covenant (Jer. 31:31-34) and Isaiah concerning the Suffering Servant (Isa. 52:13—53:12). Ezekiel saw the day when God would give the people a new heart and a new spirit. With God's Spirit within them, the people would walk in His statutes and obey His ordinances. God promised to deliver them from all their uncleanness and return them to their land. Then the people would remember their deeds and feel godly sorrow for their iniquities.

The Book of Daniel

Probably no book of the Old Testament has received more different interpretations than the Book of Daniel. Here are three major views:

- The book is eschatological and describes end-time events and the second coming of Christ.
- The book describes events of the second century B.C., including the desecration of the temple.
- The book looks forward to the coming of the kingdom of God in the person of Jesus Christ. All earthly kingdoms will crumble; God's kingdom will stand forever and ever. This is the view that I accept.

Authorship and Date

Scholars do not agree on the authorship of Daniel. One view is that it was written by Daniel in 605 B.C. and afterwards. Another view sees a later author writing it during the second century B.C. A third view is that chapters 1—6 come from the time period of Daniel while chapters 7—12 come from a later period in Israel's history.

The dating of the Book of Daniel follows the idea of authorship. The suggested dates range from 605 B.C. to 164 B.C.

Approach to the Book of Daniel

The Book of Daniel contains some of the most stirring stories in the Bible. They emphasize the sovereignty of God and the importance of being faithful to Him. Earthly kings and human tyrants cannot destroy the people of God. Faith is the key. Faith in God is the emphasis of the entire book, particularly chapters 1—6.

▶ **Choose one of the following accounts. Read the account and write what you feel is the major message for today. Be prepared to share your conclusion at this week's small-group session.**

1. The Image of Gold and the Fiery Furnace, 3:1-30.

   or

2. Daniel in the Lion's Den, 6:1-28.

Message for today: _____

_____

_____

How do you approach the symbolic visions in Daniel 7—12? As you would expect, approaches differ. One approach is to view this material as a prediction of the events surrounding the second coming of Christ. A second approach is to view these chapters as referring to events around 164 B.C.

I believe that the best way to view these chapters is in light of the coming of the Lord Jesus Christ. They are messianic passages of Scripture that look forward to the destruction of sin and the raising of the kingdom of God that will stand forever. These passages are quite involved and much beyond the scope of this general survey of the Old Testament.

▶   **To sample a part of one of these chapters, read Daniel 9:24-27. On a scale of 1 to 10, with 1 being the easiest and 10 being the most difficult, how would you rank this passage for difficulty in interpretation?** _____ .

(You may want to read the note "9:24-27 LAST THINGS, Great Tribulation" on p. 1056 of the *Disciple's Study Bible* for a summary of various interpretations of this passage.)

Daniel 9:24-27 speaks of 70 weeks of years. Notice the purpose of the passage. Seventy weeks of years is decreed for the purpose of finishing the "transgression, to put an end to sin, to atone for wickedness, to bring in everlasting righteousness" (v. 24). Our Lord Jesus Christ fulfilled this wonderful promise. Daniel may have been saying that an indefinite period of time is needed to bring in the One who will atone for sin.

The Book of Daniel promises God's blessings in difficult times. God's kingdom is coming. The Lord will reign forever.

▶   **To review this week's study of the Old Testament, see if you can mentally answer the following questions. You may want to write the answers on a separate sheet of paper. Mark your level of performance on the left: circle "C" if you can answer correctly and circle "R" if you need to review.**

C   R   1. List the Books of Law, History, Wisdom, and Major Prophets.

C   R   2. Through which three Major Prophets did God speak during 625-575 B.C.?

C   R   3. How were many of Jeremiah's messages written?

C   R   4. What are three of Jeremiah's major teachings?

C   R   5. In what two ways was the New Covenant to be new?

C   R   6. Where did Ezekiel minister?

C   R   7. What were two major themes of Ezekiel's messages?

C   R   8. What means did Ezekiel use to communicate many of his messages?

C   R   9. Explain two basic approaches to interpreting the Book of Daniel.

RESPONDING TO GOD'S WORD

★ **While we always may not be able to interpret every Scripture verse with complete assurance, we can understand the major messages of God's Word. Pause to thank God for using His Word to bless and guide your life.**

God and the Minor Prophets *(Hosea—Malachi)*

What comes to your mind when you hear the word minor? For many of us, that word, minor, speaks of lesser or inferior. We speak of the minor leagues, or of having a minor problem, or of a person who is not yet an adult. Sometimes when we hear of the Minor Prophets we apply the idea of lesser or inferior to them, as though these books were not as important as the Major Prophets. Nothing could be further from the truth. The books we refer to as Minor Prophets are packed full of meaning. They speak to the needs of our day just as they spoke to those to whom the messages were first given. The term Minor Prophets does not have reference to the quality of the books, but to their length. These books are brief, but powerful.

In this unit you will study the books known as the Minor Prophets: Hosea, Joel, Amos, Obadiah, Jonah, Micah, Nahum, Habakkuk, Zephaniah, Haggai, Zechariah, and Malachi.

Hosea proclaimed the love of God out of his own experience of heartbreak. He prophesied from 750-725 B.C.

Joel probably prophesied around 400 B.C. He proclaimed God's judgment and salvation.

Amos was one of the eighth century prophets. His preaching in Samaria confronted justice and social righteousness.

Obadiah spoke against Edom for abusing the people of Israel. He prophesied around 587 B.C.

Jonah was called by God to proclaim judgment against the Assyrian city of Nineveh. God spared the city when the people repented.

Micah prophesied from 735-701 B.C. He emphasized that God calls for justice, mercy, and love from His people.

Nahum prophesied before the fall of Nineveh in 612 B.C. His message predicted the fall of that city.

Habakkuk asked questions concerning the inactivity of God in punishing sin. He prophesied prior to 605 B.C.

Zephaniah cried out against the sins of his day, and spoke of the coming day of the Lord. His date is around 626 B.C.

Haggai and **Zechariah** prophesied after the return of the exiles from Babylon (539 B.C.). These prophets exhorted the people to rebuild the temple.

Malachi prophesied around 450 B.C. He spoke of the sanctity of marriage, and the need for true worship.

WordWatch

Watch for these words as you study this unit.

Israel—also known as the Northern Kingdom existed from the time of the division of the kingdom in 922 B.C. until the fall of Samaria, its capitol city, in 722 B.C. The Northern Kingdom was conquered by the Assyrians.

Judah—also called the Southern Kingdom existed from the division of the kingdom until its fall in 587 B.C. Jerusalem was the capitol of the Southern Kingdom. Judah was conquered by the Babylonians.

Edomites—were believed to be the descendants of Esau. The Edomites experienced long standing enmity with the Jews. They treated refugees from Judah with cruelty after Jerusalem fell in 587.

The Book of the Law—was found in the temple in the eighteenth year of Josiah's reign as king of Judah. Some scholars believe the Book of the Law contained the law code of Deuteronomy. Its discovery and reading led to revival and reform in Judah.

DAY 1   The Book of Hosea

UNIT 13

Fill in the blank:

THE MINOR PROPHETS

1. H _____
2. Joel
3. Amos
4. Obadiah
5. Jonah
6. Micah
7. Nahum
8. Habakkuk
9. Zephaniah
10. Haggai
11. Zechariah
12. Malachi

The Prophet Hosea

Hosea, whose name means "salvation," proclaimed the word of God out of the heartbreak of his own experience. Because the book seems to lack coherence (it has no obvious outline), interpretation is difficult at some points. Someone has suggested that the Book of Hosea is a succession of sobs.

We know more about Hosea's family than we know about some of the other prophets' families. Hosea married Gomer. The children were walking sermons to the people of Israel. Their first child was a son named Jezreel. Jezreel was the place where Jehu slaughtered all the descendants of Ahab (2 Kings 10). Jezreel, which means "God Sows," reflects the place of the judgment of God on Israel.

Gomer later gave birth to two other children. Some believe that Hosea was not the father of these children. One was a daughter whom Hosea named Lo-Ruhamah, a Hebrew term which means "not loved." God would no longer show love to Israel. The other was a son whom Hosea named Lo-Ammi, which means "not my people." God declared that the people of the Northern Kingdom were no longer His.

▶ **Match the following name on the left with the correct phrase on the right. Write the correct letters in the blanks.**[1]

_____ 1. Gomer	A. a place of judgment
_____ 2. Lo-Ruhamah	B. not loved
_____ 3. Lo-Ammi	C. Hosea's wife
_____ 4. Jezreel	D. not my people

Read Hosea 1:1.

---
[1]Answers: 1-C; 2-B; 3-D; 4-A.

Date of the Book of Hosea

The beginning date of Hosea's ministry is given in 1:1. He preached in the days of Uzziah, Jotham, Ahaz, and Hezekiah, kings of Judah, and during the reign of Jeroboam (II), king of Israel. By comparing these dates, biblical scholars date the beginning of Hosea's ministry about 750 B.C.

Hosea probably preached until about 725 B.C. He lived in those confused years just prior to the fall of the Northern Kingdom. Since Hosea failed to mention the destruction of Samaria (722 B.C.), the capitol of the Northern Kingdom, many Bible students believe Hosea's ministry ended before 722 B.C.

Structure of the Book of Hosea

Hosea can be divided into two sections: Hosea 1—3 and Hosea 4—14. The first three chapters of Hosea are both biographical and autobiographical. The second section of the book contains Hosea's preaching.

▶ **Fill in the blanks:**[2]

The Book of Hosea can be divided into two sections:

I. Hosea's Autobiography, chapters _____

II. Hosea's Preaching, chapters _____

God's Command to Marry an Adulterous Wife (1:2)

The central question related to the interpretation of Hosea depends on how we understand Hosea's marriage. Following are three major interpretations.

1. The allegorical interpretation. In this interpretation, the names and places found in the Book of Hosea represent spiritual and symbolic truths. This approach attempts to avoid the moral problem of God telling a prophet to marry a harlot (Hos. 1:2). However, this interpretation does not remove that problem. God still commanded the prophet to marry a harlot.

▶ **Check your response:**[3]
A. In the allegorical interpretation, the names and places in the Book of Hosea
□ 1. are factual.
□ 2. are symbols representing spiritual truths.

B. The allegorical interpretation
□ 1. avoids the moral problem of God's command to marry an adulterous wife.
□ 2. does not solve the problem of God's command to marry an adulterous wife.

2. The literal interpretation. This approach takes the book literally. God told Hosea to marry a harlot in order to teach Israel a profound lesson. The strength of this view is that it takes Hosea 1 seriously and preserves the book as it was written. This interpretation ignores the moral problem.

▶ **Check your response:**[4]
A. In the literal interpretation, the people, places, and events are viewed as
□ 1. historical facts.
□ 2. symbols.

B. The literal interpretation
□ 1. ignores the moral problem of Hosea marrying a harlot.
□ 2. takes the book seriously and preserves the book as written.
□ 3. shows the spiritual truth behind God's command to marry an adulterous wife.

[2]Answers: I, 1-3; II, 4-14.
[3]Answers: A-2; B-1.
[4]Answers: A-1; B-2.

3. A third viewpoint also holds to the literal interpretation but sees Hosea looking back on the tragic events of his marriage. This interpretation says that when Hosea married Gomer she was pure. Later she began to worship the Baal gods and committed adultery. Some conclude that she became a Baal temple prostitute. According to this interpretation, Hosea reflected on his experience and saw that God in effect had told him to marry a harlot.

The value of this view lies in its literal interpretation and in its attempt to solve the moral problem of God commanding Hosea to marry a harlot.

▶ **Check your response:**[5]

A. The literal/looking-back interpretation views Hosea as
☐ 1. seeing how misled he was about Gomer.
☐ 2. seeing his children's names had a private message just for him.
☐ 3. seeing what God was leading Hosea to do as he looked back on what had happened.

B. The literal/looking back interpretation
☐ 1. solves the moral problem of God commanding Hosea to marry a harlot.
☐ 2. tries to avoid the moral problem of God commanding Hosea to marry a harlot.
☐ 3. ignores the moral problem of God commanding Hosea to marry a harlot.

When God told Hosea to marry Gomer, she was pure. Then she began to worship the Baal, committed adultery, and broke Hosea's heart.

The Message of the Book of Hosea

Hosea, a prophet to the Northern Kingdom, preached a message that focused on the unfaithfulness of the people of Israel and the faithful love of God for His own people.

▶ **A. Read Hosea 4:1-3 for a message of unfaithfulness. Mark the following statements as T (true) or F (false).**[6]

_____ 1. Hosea 4:1-3 is a message of judgment.
_____ 2. God accused the people of not loving Him.
_____ 3. God accused the people of not being faithful to Him.
_____ 4. God accused the people of not acknowledging Him.

B. Read Hosea 14:1-7 for a message of love. Mark the following statements as T (true) or F (false).

_____ 1. God called the Israelites to repent.
_____ 2. Repentance in the heart is expressed by confession of sins.
_____ 3. God would not destroy them, but neither would He help them.
_____ 4. To the repentant, God promised that He would provide nourishment and make them flourish again.

"I will heal their waywardness and love them freely, for my anger has turned away from them."

—Hosea 14:4

As Hosea loved unfaithful Gomer, so God loved unfaithful Israel. The people of Israel committed spiritual adultery by going after other gods. Hosea suffered because of the unfaithfulness of Gomer; God suffered because of the unfaithfulness of His people. When Gomer repented, Hosea bought her back and made her his wife again. God wanted to take repentant Israel back unto Himself.

---

[5]Answers: A-3; B-1.
[6]Answers: A; 1-4 are T. B; 1-T, 2-T, 3-F, 4-T.

RESPONDING TO GOD'S WORD

★ Think of an experience when you were rejected by someone. How did you feel? What did you do? How are God's feelings and actions when He is rejected similar to yours? How do you think they are different from yours?

★ In prayer, tell God of your love for Him and ask His help and strength as you seek to be faithful to Him.

DAY 2 The Books of Joel and Amos

UNIT 13

Fill in the blanks:

THE MINOR PROPHETS

1. H _____
2. J _____
3. A _____
4. Obadiah
5. Jonah
6. Micah
7. Nahum
8. Habakkuk
9. Zephaniah
10. Haggai
11. Zechariah
12. Malachi

The book of Joel proclaims the judgment and salvation of God.

The Book of Joel

The prophet Joel described God's judgment in terms of a locust plague. A devastating locust plague took place in Ethiopia in 1978. A newspaper article reported 40 swarms of locusts in Ethiopia and 70 swarms in neighboring Somalia. Each swarm contained millions of locusts. Since each locust is capable of eating twice its weight in green vegetation each day, the devastation was severe.

▶ Read Joel 2:1-11 for the description of the plague of locusts. Write a sentence or two about how you think you would feel if you were a farmer and saw swarms of locusts approaching as described in 2:1-11.

_____

_____

Be prepared to share your response in this week's small-group session.

The Prophet Joel

We know little about Joel. Joel 1:1 indicates that he was the son of Pethuel. We do know that the word of the Lord came to Joel.

Date of the Book of Joel

Read Joel 1:1. Since this verse does not list a king of either Israel or Judah, we have difficulty dating the Book of Joel. A number of different dates have been proposed. The date that seems most likely is 400 B.C. This date was after the exile, and it was a time when the priests were in the position of leadership. At this time Judah was referred to as Israel. All of this matches the internal evidence of the Book of Joel. The book makes no reference to the Northern Kingdom, or to a king in Israel. Joel 3:1-2, 17 seems to indicate that the captivity had already taken place. Although some scholars date the Book of Joel as early as 837 B.C., the evidence seems to support the date of 400 B.C.

Message of the Book of Joel

Joel, a name meaning "the Lord is God," proclaimed judgment and salvation. In the first part of the book (1:1—2:17), Joel preached that judgment was coming by means of a locust plague. While he could have been describing an approaching army, Joel probably meant to describe a literal plague of locusts.

▶ Read Joel 1:1-14 and underline references to people whom Joel addressed—whether by status, profession, or class. After you have finished, check the references below that you underlined:

☐ 1. elders
☐ 2. all who live in the land
☐ 3. drinkers of wine
☐ 4. farmers
☐ 5. priests

What was Joel's primary counsel to the people? _____

▶ **Read Joel 2:12-17 for a full account of Joel's counsel.**
Check the statements you agree with below.[7]
☐ 1. Repentance involves a person's whole heart.
☐ 2. Outward signs of repentance are not important.
☐ 3. The character of God encourages His people to repent.
☐ 4. Because God loves His people and knows their needs, they do not have to pray.

In the latter part of the Book (2:18—3:21), Joel described God's zeal for the salvation of His people.

▶ **Read 2:18-27 for God's response to the people's repentance and prayers.**

This passage speaks of the restoration of the fertility of the land when the locusts have been driven into the sea. These verses make clear that just as God sent the locusts in judgment, He will deliver the people from the plague in His mercy.

▶ **Read Joel 2:28-32. Do you recall when and where this prophecy was fulfilled? Write your response here:** [8]

_____

"Afterward, I will pour out my Spirit on all people. Your sons and daughters will prophesy, your old :nen will dream dreams, your young men will see visions."

—Joel 2:28

The Book of Amos

Amos, one of the four great eighth century prophets (Amos, Hosea, Isaiah, and Micah), preached stirring messages of judgment to affluent people who practiced meaningless worship. Though outwardly religious, the people of Israel lacked a depth of commitment to God. In the name of religion they oppressed their fellow human beings.

The Prophet Amos

"I was neither a prophet nor a prophet's son, but I was a shepherd, and I also took care of sycamore-fig trees. But the Lord took me from tending the flock and said to me, 'Go, prophesy to my people Israel.'"

—Amos 7:14-15

Amos was from Tekoa in the Southern Kingdom. He traveled to the Northern Kingdom under God's direction. In Samaria, he preached concerning the excesses of the wealthy. They oppressed their fellow human beings in order to add to their wealth.

Amos preached in a day when a sharp contrast existed between the rich and poor. Amos called for genuine religion that would issue in ethical concerns for other people. Amos cried out against superficial worship which failed to affect the lives of the worshipers.

▶ **Read Amos 7:12-15 and check the correct answers to the following questions:[9]**
1. Where was Amos from?
☐ a. Israel
☐ b. Judah

2. Where was Amos preaching?
☐ a. Israel
☐ b. Judah

[7]Answers: Did you check 1, 2, 3?
[8]Answer: See Acts 2:1-21.

3. Before God's call, what work had Amos done?

☐ a. Fisherman

☐ b. Shepherd and farmer

Date of the Book of Amos

Amos prophesied around 755 B.C. Jeroboam II reigned during this period of unprecedented wealth in the Northern Kingdom. No one knows how long Amos proclaimed the word of the Lord. Some people assume that his ministry lasted a number of years. At least one interpreter believed that the prophet marched into the city of Samaria, proclaimed his message in 30 minutes, and left the city never to be heard from again.

▶ **Fill in the following:**[10]

1. Date of Amos' ministry: Around _____ B.C.

2. Location of Amos' ministry: _____

3. Length of Amos' ministry: _____

Structure of the Book of Amos

Amos consists of four sections that contain different messages of the prophet:

The *first section* is a prologue containing a judgment speech (Amos 1—2).

The *second section* has a series of addresses (3—6). Three of the messages begin with "hear this word" (3:1; 4:1; 5:1) and end with a pronouncement of judgment introduced by "therefore" (3:11; 4:12; 5:11,16). Two of the addresses begin with "woe" (5:18; 6:1).

The *third section* contains five visions of judgment (7—9:10).

The *fourth section* is an epilogue in which Amos described the resurrection of the nation (9:11-15).

God said to the people of Israel: "You only have I chosen of all the families of the earth; therefore I will punish you for all your sins."

—Amos 3:2

▶ **Check in the space below which of the following statements is true.**

☐ God's people are His favorites; therefore, they can get by with sin and disobedience.

☐ God's people are accountable to Him because He has chosen them.

RESPONDING TO GOD'S WORD

★ Does the Book of Amos have anything to say to us today? Think of some modern-day examples of the kinds of sins Amos' preaching condemned in Israel. Think in terms of the practice of religion, social problems, and immorality. Jot down modern day sins to which Amos speaks. _____

_____

★ Does Amos speak to your life? If so, what will you do about it?

_____

_____

---

[9]Answers: 1-b, 2-a, 3-b.
[10]Answers: 1-755 B.C.; 2-Northern Kingdom; 3-unknown.

DAY 3   The Books of Obadiah and Jonah

UNIT   13

Obadiah spoke against the cruel abuse of the people of Israel by Edom.

All we know about Obadiah is his name, which means "servant of the Lord," and his message. The Book of Obadiah is the shortest in the Old Testament, containing only 21 verses.

Date of Obadiah

A number of dates have been presented for the prophet Obadiah. The most important clue for dating the book revolves around its theme. Obadiah spoke against Edom and its abuse of the people of Israel. Therefore, the book should be dated at a time when Israel suffered and Edom rejoiced. These circumstances prevailed in 587 B.C. when Nebuchadnezzar's army destroyed Jerusalem. Almost everyone became a captive or a refugee. Apparently, the Edomites were guilty of stealing from the helpless refugees and killing them. Thus, 587 B.C. is the likely date for Obadiah's prophecy

Message of Obadiah

The message is plain. Edom abused Judah and Obadiah pronounced stern words of judgment on Edom.

▶   **A. Read verses 1-4.**[11]

1. What word best describes the Edomites' attitude?   _____

2. From whom did Obadiah's message come?   _____

B. Check the correct answer for each of the following questions.

1. In verses 5-6, what is the connection between robbers/grape-pickers and those who would ransack Edom?
☐ a. All three would pick Edom clean.
☐ b. Robbers and grape-pickers leave something; the ransackers will not.

2. In what way does verse 7 explain verses 15-16?
☐ a. Edom's neighbors will treat Edom like Edom treated Israel.
☐ b. Edom would be allied with the foreign power that took Israel.

3. What is the theme of verses 19-21?
☐ a. Vengeance
☐ b. Hope

"The day of the Lord is near for all nations. As you have done, it will be done to you; your deeds will return upon your own head."
—Obadiah 1:15

How can God, who is love, send such a strong word of judgment? As we look at the Book of Obadiah, we need to remember two key points.

First, the Book of Obadiah expresses genuine human feelings. The book obviously was written shortly after a painful event in Judah. Feelings ran high and people were still hurting. Obadiah preached his word in that setting.

Second, judgment is a legitimate message because God is a God who punishes sin even as He loves the sinners.

The Book of Jonah

The Book of Jonah may be one of the most misunderstood books in the minor prophets. If you play the word association game, the word Jonah quickly would evoke the word *whale*. We so associate Jonah with the whale that we often miss the abiding message of the book.

---

[11]Answers to A: 1-Pride; 2-the Lord. Answers to B: 1-b, 2-a, 3-b.

The Prophet Jonah

▶ **Read 2 Kings 14:23-25. Check your answer to the following questions:**[12]

1. In whose reign did Jonah prophesy?
☐ A. Joash
☐ B. Jeroboam
☐ C. Amaziah

2. In what country did Jonah prophesy?
☐ A. Northern Kingdom
☐ B. Southern Kingdom
☐ C. Syria

Like many other prophets, we know little about the prophet Jonah. Second Kings 14:25 records his optimistic words during the reign of Jeroboam II of Israel. Jonah, the son of Amittai, prophesied that Israel's border would be restored as far as Hamath in the north to the Sea of the Arabah in the south. Except for the few words of preaching in the Book of Jonah, this verse records the only known message of Jonah.

The Message of Jonah

This book differs from other prophetic books in that it is a book about the prophet instead of a book by the prophet. God used the story of Jonah to proclaim one of the most resounding messages of the Bible.

In the Book of Jonah, the message is closely related to the story of Jonah's call and his reaction to that call.

Jonah apparently lived his life as a prophet of nationalism. He thought only of Israel and the extension of its border. God called Jonah to go to Nineveh and preach repentance. Nineveh was a leading city and sometimes capital of Assyria. In the ancient world, Assyria was known as the most barbaric and ruthless of all nations.

▶ **Read Jonah 1:1-17 and mark the following statements as T (true) or F (false).**[13]

____ 1. Jonah could sincerely sing, "Wherever He Leads I'll Go."
____ 2. God sometimes uses circumstances to guide His people.
____ 3. God only uses people who sincerely worship Him in carrying out His purposes.
____ 4. On the ship bound for Tarshish, the pagan men showed more compassion for Jonah than Jonah showed for Nineveh.

When God called Jonah to go to Nineveh to preach repentance, he received the most startling call of anyone in the Old Testament. Jonah did not want God to forgive the people of Nineveh. He wanted God to condemn them.

▶ **Read Jonah 3:1-10 and check the following statements with which you agree:**[14]

☐ 1. When a person refuses to obey God, that person is disqualified from God's service.
☐ 2. God works through His Word.
☐ 3. When sinners fast, God forgives.
☐ 4. When sinners repent, God forgives.

When Jonah finally obeyed God and went to Nineveh, he warned the people of judgment. Though he never told them to repent, they turned from their sins and God spared the city of Nineveh.

The Book of Jonah reveals the sovereignty of God, the call of God, the providence of God, and the miraculous element of Jonah being swallowed by a great fish. However, it is in the fourth chapter that we discover the heart of the book.

[12]Answers: 1-B, 2-A.
[13]Answers: 1-F, 2-T, 3-F, 4-T.
[14]Answers: 2, 4.

▶ **Read Jonah 4:1-10. In each of the following pairs of statements check the one that is most accurate.**[15]

☐ 1a. Jonah was angry and depressed over the response to his preaching.
☐ 1b. Jonah was unhappy over the response to his preaching.

☐ 2a. Jonah interpreted the Lord's question in verse 4 to mean that perhaps Nineveh would be destroyed.
☐ 2b. Jonah felt rebuked by the Lord's question in verse 4.

☐ 3a. God provided a vine to shelter Jonah.
☐ 3b. God provided a vine to use in teaching Jonah a lesson.

☐ 4a. Jonah wanted God to save certain people; God wants to save all people.
☐ 4b. Jonah wanted God to save Israel and to condemn Nineveh.

☐ 5a. The primary theme of Jonah is repentence.
☐ 5b. The primary message of Jonah is a missionary message.

In anger, Jonah moved to the east side of the city to see what God would do. As Jonah sat under the blazing sun, God appointed a plant to shade him. God then appointed a worm, the same word which is used for God appointing the wind and the big fish. When the worm cut down the plant, Jonah lost his shade.

Jonah became angry because of the plant. God chided Jonah because he had love and concern for a plant, but had no love and concern for people. God cares about people. He cared even for the people of Nineveh. If Jonah could love a plant, how much more can God care for all the people of the world.

The Book of Jonah comes close to the teachings of Jesus. Jesus told us to love our enemies and to pray for them. The Book of Jonah has been called a missionary tract. It certainly encourages going to other nations with the message of hope and redemption and the warning of judgment.

"The Lord said, 'You have been concerned about this vine, though you did not tend it or make it grow. It sprang up overnight and died overnight. But Nineveh has more than a hundred and twenty thousand people who cannot tell their right hand from their left, and many cattle as well. Should I not be concerned about that great city?"

—Jonah 4:10,11

RESPONDING TO GOD'S WORD

★ Meditate on Jonah's selfish concern for losing the vine that provided him comfort. Are you more concerned with your own comfort and convenience than with helping lost people come to know God's forgiveness in Christ? Ask God to give you a concern for the lost and a willingness to follow His guidance.

---

[15]Answers: 1-a, 2-a, 3-b, 4-a, 5-b.

DAY 4   The Books of Micah, Nahum, Habakkuk

U N I T   13   **The Book of Micah**

Isn't it amazing how God uses different people to accomplish His work in the world? The prophets Isaiah and Micah served as prophets at the same time in Judah. Isaiah, a statesman who lived and served in Jerusalem, proclaimed God's message to the Southern Kingdom. Micah, a man who grew up and lived in the

Fill in the blanks:

THE MINOR PROPHETS

1. H _____
2. J _____
3. A _____
4. O _____
5. J _____
6. M _____
7. N _____
8. H _____
9. Zephaniah
10. Haggai
11. Zechariah
12. Malachi

"He has showed you, O man, what is good. And what does the Lord require of you? To act justly and to love mercy and to walk humbly with your God."
—Micah 6:8

The discovery of the Book of the Law in the temple helped bring about revival and reform when Josiah was king.

small town of Moresheth, proclaimed God's words at the same time in the Southern Kingdom.

Micah prophesied in the Southern Kingdom during the reigns of Jotham, Ahaz, and Hezekiah. Though not all scholars agree, Micah probably ministered in the years 735-701 B.C., during the significant crises of the last third of the eighth century B.C.

Message of Micah

In what is probably the best known chapter in the Book of Micah, the prophet described a courtroom scene (chap. 6). God served as judge, witness, and jury. He accused the people of Israel of disobeying Him.

▶ **Read Micah 6:1-8 and check the correct answer for each of the following questions.**[16]

1. Who were called to be witnesses to the Lord's case against Israel?
□ a. The people of Judah.
□ b. The hills and mountains.

2. What is the emphasis of verses 3-6?
□ a. The burdens God had placed on His people.
□ b. The help God had given His people.

3. Which of the following is most pleasing to God?
□ a. Burnt offerings.
□ b. Justice, mercy, and walking humbly with God.

Micah asked a series of questions. "With what shall I come before the Lord?" (6:6). Should a person give rivers of oil? Should a person give his firstborn son? What is suitable to bring before God? Micah gave a clear answer to these difficult questions. Performing acts of mercy and justice and loving God supremely fulfill the demands of God's covenant relationship.

Micah's answer demonstrates that God wants actions that please Him and devotion that comes from deep within an individual. God wants a faith that works. He wants yielded lives that produce acts of mercy and kindness.

Historical Background of Nahum, Habakkuk, and Zephaniah

Jeremiah, Nahum, Habakkuk, and Zephaniah prophesied during the seventh century B.C. Nahum and Habakkuk preached in later years but before the end of the century. In 639 B.C. Josiah became king of Judah. His reign brought hopes for a spiritual renewal of Judah and for the end of Assyrian domination. By 626 B.C., God called Jeremiah to be a prophet. His call and that of Zephaniah may have coincided. Their calls came at the same time as the death of the last strong Assyrian king. They began their ministries at a turning point in history.

Shortly after Jeremiah and Zephaniah began their public ministries, Josiah began a serious attempt at religious reform in Jerusalem. For decades, Assyria had dominated Judah. King Manasseh placed Assyrian symbols in the temple of the Lord. When Assyrian power began to wane, Josiah quickly removed those objects from the temple. His reform movement received a strong boost when workmen discovered the Book of the Law in the temple in 621 B.C.

▶ **Check the two factors that contributed to Josiah's efforts at reform:**[17]
□ 1. Assyria's decline
□ 2. Egypt's support
□ 3. Discovery of the Book of the Law

---

[16]Answers: 1-b, 2-b, 3-b.
[17]Answers: 1 and 3.

Josiah obeyed the words of the Lord (probably some part of the Book of Deut.). He destroyed the high places where the Baals were worshiped and centralized worship in the temple in Jerusalem. The reform accomplished two significant purposes: (1) it freed the people from the religious influences of Assyria, and (2) it turned the people back to a more genuine worship of the Lord.

Unfortunately, the reform failed to change the hearts of the people. Jeremiah especially demonstrated his disappointment with the reform movement's inability to change the lives of wicked or sinful people.

Josiah and many others welcomed the prophecy of Nahum concerning the destruction of Nineveh. Josiah rejoiced when word came that Nineveh had indeed fallen in 612 B.C. Josiah was killed in 609 B.C. Jehoahaz the son of Josiah became king but was deposed within three months and Jehoiakim assumed the throne. He reigned from 609 B.C. to 598 B.C.

During Jehoiakim's reign, Babylon established itself as the most powerful army of the ancient Near East. At the Battle of Carchemish in 605 B.C., Babylon defeated Egypt and began its domination in the ancient world. During this time the prophecy of Habakkuk was given.

The Book of Nahum

The name Nahum means "comforter." Nahum comforted the people of Jerusalem by decreeing the coming destruction of Nineveh. Nahum's message from God reflected the barbarous disregard of human life by the armies of Nineveh.

Nahum lived more that a hundred years after God spared the city of Nineveh when Jonah proclaimed God's message and the citizens of Nineveh repented.

Nineveh fell to the Medes and Babylonians in 612 B.C. Nahum probably prophesied shortly before Nineveh fell.

▶ **Read Nahum 1:1-14 and answer the following questions:**[18]

1. Who will bring judgment on Nineveh? _____

2. List three poetical images from nature that Nahum used to describe God's judgment:

    a. _____

    b. _____

    c. _____

Nineveh terrorized the ancient Near East from 745 B.C. when Tiglath-Pileser took the throne until its fall in 612 B.C.

▶ **Read Nahum 3:19. What would everyone who heard of Nineveh's destruction do when they heard the news?**

_____

Check your answer in the following paragraph.

Nahum reflected the feelings of all the people of that area. He said that when Nineveh fell all the people would clap their hands.

The Book of Habakkuk

Habakkuk's message revolves around a series of questions he asked God. God answered Habakkuk's questions and showed that He is the sovereign Lord who is faithful to His people. Habakkuk wondered about the inactivity of God. How could God leave Judah unpunished?

[18]Answers: 1-the Lord; 2a-c, you may have written whirlwind, storm, earthquake, volcano, or fire.

➤ **Read Habakkuk 1:1-4. Check the items that express reasons for Habakkuk's puzzlement:**[19]
☐ 1. Unanswered prayer
☐ 2. Violence
☐ 3. Injustice
☐ 4. Wrongdoing
☐ 5. Strife and conflict
☐ 6. Breakdown of the judicial system
☐ 7. Idolatry

Read Habakkuk 1:5-11.

God's response to Habakkuk only puzzled the prophet more. God revealed to Habakkuk that He would bring the Babylonians to power to serve as His instrument of judgment.

➤ **Read 1:12-17. In one or two sentences, paraphrase Habakkuk's response.**[20]

_____

_____

"The Sovereign Lord is my strength; he makes my feet like the feet of a deer, he enables me to go on the heights."
—Habakkuk 3:19

Habakkuk questioned how God could use such a wicked agent of judgment. God's answer to this question forms the central part of the Book of Habakkuk (2:1-20). God was not ignoring wickedness. God pointed to the hidden processes of judgment which are at work in the lives of the wicked. He also revealed to the prophet that the righteous lived by their faith.

Chapter three consists of the prayer of Habakkuk. This chapter is similar to a psalm. Verses 17-19 contain one of the most profound messages of faith in the Old Testament.

➤ **Read verses 17-19 and summarize them in one or two sentences.**

_____

_____

RESPONDING TO GOD'S WORD

★ **Pray Habakkuk 3:17-19 as a reaffirmation of your trust in your heavenly Father.**

---

[19]Answers: 1-6.
[20]Answer: Perhaps you wrote something like, "How could God use a wicked nation to punish a righteous or less wicked nation?"

DAY 5   The Books of Zephaniah, Haggai, Zechariah, and Malachi

U N I T   13   **The Book of Zephaniah**

Zephaniah means "the Lord hides." Zephaniah probably was born during the reign of Manasseh, the evil king of Judah. By naming their son Zephaniah, these parents may have affirmed their faith in God's watchcare.

Zephaniah arrived on the scene with a strong message of judgment about 626 B.C. Zephaniah prophesied during the reign of Josiah. He evidently began his ministry prior to the discovery of the Book of the Law in 621 B.C. since he condemned many abuses which were remedied by Josiah's reform.

Fill in the blanks:

THE MINOR PROPHETS

1. H _____
2. J _____
3. A _____
4. O _____
5. J _____
6. M _____
7. N _____
8. H _____
9. Z _____
10. H _____
11. Z _____
12. M _____

▶ **Read Zephaniah 1:4-6. Check the category of sins against which Zephaniah spoke in these verses:**[21]

☐ 1. Sexual immorality
☐ 2. Unethical business practices
☐ 3. Idolatry
☐ 4. Murder

Zephaniah described the sins of the people of his day. They worshiped the heavenly bodies. They bowed down on their knees to the host of heaven. They worshiped other gods, like Molech, while worshiping the Lord at the same time. Zephaniah accused this group of turning back from following the Lord.

▶ **Read Zephaniah 1:7-18.**

Zephaniah spoke of the coming judgment in terms of the day of the Lord. The concept of the day of the Lord went back at least as far as Amos. It was a day of God's judgment against His people who rebelled against Him. In earlier times, the day of the Lord may have been seen as a day when God would judge Judah's and Israel's enemies. Amos turned the concept around to describe the day of the Lord as the day when God would judge His own people for their rebellion against Him. The fulfillment of Zephaniah's prophecy probably came with the destruction of Jerusalem in 586 B.C.

▶ **Mark the following statements as T (true) or F (false).**[22]

____ 1. The day of the Lord refers to the second coming of Christ.
____ 2. The day of the Lord in Zephaniah refers to God's judgment on Judah.
____ 3. The day of the Lord is a day of hope and comfort.

The Historical Background of Haggai and Zechariah

Haggai and Zechariah prophesied after the return from exile in Babylon (539 B.C.). Soon after the decree of Cyrus, Jews began to leave Babylon to return to Jerusalem. Haggai, Zechariah, and Zerubbabel made up part of that exodus.

In 534 B.C., the people began work on the temple. They laid the foundation and hoped to complete the temple speedily. That was not the case. For a number of reasons - their poverty, their preoccupation with their needs, and opposition - they were not able to complete the temple. In the second year of Darius, God raised up two prophets, Haggai and Zechariah, to exhort the people to rebuild the temple.

Their preaching prompted renewed efforts to build the temple of the Lord. The people began work on the temple while the prophets were prophesying. In 516 B.C. they dedicated the temple.

▶ **Check the correct answer for each of the following questions.**[23]

1. In what period did Haggai and Zechariah prophesy?
☐ a. During the Babylonian exile.
☐ b. Before the Babylonian exile.
☐ c. After the Babylonian exile.

---

[21]Answer: 3.
[22]Answers: 1-F, 2-T, 3-F.

2. What did their preaching help accomplish?
☐ a. Returning to Jerusalem.
☐ b. Completing the temple.
☐ c. Completing the city walls.

The Book of Haggai

The name Haggai means "festival," a quite appropriate name for the prophecy of this book. Haggai preached in 520 B.C., the second year of Darius (1:1). All of Haggai's messages came within that year from the sixth to the ninth month. Haggai's message contains the exhortation to rebuild the temple. His messages dealt with several obstacles.

▶ **Read Haggai 1:2-4 and answer the following questions:**

1. According to the returned exiles, was the time right for building?

_____

2. What was God's response to their attitude? _____

_____

Some people said that it was not time to build the temple (1:2). The people said that they were unable to build. Too many problems existed. Haggai responded by reminding them that their problems had come from their neglect.

▶ **A. Read Haggai 1:5-11. Explain in two or three sentences how God had sought to attract His people's attention concerning their neglect of His Temple.**[24]

_____

_____

_____

B. Read 1:12-15 to discover the people's response and a promise from God. In a few words, write:

1. The people's response: _____

2. God's promise: _____

▶ **Read Haggai 2:3-9.**

Some of the people were discouraged because the temple they built did not compare in splendor to the first temple. Solomon built the first temple in an age of wealth; the people who rebuilt the temple were poor. They could not construct a building that could compare with that of Solomon's temple. Haggai responded that one day the splendor of the new temple would be greater than the temple of Solomon. In one sense, this was wonderfully fulfilled. Our Lord taught in the temple rebuilt during the time of Haggai and Zechariah.

The Book of Zechariah

Zechariah preached the same message at the same time as Haggai. He exhorted the people to rebuild the temple. His ministry extended from 520 to 518 B.C.

Zechariah 1—8 is a series of visions which encouraged the builders to begin and complete the work. Chapters 9—14 contain material that foretells establishing the kingdom of God. The Gospels quote several verses from Zechariah in relating Jesus' last days.

---

[23]Answers are 1-c, 2-b.
[24]Answers: A-Your answer; B,1-The people began to rebuild the temple; 2-God promised to be with His people.

▶ **Read Zechariah 1:1-17. Fill in the blanks in the short outline of this passage with the appropriate verse numbers:**

The Punishment (Zech. 1:1-___)

The Promise (Zech. 1:___-___)

Write in one or two sentences how you think you would have reacted to this message if you had been one of the exiles who had returned.

_____

_____

The Book of Malachi

Malachi fits at the end of the Old Testament. Most biblical scholars date his prophecy around 450 B.C., making him a contemporary with Ezra and Nehemiah. His prophecy and the conditions in Jerusalem seem to reflect that time period.

The name Malachi means "my messenger." Some scholars believe the name is not the personal name of the prophet but one that describes the nature of the book, as in 3:1 where the words "my messenger" are used. The message of the book is rich and varied. It contains the highest view of marriage found in the Old Testament except possibly for Genesis 2:24.

▶ **A. Read Malachi 2:13-16. Write a brief summary of what this passage teaches about marriage.**

_____

_____

B. Read 3:1; 4:5-6, and compare with Matthew 17:11-13.

In Malachi we find passages concerning Elijah, the prophet who was to come before the great and terrible day of the Lord. Jesus said that the passage was fulfilled in John the Baptist.

▶ **Read Malachi 1:6-14.**

God expressed concern through His prophet about the service of the priests and the worship of the people. Their offerings were not pleasing to the Lord, because they did not represent the best that the people had to offer. The attitude of the people was negative. They only seemed to go through the motions of worship. They, and their priests, were not concerned with the manner in which they approached the God of all nations.

The Book of Malachi, which marks the end of our Old Testament, ends with the exhortation to "Remember the law of my servant Moses, the decrees and laws I gave him at Horeb for all Israel" (4:4). As we have studied and as we study in the future, let us remember that the Lord has taught us to obey His words and to do His will each day.

▶ **SUMMARY REVIEW**

To review this final week's study of the Old Testament, see if you can mentally answer the following questions. You may want to write the answers on a separate sheet of paper. Mark your level of performance on the left: circle "C" if you can answer correctly and circle "R" if you need to review.

C R   1. List the Minor Prophets.

C R   2. What is unique about Hosea's prophecy?

C R   3. How did Joel describe God's judgment?

C R   4. What is one major theme in the Book of Amos?

C R   5. Obadiah pronounced judgment on what nation?

C R   6. Jonah preached to what nation?

C R   7. The Book of Micah is best known for what kind of scene?

C R   8. Nahum's prophecy dealt with what city?

C R   9. Name one thing that disturbed Habakkuk.

C R 10. What concept did Zephaniah use to describe God's coming judgment on Judah?

C R 11. In what project did Haggai and Zechariah play a key role?

C R 12. What New Testament figure fulfilled a prophecy in Malachi?

STEP BY STEP THROUGH THE OLD TESTAMENT
GROUP COVENANT

I, _____

covenant with my Step by Step through the Old Testament group to:

1. *Complete the Bible study and learning activities in the workbook each week before the group session.*

2. *Pray regularly for my fellow group members.*

3. *Participate in all group sessions unless circumstances beyond my control prevent my attendance. When unable to attend, I will make up the session at the earliest possible time with the group leader or group member assigned.*

4. *Participate openly and honestly in the group session.*

5. *Keep confidential any personal matters shared by others in the group.*

6. *Study to show myself approved unto God as a disciple that doesn't need to be ashamed regarding the word of truth.*

Others: _____

_____

_____

_____

_____

_____

_____

Signed: _____ *Date:* _____

Step by Step through the Old Testament Group Members

_____ _____

_____ _____

_____ _____

_____ _____

_____ _____

CHRISTIAN GROWTH STUDY PLAN
Preparing Christians to Serve

In the **Christian Growth Study Plan (formerly Church Study Course),** this book **Step by Step Through the Old Testament** is a resource for course credit in the subject area Bible Studies of the Christian Growth category of diploma plans. To receive credit, read the book, complete the learning activities, show your work to your pastor, a staff member or church leader, then complete the following information. This page may be duplicated. Send the completed page to:

**Christian Growth Study Plan
127 Ninth Avenue, North, MSN 117
Nashville, TN 37234-0117
FAX: (615)251-5067**

For information about the Christian Growth Study Plan, refer to the current Christian Growth Study Plan Catalog. Your church office may have a copy. If not, request a free copy from the Christian Growth Study Plan office (615/251-2525).

Step by Step Through the Old Testament
COURSE NUMBER: CG-0104
PARTICIPANT INFORMATION

Social Security Number (USA Only) | Personal CGSP Number* | Date of Birth (Mo., Day, Yr.)

Name (First, MI, Last) ☐Mr. ☐Mrs. ☐Miss ☐ | Home Phone

Address (Street, Route, or P.O. Box) | City, State, or Province | Zip/Postal Code

CHURCH INFORMATION

Church Name

Address (Street, Route, or P.O. Box) | City, State, or Province | Zip/Postal Code

CHANGE REQUEST ONLY

☐Former Name

☐Former Address | City, State, or Province | Zip/Postal Code

☐Former Church | City, State, or Province | Zip/Postal Code

Signature of Pastor, Conference Leader, or Other Church Leader | Date

*New participants are requested but not required to give SS# and date of birth. Existing participants, please give CGSP# when using SS# for the first time. Thereafter, only one ID# is required. *Mail To:* Christian Growth Study Plan, 127 Ninth Ave., North, MSN 117, Nashville, TN 37234-0117. Fax: (615)251-5067

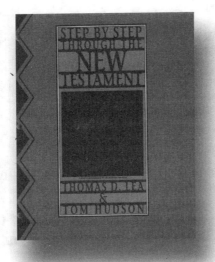